Christianity and Culture

John Cogley

Christopher Dawson

Thomas P. Neill

Barbara Ward

Jacques Maritain

Sir Robert Falconer

Lawrence E. Lynch

Friedrich Wilhelm Foerster

Frank O'Malley

Noël Mailloux

Ruth Nanda Anshen

Etienne Gilson

Charles Malik

Sigrid Undset

Dorothy Donnelly

Ivan Mestrovic

Hugh Kenner

Robert Speaight

Marshall McLuhan

Peter Drucker

Christianity
and
Culture

Edited by J. Stanley Murphy, C.S.B.

with an Introduction by Donald McDonald

1960
HELICON PRESS
Baltimore

Nihil obstat: EDWARD A. CERNY, S.S., S.T.D.
Censor Librorum

Imprimatur: † FRANCIS P. KEOUGH, D.D.
Archbishop of Baltimore
January 4, 1960

The *Nihil obstat* and *Imprimatur* are official declarations that a book or pamphlet is free of doctrinal or moral error. No implication is contained therein that those who have granted the *Nihil obstat* and *Imprimatur* agree with the opinions expressed.

Library of Congress Catalog Card Number: 60-15488

Printed in the United States of America
by North Central Publishing Co., St. Paul, Minnesota

Foreword

THE TWENTY contributors to this anthology include ten from the list of Christian Culture Award medallists and ten from hundreds of participants in the Christian Culture Series of platform presentations during the past twenty-six years.

The gold medal for the Christian Culture Award, presented once a year by Assumption University of Windsor to some "outstanding lay exponent of Christian ideals," started with the Series in 1941 and is one of the high peaks of each season. The design combines the artistry of Adé Bethune, Graham Carey, and Ference Varga: the inscription on one side "Simile est regnum caelorum grano sinapis" encircles a replica of a human hand and the symbolic mustard plant; on the other side "Christian Culture Award, Assumption University" surrounds the engraved name of the medallist and the year. The twenty recipients to date have been Sigrid Undset, Jacques Maritain, Philip Murray, Frank J. Sheed, Arnold M. Walter, George S. Sperti, Richard Pattee, Henry Ford II, Etienne Gilson, Paul Doyon, Christopher Dawson, John C. H. Wu, Charles Malik, Ivan Mestrovich, Friedrich Wilhelm Foerster, Paul Martin, Robert Speaight, Allen Tate, Barbara Ward, and John Cogley.

The idea of the Christian Culture Series germinated in the mind of the founder, a young Basilian Father, not three years ordained, assigned to an institution valiantly struggling for survival in an industrial milieu still paralyzed by the Depression. Nourished by reading begun in his parental home, and furthered in his years of academic training, his impractical dream grew with the enthusiastic acquaintance of the works of Newman, Chesterton, Papini, Belloc, Jörgensen, Dawson, Maritain, Noyes, Gilson, and a harvest of other new authors. It was definitely enhanced still further by the early work of Bishop Fulton J. Sheen as well as by the inspiration from the classroom presence of the Very Reverend Henry Carr, C.S.B., L.L.D., then Basilian Superior General. Father Carr was the man who was most responsible for the advent to North America, with long periods of teaching in Toronto, of scholars like Maurice DeWulf, Léon Noël, Sir Bertram Windle, Etienne Gilson (with whom he co-founded the Pontifical Institute of Medieval Studies), and Jacques Maritain. Fresh in memory is some of the incomparable lecturing of Dr. Gilson in those days and the lasting effect of some of his insights into the work of the Fathers and the great Christian thinkers of the past — such as St. Justin Martyr of the second century, who felt that Christians should welcome as part of their inheritance with Christ the pagan past and baptize whatever of truth or beauty or goodness had come to them from it.

On November 25, 1934, Bishop Sheen opened the first Christian Culture Series, and he has been the scheduled opening speaker for twenty-seven consecutive seasons since. Over five hundred presentations in twenty-six years, stressing almost every phase of Christian culture, were completely subsidized by, and open to, all men of good will regardless of class, color, or creed. This testifies to the enduring vitality of the founder's dream: an evidence that "the re-invention of a true civilization" can be appropriately promoted by a Catholic university or kindred institution, where "things of the spirit gather together . . . art and poetry among them, and metaphysics and wisdom, the charity of the Saints [leading] the choir." *

The necessity for brevity precludes the acknowledgment of thanks to all the persons and groups to whom it is due, such as: my late parents; my brother; my Basilian family; the abidingly loyal and keenly interested Bishop Sheen, whose advice to "keep the standard high and the purpose unobscured" we have tried to follow since he gave it in 1934; the sponsors of the Series, the University; the ecclesiastical and civil authorities of Michigan and Ontario where the presentations take place; the generous contributors; and Donald McDonald, editor of the new *Marquette University Magazine*, who courteously found the time in a very busy schedule to write the Introduction; to all who directly or otherwise helped in the preparation of this anthology. It is indeed "light alone that gathers men together"† in such projects.

We wish to express our gratitude, also, to the staff of Assumption University Library; to Jeannine and Leo Shanley for renewing my

* Jacques Maritain, *Art and Scholasticism* (London: Sheed and Ward, 1930), p. 82.
† *Ibid*, p. 26: "Once we touch a transcendental . . . the good and Love, like the Saints, or the true, like an Aristotle, or the beautiful like a Dante, a Bach or a Giotto, then contact is established and souls communicate. Men are only really united by the spirit: light alone gathers them together."

contact with Dr. F. W. Foerster in New York City; to the *University of Toronto Quarterly* for the reprinting of Sir Robert Falconer's essay; to *Commonweal* for permission to use the essays by Barbara Ward and Peter Drucker; to the Canadian Broadcasting Company for use of the essays of Etienne Gilson and Noël Mailloux; to *Review of Politics* for the excerpts in Frank O'Malley's contribution; to the *Dublin Review* for large sections of Robert Speaight's article; to Oxford University Press for the use of the Gerard Manley Hopkins excerpt in Mrs. Donnelly's essay and to Random House, New York, and Faber and Faber, Ltd., London, for the excerpt from W. H. Auden's "September" in the same essay; to Image Books and Doubleday of New York for most of the Gilson essay; to *Pastoral Psychology* for many paragraphs in the Mailloux essay.

Joseph Stanley Murphy, C.S.B.
Founder and Chairman, Christian Culture Series
Assumption University of Windsor, Windsor, Ontario

Contents

Christianity and Culture

Introduction

THE GREAT temptation for Christians, when they speak of "Christian culture," is to let their criticism of "secular culture" become a condemnation. One cannot, of course, analyze Christian culture without critically comparing it with secular culture. The temptation to condemn the latter is natural and understandable. Sometimes the spokesmen for the secular act as if their culture were a terminal good. Sometimes they act as if their culture owed no debt to Christian sources and Christian inspirations. And sometimes, in the competition for adherents, secular culture seems to be winning the day.

But condemnation of secular culture is, for the Christian, impermissible — on intellectual, historical, psychological and, above all, theological grounds. Grace does build on nature, and while Christian culture is, in one sense, an aggregate, a cumulative development of many energies and impulses (some of them far removed from the direct influence of grace), what makes the resulting culture "Christian" is that these energies and impulses have been and are lodged in grace-filled Christians. We can speak, then, I believe, of Christian culture as being "grace-charged." And, just as grace cannot, in Christianity that is specifically and by definition incarnational, and in a context which is by nature secular, dispense with the natural and the secular, so a grace-charged Christian culture cannot, if it is to be genuine and real, exist apart from an organic relationship with the natural and the secular.

The first value of the present collection of essays and addresses on Christian culture is precisely this negative thing: none of the contributors, so far as I can see, is guilty of what one of them, John Cogley, criticizes — a kind of "pseudo withdrawal" from the world and a "sniping at the world from some sectarian fox-hole."

If one of the marks of a mature Christian is that he is able to discern and assimilate what is good and true in the secular culture — as Aquinas, in his day, was able to discern and assimilate what was true

3

and good in the philosophic thought of non-Christian thinkers; if he, like Aquinas, is more delighted with the truths he finds in secular thought than he is with unmasking the errors it contains, then the contributors to the present volume must be reckoned mature Christians.

For even, as in the case of Foerster, Dawson, Donnelly and Undset, where criticism of the secular is most pointed and most cutting, the criticism does not become condemnation; no one is advocating a divorce of the Christian and the secular. One can, it is clear, speak of the "superstitious divinization of reason," or one can picture modern life being "enameled over with an arrogant gaiety," or one can describe "fate's most exquisite irony" — today's "enlightened" leaders who scorn the "superstitions" of the Dark Ages and the Middle Ages, but who "deliberately propagate superstition in which they themselves cynically disbelieve." One can speak of these realities, as some of this volume's contributors do, and still preserve, implicitly or explicitly, the understanding that the aberrations of secularism do not justify the dismissal of the secular. One can speak of them without denying, again quoting from Mr. Cogley, that one "must establish a relevance between the natural and the supernatural, between the secular and the sacral, between the actually existing culture and Christianity.

Certainly a second mark of the mature Christian is his willingness to criticize himself and, when his culture is criticized by others, his restraint, his steady refusal to resort to invective or to pretend that anything Christian is beyond criticism. Mr. Cogley, Barbara Ward and others sustain the self-critical tradition which is indispensable to not only the maturity of the individual Christian, but to the progress and vitality of the culture itself. And this, for me, is the second great value of this book.

When Miss Ward, for example, speaks of the modern Christian's "limitation of compassion" or when she observes that today the "good Samaritan asks to see a passport before he sets to work," her indignation is that essential moral element which is inseparable from Christian culture.

And when Christopher Dawson notes that the "old domination of classical humanism has passed away," that "nothing has taken its place except the scientific specialisms which . . . tend to distintegrate into technologies," he does so, not for the sake of fox-hole sniping, but rather because he wants to underline a more fundamental point, that Christians must "realize" their "spiritual and historical identity" and they must restore that "missing link" of Christian culture without which Western culture and Western education cannot survive.

A third value of the present collection is what it tells us about Christian culture itself. The scope of Christian culture, as I say, emerges as necessarily catholic, as universal. The spirit of that culture is healthily introspective. And the content and orientation of that culture are personalist. The personalism is communicated at times directly, most often obliquely. One learns a great deal about Christian culture not only through immediate instruction but also from witnessing Christians at work within that culture, as, for example, when we read Dorothy Donnelly's "Men and Symbols" or Hugh Kenner's "The Book as Book." Christian culture, as such, is seen from the viewpoint of each of the writers in this book, and, while no one of the viewpoints exhausts the meaning of that culture, together they form a fairly comprehensive treatment.

The appearance of this volume at the present juncture in human history is particularly significant. Times have not changed so greatly since Sigrid Undset's lecture ("Amid the Encircling Gloom") that we cannot still profit from her observation: "Far worse than all the horrors (of war) is the evidence that men who have felt called upon to be leaders have chosen lies as their chief weapon."

But this alone does not say all that can be said about the timeliness of this collection of humanist and cultural statements. In the world at large, the evidence is impressively massive that Western man, who had been told to pin all his hopes and ground his deepest aspirations exclusively on intellect, science, technology, has begun to look elsewhere for the answers to his ultimate questions, to the questions that reach, as Etienne Gilson notes, beyond science and into the realm of wisdom. Even the scientists, says Gilson, "on the basis of their science, are beginning to ask metaphysical and theological questions."

Marxian man and capitalistic man are also disappointing. The horizon, the dream and promise of both is terminal in this life.

Esthetics, as Miss Donnelly says, can correct, with its own "magical distortion" the "distortion in the direction of the commonplace and the ugly which misdirects us as to the quality of life by seeming to make little of it." But beauty, of itself, cannot be the ultimate satisfaction of man's primordial thirst — beauty's purpose, says Miss Donnelly, is to send out a ray "which points to beauty's source."

What the present collection of articles and addresses seems in a fair way to accomplish is the transmission of its own ray pointing back not to all the answers to all the questions which today perplex man and which seem to have pushed him to the brink of hopelessness; but it points to at least some of the answers to some of the questions.

It points, too, to the presence of an intelligent, articulate and thoughtful group of Christian men and women (of whom the contributors to this book are a representative sample) who are themselves concerned with the same fundamental problems and questions which trouble thoughtful men and women of every faith, or of no faith.

It is important, I think, that Christians contribute what they can of truth to the common striving and efforts of all men for a better world in which the human person might flourish and mature. It is no less important that Christians disclose their fundamental sympathy in and for that common striving.

Too often, whether consciously or not, we tend, as Senator Eugene McCarthy of Minnesota once said, to "judge" the world rather than contribute to it. While judgment is certainly indispensable, if that is our sole interest in the world, it is safe to predict that the world will have little time and less patience for our pronouncements. What the writers in this book seem to have achieved vis-à-vis the world is identification without assimilation; they are sympathetic, but not sentimental.

Ordinarily a Preface is not a vehicle for personal encomiums, but I cannot resist a word of praise for the editor of these essays and lectures, Father J. Stanley Murphy, C.S.B.

It has always seemed to me that a major lecture on an important subject deserves a far greater audience than that which was in the lecture hall at the time it was delivered. Indeed, I have written several columns on this subject in the American Catholic diocesan press.

It is with personal satisfaction, then, that I thank Father Murphy for extending the life and the influence of a number of the Christian Culture lectures given at Assumption University in Windsor through the publication of this volume. As a matter of fact, in reading these lectures, I realized anew that, had it not been for Father Murphy's enterprise and the Helicon Press' interest and support, I would undoubtedly never have had the opportunity to read most of the material in this book.

Perhaps the present volume will be the beginning, by the editor and the publisher, or by others, of a series of books of "vital speeches" by the leading thinkers of our time. Surely a problem which can engage for several months or longer the serious efforts of a Christian humanist and intellectual as he prepares his lecture, is important enough, once the lecture is given, to be given extended consideration through the wider distribution of that lecture in book and/or magazine form. The book herewith presented, in addition to its other merits, shows, I think, that the amplified consideration and distribution is both feasible and desirable.

Donald McDonald

On Christian Culture

John Cogley

John Cogley was born in Chicago, Illinois, in 1916, and at present makes his home in Santa Barbara, California with his wife and six children. He is director of the Center for the Study of Democratic Institutions of the Fund of the Republic. As founding editor of Today, *he has been prominent in journalism. He was executive editor of* Commonweal *for six years and has been a regular columnist for that magazine for the past fifteen years. Under the auspices of the Fund of the Republic he edited the two-volume* Report on Blacklisting *in 1956. He was editor of the books,* Catholicism in America *(1954) and* Religion in America *(1958). He belongs to the Board of Trustees of the Church Peace Union, is a member of the advisory board of the National Student Association and also is a consultant for the Jacques Maritain Institute of Notre Dame University. John Cogley is unusually well fitted for his role as a spokesman to clarify issues touching on the spiritual and the temporal. After majoring in philosophy at Loyola University, Chicago, he pursued further studies in philosophy and theology at Fribourg, Switzerland. He knows that the primacy of the spiritual need not, and should not, mean the neglect of the temporal. John Cogley, the twentieth annual recipient, accepted the Christian Culture Award for 1960 on April 10th and spoke specifically on Christian culture.*

Is THERE such a thing as Christian Culture anymore, and if there is not, what can we do about it? These are the questions I have assigned to myself.

In reply to the first, I cannot claim to be either as pessimistic as those who see nothing but "secularism" when they look out at the world, or as optimistic as those who believe that the renaissance of the older Christian culture and the revival of a world long dead remains a possibility. Even if I could summon such optimism, I do not believe I would await the "revival" with enthusiasm.

First, let us take the argument of the pessimists. They say that Christian Culture is totally gone and has been replaced by the cursed thing they call "secularism." To a degree, I have to tell them they are right, for I would not go so far as to say that the culture "out there" is Christian in the sense that is is shaped exclusively, or even primarily, by Christian dogmas and beliefs. At best, ours is a pluralistic culture in this sense. Christianity is only a strand, albeit a very strong strand, of the whole.

But while granting all that, I cannot agree that our culture is as cut off from Christianity as we sometimes claim it is. For in some important ways the very "secular" values which have replaced earlier "religious" values may be more authentically Christian than the "religious" values ever were. For instance, consider our advance in science, not only physical science but the social and biological sciences as well. Certainly we can exaggerate their importance, and frequently do, but haven't they widened our knowledge of God's universe and revealed to us great stretches of natural truth, which is no less God's truth than those truths received through His revelation? Would anyone argue that a true knowledge of science is more "Christian" than the hodgepodge of science and theology which held back man's knowledge of the universe in the ages of faith? Or take the development of political liberty, another important element of our culture. Could it not well be argued that the modern "secular" state, granting freedom to its citizens, constitutionally calling a halt on its own powers and scrupulously safeguarding the human rights and dignity of those who live under it, is far more "Christian" than anything the "sacral" societies produce? Or would anyone deny, to move to another field, that modern psychiatry is more "Christian" than witch-burning; that the First Amendment to the American Constitution is a more "Christian" institution than the Spanish Inquisition; that the Fourteenth Amendment, banishing slavery, is more "Christian" than the canonization of medieval serfdom?

Of course we would all have to acknowledge, sadly and contritely I hope, that many of the elements of modern culture were seeded in religious rebellion and brought forth in pride of intellect. In a manner of speaking, then, we would have to acknowledge that the culture we have was, in a sense, conceived in sin. But I do not believe we should despair of it or deny the possibility of its redemption for that reason. There is always baptism to wipe away the Original Sin, and from the beginning the Church has been baptizing the cultures she found herself in.

As for the optimists who talk of "revivals" and "renaissances" of the older Christian culture, it seems to me that they have mistaken the basic problem. They talk endlessly of "secularism" as the disease that infected our present culture. I tend to think that they have chosen the wrong word, or at least that they put their emphasis in the wrong place. It is not so much an exaggeration of the secular that characterizes modern culture as a misplaced "sacralism," if I may invent a word to describe what happens when the secular is given the place that belongs to the sacred. Our problem will not be solved by despising secular values or denying the truths discovered under secular (or even secularist) auspices. That will only widen the breach between Christianity and modern culture. Our problem is to challenge the modern idolatry, for it is idolatry more than godlessness that poisons cultural life today. What we often identify as godless is really not that at all; it is the worship of false gods. The secular has been turned into the sacred. It would be foolish to try to undo that by replacing the secular with the sacred. In fact, to do so would only compound the problem. The challenge, rather, is to show the relevance between the authentically secular and the authentically sacred. Until that is done, many Christians will continue to feel ill at ease in modern culture, as Christians would feel out of place in any idolatrous atmosphere.

We know that there are Christians who experience this alienation more than others and who, feeling obliged to create a kind of underground culture in their pursuit of perfection, cut themselves off from the central stream of cultural life. Even among the laity, a few Catholics have virtually withdrawn from the world in pursuit of integralism of this kind. They have organized little enclaves of Catholic culture here and there. For temperamental reasons if no other, I personally could never feel a vocation to such a calling, but would not want to seem to be belittling its importance in the total scheme of things. Even though the groups I have in mind may be layfolk, their wisdom is essentially monastic, and after two thousand years of Christian history we know that the monastic response serves the world better than the world has usually realized. Saint Benedict, centuries ago, practiced a kind of withdrawal — or to use a word invidious in today's context, a kind of separatism — and Benedict, after all, is a hero of Christian civilization. In the long run he contributed more to the life of the world than any dozen of the earnest *engagés* who involved themselves in the world's immediate problems.

But monasticism, even for a Benedict, must be a special vocation. The Church itself, while it encouraged him and his disciples, could not follow the same policy of withdrawal. Nor can the Church withdraw from the world today. For most Christians, whether they be in the lay state, the religious or the clerical, withdrawal is out of the question. Our deepest problem, then, arises from the fact that while we are required to remain *in* the world, we have been solemnly warned not to become *of* the world, worldly. Here, probably very few of us succeed, for the culture of the world is imperialistic and all of us more or less succumb to it at times. But we have to keep trying. And the effort required, I take it, must be so constant, so indefatigable, that no Christian can escape the true anguish of his essential vocation — which after all is first and foremost to be a Christian and only secondarily to succeed in his state of life.

I have spoken sympathetically of the few who have been called to withdrawal so that they may, as it were, be like lighthouses seated on a mountain top. I have no such sympathy for the pseudo-withdrawal which conceives of the Christian vocation in terms essentially negative and carping. The genuine monastic vocation is to withdraw from the world in order to serve the world. The pseudo-withdrawal I am thinking of requires one to stay in the world in order to snipe away at it from some sectarian fox-hole. It apparently conceives of the Christian as the eternal enemy of the natural world and of Christianity as unremittingly hostile to every manifestation of secular culture. It has succeeded in getting across the idea that the believing man has no concern for values of truth and beauty which are not specifically "religious" — in the theological or, what is worse, in the institutional sense. As a result, we find too often that there has been a break between the men of culture and the men of the Church. It is a tragic break. It is tragic, most of all, because it is unnecessary. We know, as Saint Thomas Aquinas taught, that every genuine truth proceeds from the Holy Spirit. The Church can never be the enemy of the true and the beautiful, no matter how alien their apparent source or how "secular" their uses. And he who makes it appear as if such is the case, seems to me guilty of a terrible mischief, for in a manner of speaking he is smashing the only mirrors in which men without faith can see the image of God.

Let this be said, too. The Church is not the bearer of a cultural imperialism, though we must admit that the greatest missionary failures in the past arose from the fact that some of its apostles, with every good intention in the world, behaved as if it were. They could not conceive of a genuinely Christian culture that was not an adaptation of the Western European. But other missionaries, more foresighted men in my opinion, have held that the Church is neither to be identified with a cultural form nor to be regarded as the enemy of any manifestation of human genius. Rather, the Church stands ready to purify and to respect the forms of even the most exotic cultures. Men like Dom Bede Griffiths, the English Benedictine who is now pioneering in the Orient with a missionary monasticism typically Indian, have written eloquently of the need to adapt the Christian apostolate to what one finds "out there," as the early Church spoke of the West in terms which the West understood. As the Jesuit Father Karl Rahner points out, when it became possible for Christianity as a social force to move out beyond the European continent, the idea of a single manifestation of Christian culture became out of the question. Even if this uniformity were possible, it would not be desirable. In the sense that grace is built on nature, in that sense every genuine Christian culture is built on the pre-existing forms and genuine values already accepted.

All this may be clear enough in the case of pre-Christian civilizations — the Roman Empire of old, the Orient and Africa of today. But what of our post-Christian culture in the Western world? Does the same principle apply? Now, obviously, it cannot be applied in any univocal sense. The situations confronting a Dom Bede in pre-Christian India, his adopted land, and a Dom Bede at post-Christian Oxford, his alma mater, are quite different. It is not necessary to consider the difference between a culture which was developed without the influence of Christianity, such as one finds in India, and one which has followed after a once-thriving Christian culture.

Here in the West, we are not starting from scratch, as it were; and the Christian influence is still strong. Our educated elite is familiar with an age when Christianity was the unchallenged cultural force. There was much in those ages, of course, that we are still delighted to see pass away, and other things that we wish had been retained. But however we feel about it, there is no hope of restoring a Christian culture in its ancient form. As Thomas Wolfe said, "You can't go home again," and that applies to mankind as equally as it does to individual men.

So in the post-Christian West, we have a problem somewhat different from, and yet somewhat the same as, the problems facing Dom

Bede Griffiths of India. It is different insofar as the Orient is not the West where a recognizably Christian culture is our oldest ancestral memory. It is the same, insofar as the problem is one of establishing *relevance* — the relevance of what the world already knows of the good, the true and beautiful to the Goodness, Truth and Beauty which Christianity proclaims in the name of God. We have a kind of double problem: first, to show the relevance of our actual existing culture to Christianity; and, second, to show the relevance of Christianity to our actual existing culture. This twin assignment faces anyone concerned with Christianity and Culture.

It is not an easy assignment. I confess I would be thoroughly suspicious of any formula which promised to show precisely how it can be done. The movement for a Christian culture — or for Christianizing (or re-Christianizing) the culture we have — will have to move slowly on many fronts. So please do not think that I feel I have The Big Answer if I make one suggestion. I am acutely aware that the proposal I am about to make covers only one aspect of the problem. Still, I believe it is an important aspect.

It has to do with theology, theology as an academic discipline, an important branch of university studies. Let me say, first of all, that I believe theology belongs in the university, whether the university be a religious or a secular institution. It belongs there as a branch of learning. Mind you, I am not speaking of apologetics or of glorified catechism classes or of boy-scoutish training in moral and spiritual values. All these have their place, somewhere if not in the university. When I use the word "theology," however, I am not thinking anything like this. Rather, I am claiming that theology as an intellectual discipline deserves a place in any serious academic curriculum — on its own merits as it were. I know that from time to time we hear plaintive pleas that theology be reinstated as queen of the sciences, and all that. But I would be happy enough if it were merely restored to a respectable place in the university.

It may be worth spelling out that when I speak of theology in the university, I do not have in mind extending the theological course which is taught to students preparing for the priesthood. Certainly the seminary must remain as a specialized form of theological education, rather like the law school or the medical college, designed to turn out competent professional men — not professional speculative theologians, necessarily, but professional clergymen, professional practitioners, as it were. However, the university theology I am pleading for would have no such immediate practical end in view. I would like to see it treated, instead, as an academic discipline whose foremost end is to contribute to the cultivation of genuinely educated men. In a word, I would like to see it take its place as a normal part of the liberal-arts curriculum. And let me stress again that I do not have in mind anything like the traditional college religion class, which is necessarily didactic. What I do have in mind is exposing students to theological speculation, as they are exposed to philosophic and scientific speculation.

You can see, then, that I am calling for a lay theology — "lay" not in the sense that it is directed to the layman as such but in the sense that it is not thought of primarily in trade-school terms at all, either as a preparation for the sacred ministry, or for the lay apostolate. "Academic theology," as I use the phrase, would be just as suitable to clerics as to the laity, for there is no reason in the world why the clergy should not be as liberally educated as their parishioners. The whole question of lay and cleric in such a class would be fairly beside the point.

I think I have said enough to indicate how I feel about the subject. I would like to see a flowering of what might be called academic theology — as distinct from seminary theology — in all Catholic institutions of higher learning. I would like to see Graduate Schools of Academic Theology established in the larger institutions, departments open to the laity of course and ultimately conducted in great part by competent laymen who have their doctorates in the sacred science. And, incidentally, if it is necessary to establish a new academic degree to distinguish these university theologians from seminary theologians — well, then, by all means, let us establish the new degree. But however it be done, it is important that theology be installed in the Catholic universities as an important intellectual discipline. It is equally important that, in time, Catholic theology find a place in the secular universities as well.

If the Catholic institutions can produce academically qualified scholars, enough to place at least one and hopefully more theologians in all the major secular universities, would not the Catholic universities thereby be making a tremendous contribution to the nation's intellectual life? And this contribution can only be made by the Catholic universities; no one else can do it.

Should these theological scholars be priests or laymen? I suppose it really does not make a great deal of difference so long as they do not regard themselves either as missionaries or as pastors-on-campus but simply as academics who are neither specially privileged nor specially burdened beyond their confreres in the university community. Yet I must confess that this kind of assignment might normally be done more easily by a layman than by a priest. The layman could come to it with fewer demands on his life and more ample space to move around in the intellectual give-and-take of modern university life. Moreover, if theology is to be related to life and life to theology — which I take it is the *sine qua non* of Christian culture — the training of laymen-theologians has to be developed more systematically than it has been. If the times have taught us anything it is that theology can no longer be the exclusive preoccupation of churchmen. The advance of the physical sciences, the development of the social sciences, even the turn literature has taken, all these changes have made it impossible for the thinking man on any campus to avoid asking theological questions. And should not we Catholics be a little ashamed of the fact that every conceivable answer to modern man's difficulties is found in the American university except the response offered by Catholic theology? At the same time, questions are arising in every phase of modern life with which theology, theology-as-an-intellectual-discipline, alone can deal.

I realize this fact may have escaped the attention of our present theologians. I take it they may have missed it because the questions that haunt men of the world do not ordinarily arise in the seminaries as they do on other campuses. That happy situation may be due to the fact that seminary theology is satisfactorily answering the questions seminarians ask. Remember, though, that the questions seminarians ask are not the kind of questions being asked, and going unanswered, elsewhere.

Ploughing a Lone Furrow

Christopher Dawson

Christopher Dawson was born in Yorkshire, England, in 1889. He engaged in studies first at Winchester and later at Trinity College, Oxford. A sensitive and fastidious scholar, well-read in many fields, including theology, he is equally at home, like Newman, in the great movements of history. Having foreseen long ago the advent of the totalitarian state and the present crisis in the world, he has done much to arouse interested men, especially scholars, to think about solutions. During the years of World War II, his inspiration given to the great "Sword of the Spirit" movement will never be forgotten. Someone once said that this movement was "born of the intellect of Dawson, the vision of Cardinal Hinsley, and the energy of Barbara Ward." Dawson might be called a constitutional democrat. Fortunately in this volume there is a study of Dawson, along with Arnold J. Toynbee, that other well-known historian of culture of our century. Some of Dawson's great studies include Progress and Religion, The Age of the Gods, The Making of Europe, Enquiries, Understanding Europe, The Judgement of the Nations, Beyond Politics, Christianity and the Rise of Western Culture, Movement of World Revolution, Dynamics of World History, *and* The Historic Reality of Christian Culture. *Aberdeen University accorded Dawson in 1947–48 a most unusual honor by appointing him to give the famed Gifford Lectures for two successive years. In 1958, Dawson came to Harvard University Divinity School to become the first occupant, for either a three- or five-year period, of the Charles Chauncey Stillman chair of Roman Catholic Studies. Christopher Dawson was the Christian Culture Award Medallist for 1951. The following essay is an expansion of his acceptance address.*

WHEN I SAY that I am deeply grateful for the honor conferred on me, I wish to convey more than a conventional expression of thanks. In the world of the universities and of organized scientific research,

such awards are not unfamiliar, although they must always be grati-
fying. But the individual who works alone in his own little field, and
not as a member of a team, seldom has an opportunity of getting this
kind of public recognition, so when it comes it means more to him
than to others.

No doubt, in England there has always been a tradition of private,
unorganized individual study, and English history in the past has
owed no less to it than to the professional historians.

But there is no longer any room for this tradition in the modern
world, where modern methods of co-ordinated research combine with
social and economic conditions to make it impossible. If, therefore, I
have had to follow my own line of studies and plough a lone furrow
for thirty-five years, it is not because I could afford to dispense with
the help of others, but simply and solely because the subject to which
I have devoted myself — the study of Christian culture — has no
place in education or in university studies. [1] Although the range of
modern university studies has been extended in every direction for
the past hundred years, this subject, which is certainly not the least
important, still remains almost unrecognized.

What is the reason for this state of things ? Chiefly I think the idea
that religion is essentially subjective — an affair of private opinion and
personal feeling, while education must concern itself only with the
world of objective reality, with facts and events and economic forces.

Actually this idea is irreconcilable with the nature of history, and
no true historian has ever accepted it in practice, whatever his theories
may be. For Christian culture is just as much a part of historical reality, as classical culture or the culture of Islam, while it is a great deal
more important for us, since we cannot understand our own past
without it.

Beyond religious and secularist prejudices, however, there exists a
great obstacle to this study that is strictly cultural. It has its origins in
the idealization of classical antiquity by the humanist scholars and
artists who rediscovered the beauty of nature. And it followed from
this conception that the period that intervened between the fall of
Rome and the Renaissance offered the historian as Voltaire says, "the
barren prospect of a thousand years of stupidity and barbarism." They
were "middle ages" in the original sense of the word — that is, a kind
of cultural vacuum between those two ages of cultural achievement

---

[1] Since this statement was made, St. Mary's College, Notre Dame, has inaugurated
a major course in Christian Culture [Ed. note].

which (to continue the same quotation) "vindicate the greatness of the human spirit."

This view, which necessarily ignores the achievements and even the existence of Christian culture, was passed on almost unchanged from the Renaissance to the 18th-century Enlightenment, and from the latter to the modern secularist ideologies. And though today every instructed person recognizes that it is based on a completely erroneous view of history, and very largely on sheer ignorance of history, it still continues to exert an immense influence, both consciously and unconsciously, on modern education and on our attitude to the past.

It is therefore necessary for educators to make a positive effort to exorcise the ghost of this ancient error and to give the study of Christian culture the place that it deserves in modern education. We cannot leave this to the medievalists alone, for they are to some extent tied to the error by the limitation of their specialism. For Christian culture is not the same thing as medieval culture. It existed before the Middle Ages began and it continued to exist after they had ended. We cannot understand medieval culture unless we understand its foundations in the age of the Fathers and the Christian Empire, and we cannot understand the classical vernacular literatures of post-Renaissance Europe unless we study their roots in medieval culture. Even the Renaissance itself, as Konrad Burdach [2] and E. R. Curtius [3] have shown, is not intelligible unless it is studied as part of a movement which had its origins deep in the Middle Ages.

Now it seems to me that the time is ripe for a new approach to the subject, since our whole educational system — and not in one country alone, but throughout the Western world — is passing through a period of rapid and fundamental change. The old domination of classical humanism has passed away, and nothing has taken its place except the scientific specialisms which do not provide a complete intellectual education, but rather tend to disintegrate into technologies. Every educator recognizes that this is unsatisfactory. A scientific specialist or a technologist who has nothing but his specialty is not an educated person. He tends to become merely an instrument of the industrialist or the bureaucrat, a worker ant in an insect society, and the same is true of the literary specialist, though his social function is less obvious.

[2] Konrad Burdach, 1859–1936, an eminent German scholar; his voluminous works on language, culture and criticism have not been translated [Ed. note].

[3] *European Literature and the Latin Middle Ages* (London: Routledge and Kegan Paul, 1952); trans. from German ed., 1948, by W. R. Trask [Ed. note].

But even the totalitarians do not accept this solution; on the contrary, they insist most strongly on the importance of the cultural element in education whether their ideal of culture is nationalist and racial as with the Nazis, or cosmopolitan and proletarian as with the communists. No doubt from our point of view this totalitarian culture means the forcible indoctrination of scientist and worker alike, with the same narrow party ideology, but at least it does provide a simple remedy for the disintegrating effects of modern specialization and gives the whole educational system a unifying purpose.

Some cultural education is necessary if Western culture is to survive, and we can no longer rely exclusively on the traditional discipline of classical humanism, though this is the source of all that was best in the tradition of Western liberalism and Western science.

I believe that the study of Christian culture is the missing link which is essential to supply if the tradition of Western education and Western culture is to survive, for it is only through this study that we can understand how Western culture came to exist and what are the essential values for which it stands.

And when I speak of Western culture I am not using the word in the limited sense in which it was used by Matthew Arnold and the humanists who were concerned only with the highest level of cultivated intelligence, but in the sense of the anthropologists and social historians who have widened it out to cover the whole pattern of human life and thought in a living society. In this sense of the word, a culture is a definite historical unit, but as Dr. Toynbee explains so clearly in the Introduction to his *Study of History*,[4] it has a much wider expansion in space and time than any purely political unit, and it alone constitutes an intelligible field of historical study since no part of it can be properly understood except in relation to the whole.

Now, behind the existing unity of Western culture we have the older unity of Christian culture which is the historic basis of our civilization. For more than a thousand years, from the conversion of the Roman Empire until the Reformation, the peoples of Europe were fully conscious of their membership in the great Christian society and accepted the Christian faith and the Christian moral law as the ultimate bond of social unity and the spiritual basis of their way of life. And even after the unity of Christendom had been broken by the Reformation, the tradition of Christian culture still survived in the

[4] Arnold J. Toynbee, *A Study of History, Vol. IV* (London: Oxford University Press, 1936).

culture and institutions of the different European peoples, and in some cases exists even in the midst of our secularized culture, as was apparent in the English coronation rite of Queen Elizabeth II, June 2, 1953.

Consequently anyone who wishes to understand our own culture as it exists today cannot dispense with the study of Christian culture, whether he is a Christian or not. Indeed in some ways this study is more necessary for the secularist than for the Christian because he lacks the ideological key to the understanding of the past which every Christian ought to possess.

The more we can realize our spiritual and historical identity by the study of Christian culture, the better we shall be able to withstand the forces of secularization. For behind all the temporal vicissitudes of Christian history and the changing fortunes of Christendom there stands the reality of the one great society which is the hope of humanity and which St. Peter defined in a memorable sentence as a "chosen race, a royal priesthood, a holy nation, a special people . . . who in times past were not a people but are now the people of God." [5] All through the ages we see the creative process of sifting and regeneration and re-education out of which a new humanity is being formed; and the history of this process is the only history that really counts for the Christian.

The Christian Culture Award, then, is doubly welcome to me, if I can regard it as a sign that the educationalists of the New World are beginning to revise these old ideas and preparing to take a wider and more scientific view of the nature and significance of Christian culture. At Assumption University of Windsor, Canada, you stand at a strategic point on the frontier of two great nations and are therefore in a good position to survey all that is being done for higher education in the United States, while retaining the freedom and initiative of an independent society with its own political and educational traditions.

[5] 1 Peter 2:9.

Toynbee and Dawson on the Meaning of Contemporary History

Thomas P. Neill

Dr. Neill is professor of History at St. Louis University. Formerly he taught at Aquinas College, Grand Rapids. He is a prolific but meticulously accurate writer, and his books include such titles as Weapons for Peace, Makers of the Modern Mind, They Lived the Faith, The Rise and Decline of Liberalism, Religion and Culture, *and* 1859 in Review. *He was elected President of the American Catholic Historical Association for 1954. He is co-author of* History of the Catholic Church. *He was born in 1915 in Colorado. He received his B.A. from St. Louis University, his M.A. from the University of Notre Dame, and his Ph.D. from St. Louis University. He lives in St. Louis with his wife and nine children.*

IN THIS discussion we are concerned not with the totality of Arnold Toynbee's and Christopher Dawson's thought but rather with how their analyses of the historical process cause them to see contemporary civilization differently and propose different resolutions of the "modern dilemma." Both Toynbee and Dawson believe that we live in a time of crisis. Neither takes the superficial view that this crisis came about because of atomic bombs and the possibility of mass destruction, nor do they hold that it is basically the threat of communism. Both see it a long time in developing, several centuries in fact, and both analyze it in spiritual and social terms rather than technological and economic. Neither Toynbee nor Dawson is a determinist; both insist on individual freedom and on the freedom of a civilization to solve problems in one way or another, and thus they both leave the future open. Here Toynbee has more difficulty than Dawson, for he finds that twenty civilizations have followed the same course and — despite his protests that he is not a determinist — is not convincing when he insists that the twenty-first civilization need not follow the same course of disintegration.

Toynbee and Dawson both take a theological view of history. Strictly speaking, neither works as an historian but rather as a scholar who uses historical data to generalize about the meaning of history and of life. Dawson is considerably more Christo-centric in his view of history than is Toynbee — a decisive fact in their differing interpretations of the contemporary crisis — for Dawson accepts Revelation and considers the Incarnation and Redemption as the unique personal intervention by God in human history. Toynbee, on the other hand, attempts to arrive at a knowledge of God empirically from a study of history. Dawson thus puts Judeo-Christian history in a central position, pivotal to all history, whereas Toynbee considers it one among many histories, all of which are fundamentally similar and equal.

A further preliminary comparison involves the areas in which these two men work and their respective methods of arriving at interpretations of the historical process. Dawson confines himself to smaller areas of history than does Toynbee, although he is well informed on Asiatic and African developments and makes use of his knowledge for revealing comparisons. Dawson is concerned primarily with Western history. Toynbee, on the other hand, ranges through all ages and all cultures, apparently as much at home in one as in another. Whereas Dawson treats the data of history as a sociologist and anthropologist who occasionally uses the wisdom of Revelation, Toynbee's treatment of history is essentially poetic. He relies, he tells us, on flashes of insight or private revelations to see the meaning behind the facts of history. Dawson is more the plodding scholar whose generalizations are cautious, whereas Toynbee is the man of imagination who relies on intuition as much as on empirical evidence to arrive at his conclusions.

Toynbee is a many-sided man. He was first an historian of the Hellenic civilization who was led to a wider study of history to "feel after Him (God) and find Him." [1] His inquiry led him to compare twenty civilizations, including our own Western, with Hellenic civilization to see whether the same course is always followed — but ultimately to find the God of History Who works through time to achieve His design. "The meaning behind the facts of History towards which the poetry in the facts is leading us is a revelation of God." [2] History is "a vision — dim and partial, yet true to reality as far as it went — of

---

[1] Arnold J. Toynbee, *A Study of History*, (Oxford University Press: London, New York, Toronto, 1954) X, p. 1, quoting the *Acts of the Apostles*, 17:27.

[2] *Ibid*, X, p. 126.

God revealing Himself in action to souls that were sincerely seeking Him . . . History's contribution is to give us a vision of God's creative activity on the move.[3]

Toynbee's *A Study of History* is therefore basically theological. It was conceived and planned when three "philosophies" of history competed for acceptance: the optimistic late-nineteenth century Progress view of history, the early-twentieth century Organic theory of Spengler, and the Marxian dialectic materialism. All three pretended to give an ultimate explanation of the meaning and the direction of history. All three eliminated the traditional God of Western culture from history as Creator, End, and Sustainer of history. All three, moreover, were materialistic and ultimately deterministic. Against these explanations of the ultimate meaning of history Toynbee renewed — in a strange and somewhat distorted way — the older Christian tradition, more in the fashion of Vico than of Augustine or Bossuet. This renewal coincided with an apparent Christian revival that made it fashionable to talk in theological terms and to speak seriously of Providence again. Thus Toynbee succeeded, with vast erudition and a world-encompassing urbanity, to reintroduce God into historical thinking, not merely as the Creator of the deists but as the Providential God Who weaves the cloth of history on the loom of time.

Although Toynbee is a specialist in Hellenic history, he writes his voluminous *Study* as a humanist who is at home with modern science, with the literature of all ages and all cultures, who is intimately acquainted with the Bible (which he cites several thousand times in his ten volumes), with classical literature, and with the classics of other cultures. The work he has produced is therefore rich. But underneath it lies a skeletal pattern to which he faithfully adheres. The intelligible unit of history is a civilization (through the first seven volumes), and the purpose of the inquiry is to discover the meaning of history through a comparative study of the world's civilizations. The first three volumes, published in 1934, deal with the genesis and growth of various civilizations. After examining the racialist and environmentalist explanations of the genesis of civilizations, Toynbee rejects them as explanations in physical-science terms of a problem that is really spiritual. He finds that the genesis of any civilization can best be explained in terms of response to a challenge presented by the physical or human environment. If the challenge is sufficiently strong, but not overwhelming, a society's response to it brings a civilization

[3] *Ibid*, X, p. 1-2.

into being. Civilizations grow, Toynbee tells us, by continuing to meet successfully the challenges which confront them, challenges which are internal rather than external, spiritual rather than material. He finds that growth originates with creative individuals or minorities who generally pass their creative discoveries on to the masses through the process of "mimesis" or imitation.

The next three volumes, published as a unit in 1939, trace the pattern of breakdown and disintegration of civilizations. Here Toynbee enters on a more difficult field, but one of greater interest to our age because Western civilization is seen to be somewhere in the process of breakdown and we are anxious to know what Toynbee's prognosis, explicit or implicit, is for our future. He sums up breakdown under three main points: 1) a failure of creative power in the creative minority, which becomes a dominant rather than a creative group accepted by the rest of society; 2) a resulting withdrawal of allegiance and mimesis by the majority; 3) a consequent loss of social unity within the civilization.

Toynbee examines and rejects the deterministic explanations, such as Spengler's, that the breakdown of a civilization is inevitable and is outside human control. He also rejects the explanation that it is due to aggression from outside. In each case he tries to show that decay of technical achievement and failure against outside aggressors are the result of breakdown that has already occurred rather than a cause of breakdown. This involves a readjustment of the timetable, on the growth and decline of civilizations, that has been challenged by many historians. Nevertheless it includes several suggestive "laws" which implicitly apply to Western civilization in its "time of troubles." The most important of these are three forms of the "nemesis of creativity," idolization of an ephemeral self, idolization of an ephemeral institution, and idolization of an ephemeral technique. The basic point in each case is that an institution or a technique, that is once successful ensnares a people into using it when it becomes outmoded.

Disintegration follows breakdown when the body social breaks into three fractions: the dominant minority, the internal proletariat, and the external proletariat. After discussing the characteristics and the role of each of these bodies, Toynbee rather arbitrarily sets forth alternative ways of behavior, feeling, and life: abandon and self-control, truancy and martyrdom, the sense of drift and the sense of sin, the sense of promiscuity and the sense of unity, archaism and futurism, detachment and transfiguration. A considerable section is

24

also devoted to the role of creative individuals who, in the disintegration stage, appear as saviors of one form or another (the military man, for example, the philosopher, and the religious leader) to rescue the disintegrating society.

Two last points remain in the section on disintegration. One is that standardization is the mark of disintegration, as differentiation is a mark of growth. The second is that disintegration does not proceed by a straight-line process but rather by a series of "routs" and "rallies." In tracing out these routs and rallies Toynbee seems quite arbitrary, and most historians agree that he does considerable violence to history. At any rate, he concludes that the normal pattern is three-and-a-half beats: rout-rally-rout-rally-rout-rally-rout. The time of troubles which the West has been experiencing is an example of the "rout" beat, and the universal state is a "rally" beat.

The last four volumes of Toynbee's *A Study of History* differ markedly from the first six. The change in outlook is due partly to the world upheaval between 1939 and 1946, when Toynbee returned to work on the *Study*. It is also due partly to a crisis in Toynbee's personal affairs. "At the same time," he tells us after alluding to the Great War, "my inner world had been undergoing changes which, on the miniature scale of an individual life, were, for me, of proportionate magnitude." [4] Finally, the change is due partly to the very nature of Toynbee's inquiry, for he is led to see that civilizations are no longer intelligible units of study in an age of disintegration and his quest for the meaning in history leads him to study universal states and higher religions.

The last four volumes deal with the products of the three fractions of the body social during the period of disintegration: the universal state, created by the dominant minority; the universal religion created by the internal proletariat; and the pressures created by the external proletariat. Here Toynbee says that the universal state is not an end in itself but that it serves as a means, primarily for the birth and progress of a universal religion. Here Toynbee leaves the reader — and the civilization under consideration — hanging in mid-air. For when a civilization has served its function of generating a new religion it is not going to wither quietly away. Moreover, a religion must take embodiment in a civilization. A religion cannot be indifferent to civilization, as Toynbee seems to think it should, and Christians cannot subscribe to the theological equivalence of the higher religions

* *Ibid*, VII.

that Toynbee substitutes in these volumes for the philosophic equivalence of civilizations in the earlier volumes.

Despite his "distaste" for the task, Toynbee felt compelled to write a 240-page chapter on "The Prospects for the Western Civilization" because it "was perhaps the only extant representative of its species that did not show indisputable signs of being already in disintegration." [5] and because Western civilization had become for all practical purposes world-wide by 1950. Toynbee sees our own civilization as being in the breakdown stage, more precisely in its "time of troubles." But there are no "indisputable signs of being already in disintegration. . . . In A.D. 1952 the plot of this Occidental drama had not yet arrived at its denouement." [6] Toynbee's hope is that "a transfer of energy from Economics to Religion . . . might ultimately come to a self-stultified Western *Homo Economicus'* rescue." [7]

More specifically, Toynbee offers suggestions for the direction Western civilization can take, and these are based on a political and spiritual analysis of its problems. Following his general scheme, he sees the coming of the universal state, but this time the world is dividing around the United States and the U.S.S.R. into two such states. "In these perilous circumstances," he says, "the best hope for the future of Mankind lay in the possibility that the governments and peoples of the United States and the Soviet Union might have the imagination, wisdom, tolerance, self-restraint, patience, and fortitude to seek and ensue the one alternative to a third world war that, at this state, was practical politics: that is to say, a pacific partition of the *Oikoumenê* (human habitat) between these two surviving Powers for an indefinite time to come." [8]

On the spiritual plane Toynbee sees some grounds of hope for Western civilization in that it has done a better job of social amelioration than any previous civilization, as in a material way it has outstripped all civilizations in mastering nature. The spiritual problem is to find some way of avoiding self-destruction without falling into self-stultification. Ultimately, this requires a true religious revival which will avoid the Christian heresy of communism, as well as "a backward-looking ecclesiastical tradition" which Toynbee apparently associates with Rome. To weather their "time of troubles" successfully men of the Western world are required to show contrite humility and

[5] *Ibid*, IX p. 411.
[6] *Ibid*, IX, p. 411.
[7] *Ibid*, IX, p. 641.
[8] *Ibid*, IX, p. 525.

indomitable endurance in the spirit of St. Francis Assisi, "the most god-like soul that had been born into the Western World so far." [9]

Whereas the Toynbee we have been discussing is a man of one ten-volume book, Dawson is the author of many short studies. But through them runs a remarkable consistency of thought which is well summed up in his three most recent publications: *Dynamics of World History*,[10] a collection of previously published essays and reviews; *Movement of World Revolution*,[11] which studies the spread of Western culture throughout the world; and *The Historic Reality of Christian Culture: A Way to the Renewal of Human Life*,[12] which succinctly restates the theses Dawson developed in his earlier works.

From Dawson's works we can extract three theses which bear on the nature of contemporary history and the prospects for Western civilization. These theses can be stated this way: 1) a religion lies at the core of every culture, and the Christian religion has informed Western culture; 2) the Western world has been losing its religion in recent centuries; 3) Western civilization has been spreading over the globe in recent decades, and therefore the future of world history depends intimately on what happens in Western civilization in the immediate future.

The first of these has been brilliantly defended by Dawson in many works, especially in his lectures on *Religion and Culture*[13] and *Religion and the Rise of Western Culture*.[14] One can indeed say that all Dawson's work centers around the key thought that religion is the dynamic element in culture. As Dawson uses the term, a culture — or a civilization — is a way of life embodied in institutions and accepting certain moral principles and basic beliefs. These have historically emanated from a religion, and this was true of Western culture in the past, for, Dawson points out, in its creative phase the West considered the religious community as absolute and other communities as relative. Sacred learning was the highest form of wisdom, and the first social duty was the public act of worship. Christian culture was essentially sacramental, for it embodied the great religious truths in visible form, in drama, architecture, literature, painting, and music.

[9] *Ibid*, IX, p. 644.
[10] Editor, John J. Mulloy, (New York: Sheed and Ward, 1956).
[11] (New York: Sheed and Ward, 1959).
[12] (New York: Harpers, 1960).
[13] Gifford Lectures at Aberdeen University, Scotland, 1947–48, (London: Sheed and Ward, 1948).
[14] Gifford Lectures, 1948–49, (New York: Sheed and Ward, 1952).

Social institutions, such as Western man's respect for women, ultimately derive from the Christian religion and from the cult of the Blessed Virgin, as such political institutions as limited government and inalienable human rights have an ultimate religious basis.

The second of these three theses can most easily be summarized under the two headings of secularization and depersonalization. The former consists of eliminating the distinctively Christian institutions and standards from the Western cultural matrix. Put more bluntly, secularization means pushing God and religion out of Western culture, replacing Him by worldly duties, and substituting secular standards for religion. In his most recent work, *The Historic Reality of Christian Culture*,[15] Dawson summarizes the process of secularization he has worked out more thoroughly in previous studies. One big step was the loss of Christian unity at the time of the Protestant Reformation, for when there came to be several competing religious sects within the culture and within each national state it became impossible for religion to speak with authority on matters of public policy, personal morality, or basic beliefs. More and more the only institution encompassing all persons in the community and possessed of authority to enforce its will was the national state, which therefore took over many functions formerly reserved to the Church.

Another big step in secularization took place as Christians abdicated their social responsibilities. Thus there grew up a body of political thought and a science of economics disassociated from and unconcerned with religious principles. Religion became more and more a private affair, and the clergy were told that social and political matters were outside their province. A third step in the process of secularization was loss of belief in a personal, providential God Who is the sustainer of history. God was replaced in many Western men's hierarchy of values with such "isms" as nationalism or communism, secularized religions in the full sense of that term. And new moral criteria, such as pragmatism and instrumentalism, were formulated to take the place of the Christian standards of morality.

Depersonalization accompanied the process of secularization and to some extent followed it with the development of empirical science and positivism, as well as the new social organization brought about by the industrial and technological revolution. Personal relationships have come to be minimized and even eliminated in many cases in industry, education, social work, medicine, and other fields. There is

[15] (New York: Harpers, 1960).

something to be gained in efficiency from automatic and semi-automatic processes, but there is always the danger of treating the human person as a thing instead of a person. In a certain sense, man, created to the image and likeness of God, has been remaking himself to the image of the machine. For depersonalization involves an implicit or explicit denial of those qualities which are distinctly human and personal. Industrialization is creating a new environment for Western man as he moves from a natural to a technical environment. He must gear his living to the rhythm of the machine and the factory instead of to the rhythm of the day and the season. Such a readjustment of life is difficult to accomplish without minimizing personal relationships and violating the mysterious inner recesses of the human person.

Dawson's third key thesis bearing on the problem of contemporary history is most succinctly stated in his *Movement of World Revolution*,[16] in which he throws light on the problems involved in the spread of Western ideas and techniques and values over the rest of the world. The important and disturbing point here is that it is a secularized Western culture which is being spread by both the Western countries and the Soviet Union, as Western industrial, military, and medical techniques are exported along with secularized Western ideas like nationalism and socialism. Dawson shows how the great awakening in Asia and Africa is directed against the older cultures of India, China, and Islam, as well as against the Western countries which bear the taint of imperialism throughout the African and Asiatic worlds. Thus the problem of revitalizing a secularized Western culture takes on a universal rather than merely a parochial importance at the middle of the twentieth century.

In facing the prospects of the future Dawson exhibits neither despair nor naïve optimism. Various recent developments give him certain grounds for hope, as is also the case with Toynbee. The renewed interest in and appreciation of religion in the West is one of these developments, and especially the intellectual and liturgical stirrings within the Catholic community. "I feel," he wrote in 1960, "that the outlook for Christian culture is brighter than it has been for a considerable time — perhaps even two hundred and fifty years." [17] The immediate problem confronting us is given by Dawson as twofold: 1) how to maintain a unity of culture in an age of increasing

[16] (New York: Sheed and Ward, 1959).
[17] *The Historic Reality of Christian Culture, op. cit.*, p. 25.

technical specialization; 2) how to preserve the tradition of Christian culture in an age of secularism. The only salvation for a Christian culture in this age of breakdown (from which time may show we may already be recovering) therefore lies an intensification and extension of the Christian religion. It lies in Western society's recapturing the vision which moved the early Christians in the Roman Empire — and Dawson makes the interesting observation that today the social stage is set in remarkably similar fashion to the way it was in early Christian times, when the future of the Church lay in the cities rather than the rural "pagan" areas. Although Dawson does not state it this way, it is consistent with his thought to say that he believes the future lies with diocesan priests in the suburbs and missionaries in the non-Western world.

Toynbee and Dawson agree in seeing our society as going through what Toynbee calls "its time of troubles" and Dawson its "period of disintegration." They also agree that we are moving into a period of universal history as the world is becoming Westernized. The approach to this generalization is made by Toynbee according to his schema, whereby in the period of disintegration a civilization is no longer an intelligible unit of history but must be studied in relationship with other civilizations with which it has made contact. Dawson sees the present moment rather as a unique period in history when the Christian dispensation, which historically had been confined to the Western world, is now enabled to move into all cultures and make a future of universal history.

Dawson differs from Toynbee in insisting on the uniqueness of Christianity. This is not in the narrow or parochial sense of a Belloc saying that Europe is the Faith and the Faith is Europe, but in the sounder sense of seeing that somehow — in the inscrutable design of God — the Christian religion took root in and was nourished in the Western culture and now it seems at the point of taking root in the other cultures of the world, or rather that this is the moment for the creation of a truly world-wide civilization and the West's providential contribution is not only its material accomplishments but especially its religion. Put another way, the mission of the Jewish nation in the Mediterranean world has two thousand years later become the mission of the West in the world as a whole.

Toynbee sees Christianity as one of the four "higher religions," each fitted to a particular type according to the Jungian analysis of psychological types. Apparently these four higher religions are destined to co-exist like a quartet, each praising God in its own way and with its own voice, each a valid approach to the God Who is bigger and more approachable than any religion. Toynbee is right in saying that Christians were parochial in their historical view in the past and in implying that God was unconcerned about the rest of humanity. But unlike Dawson he fails to see that in some mysterious way the central thread of history is the story of the Jews and, after the Incarnation, of the Christians, and that in a very real sense the apparently meaningless history of other civilizations takes on meaning as they make contact with the Judeo-Christian culture. In a sense which Toynbee implicitly denies and Dawson accepts they take on an added measure of reality as they make contact with the God of history.

Finally, there is another Christian virtue — not much exhibited in our time of troubles — which Dawson exercises confidently and Toynbee, with lack of conviction. This is the Christian virtue of hope. When Dawson speaks of the future he is not presumptuous, but he is convincing in seeing the likelihood of better times to come. Toynbee tries not to be the sort of pessimist Spengler was and he insists on keeping the future open, but his optimistic statements are somehow hollow and unconvincing, for they do not fit in with the pattern he finds in twenty other civilizations and which is followed, though not perfectly, by our own. On the other hand, Dawson carries conviction when he speaks of the troubled times in which we live out of the possibility that this is the beginning of a new era. These different outlooks come, it seems to me, from Toynbee's view of the philosophic equivalence of civilizations and the theological equivalence of higher religions as contrasted with Dawson's view of the uniqueness of the Judeo-Christian dispensation and the culture in which it took place.

Two Worlds

Barbara Ward

Barbara Ward is the wife of Sir Robert Jackson, a British Treasury official currently on loan as Commissioner of Development to the Government of Ghana. She was born in England forty-four years ago, and she was educated at the Sorbonne in Paris. She also studied philosophy, politics, and economics at Somerville College, Oxford, where she took a First-Class Honors degree. As a former Foreign Affairs editor of the London Economist *and as a frequent essayist in the* New York Times Magazine, *as well as occasional lecturer at Harvard, Cornell, and other universities, she has wielded a great influence. It has been said that at the age of 44 Barbara Ward has "collected more honors than most people do in a whole lifetime." Many universities have bestowed honorary degrees on her. She is a member of the Royal Institute of International Affairs Council, and she is also a Governor of the B.B.C. and of the Old Vic Theatre and the Royal (formerly Sadler Wells) Ballet. She is also an influential radio and television personality whenever she is invited to appear. Among her books, so widely read by highly intelligent citizens in many parts of the world, are* Faith and Freedom, The West at Bay, Policy for the West, Inter-play of East and West, *and* Five Ideas that Changed the World. *She was the Christian Culture Award medallist for 1959.*

THE IDEA of mankind as a single family under the Fatherhood of God is so much a foundation of Christian thinking that, like many other fundamental ideas, it is simply taken for granted and not thought about at all. Certainly no one could say that its implications are constantly studied or that a steady effort is being made to ask what, in this second half of the twentieth century, the fact of a single humanity means in terms of moral obligation and Christian duty.

In the past, the excuse could lie in the gulf between the metaphysical idea of mankind's unity and the physical division of the universe. A man could hardly feel that the inhabitants of the Americas were his brothers if he did not even know that America existed. Anyone reading Marco Polo's account of the Mongol Empire in the thirteenth century must be struck by his efforts to counter the plain incredulity of his readers. Medieval Christians could hardly conceive of the existence of China. To have convinced them, in addition, of its enjoying a high degree of civilization was virtually beyond Polo's skill.

Even after the great age of Western discovery which brought the whole world onto a single map, physical distances still countered the idea of a common humanity, and physical interdependence had no meaning for a world in which the basic unit of production still tended to be the river valley, and the center of commerce, the small market town. Until the nineteenth century, therefore, the physical preconditions of recognizing all men as brothers did not exist. The idea remained a metaphysical truth with no general possibility of concrete application.

Ours is the first century in which men move round the world as they once moved round New and Old England. Ours is the century in which the livelihood of a Malayan peasant can be determined by a Congressional decision to maintain synthetic rubber factories in the United States. Physical interdependence has become a fact for a large part of humanity. What has not accompanied this sudden development is an enlargement of the sense of mankind's moral interdependence. In other words, the physical realization of Christianity's deepest insight has come about. But the truth itself — that men are brothers and that we all are our brother's keeper — is as shadowy and remote as it was when Marco Polo arrived at the court of the Great Khan or Columbus set sail for the Indies.

This failure of moral sense to keep pace with physical fact should be of particular concern to Christians. They believe that material society unenlightened and unredeemed by grace tends to become a vessel of destruction. A society which, while physically one, lacks any principle of moral order is hideously dangerous and Christians should be the first to perceive that danger and to discern its cause.

Physical charity

But there is another and more pressing reason for concern among the Christian and post-Christian peoples of the West. It is not only that they carry the responsibility of having created the world's new physical unity. Theirs is the deeper responsibility that springs from having profited most richly from that unity.

However sophisticated our moral analysis or refined our metaphysical speculations be, Christ's own parables constantly stub us against the fact that the rich have a hard time of it. They can make their riches work salvation. They can make friends of the mammon of iniquity. But the line of least resistance carries them to the fate of Dives or of the fool who filled his barns.

It is, or should be, a disturbing fact that Our Lord's clearest discrimination between those who will enjoy eternal life and those who will not is based solely upon physical charity in the most material sense. Those who feed the hungry may expect the Beatific Vision. Those who neglect "the least of these little ones" may not. Our Lord even suggests that this physical expression of neighborly love will more than offset the ignorance of His Name. Many of the compassionate providers of bread and shelter may not have known the Lord, while they were loving and serving Him through His creatures. But there is no salvation for those who say "Lord, Lord" and do not the things that He says. All this is so elementary, so starkly clear in the Gospels, that the Christian knows it as soon as he can read, and often forgets it again almost as soon.

In the world community of today, there is no doubt who is cast for the role of Dives, who for Lazarus. Comparative standards of wealth are, admittedly, difficult to establish. Most undeveloped countries have undeveloped statistics as well, but a reasonable basis may be found in recent estimates made by Colin Clark. He establishes a unit of comparison — called an "oriental unit" — based upon the goods and services which could be purchased by an Indian rupee in 1948/49. On this basis, he establishes a comparative table which shows that, broadly speaking, the "Atlantic Community" of the United States, Western Europe and the white members of the British Commonwealth have a standard of living of over 1,000 oriental units per head of population, while the vast bulk of Asia and Africa have a standard of below 200.

This broad generalization masks even sharper individual differences. The United States and Canada, for instance, may well be in the category of 7,000 oriental units per head. The debatable lands of Southeast Asia — Burma, Indonesia, etc. — have under 150.

A privileged class

This absolute disparity is matched by further comparative advantages enjoyed by the West. Since the year 1500 the Atlantic peoples have systematically occupied the best and most fertile uninhabited areas of the earth. This taking over of temperate lands by the men of Europe is probably the most significant Völkerwanderung of the Christian era. In North and South America, in Australia, in Siberia, the white peoples have pressed outwards, exterminating or driving back or reducing to subordinate status the aboriginal inhabitants. This white flood has even filtered into the few temperate areas in otherwise unwholesome and hostile continents such as Africa. In East Africa, the highlands of Kenya have the most congenial climate for human settlement. They have been taken over by the white man.

This appropriation of the temperate belt is not simply a matter of health, comfort and convenience — although it is all these things. It is a matter of controlling for the future the bulk of the world's best resources. The greatest increases in farming output are possible in the temperate zones of North and South America. Canada, Australia and Brazil are the most obvious areas of under-population, but the population of the United States could be trebled in relation to its resources. The mineral reserves of Canada are among the largest in the world and where, as in the Belgian Congo, tropical climate is combined with great potential mineral development, the territory is, once again, under Atlantic control.

The instances could be multiplied endlessly. They all amount to the same thing — that the Atlantic peoples, in relation to the rest of the world, are an elite, a privileged class, a group enjoying a quite disproportionate share of the world's resources, and in certain cases (petroleum, for instance) using them up so fast that the reserves may be exhausted by the end of the century. Moreover, at present, the disparity is tending to grow greater. In the circulation of wealth in the modern world, new wealth tends to follow old wealth. The opportunities for reliable investment are inevitably greater in the rich stable communities of the West rather than in backward areas, to whose poverty is now added the risk of political instability.

The case is perhaps most tragic in relation to man's basic need — food. The latest report of the Food and Agriculture Organization shows that while food production has increased by nineteen per cent above pre-war in North America, in the Far East production is thirteen per cent lower. The rich countries thus have more to eat than ever before. Many of the poorer countries are eating less than before. Nor, without extraordinary measures, will the picture change.

Many peoples in Asia and Africa are poor because they occupy the worst land and suffer the worst climates in the world. Unable to move on to better land which is still underpopulated, they must remain where they are, hungry, disease-ridden and short-lived, while the Western people continue to add calories to their diet and decades to their living span. The Marxist prediction of the rich growing ever richer and the poor growing ever poorer, which has been disproved in the democratic countries of the Atlantic world, nevertheless shows signs of being realized in the world as a whole.

Distributive justice

One must therefore ask whether, since Christian peoples are the overwhelming beneficiaries of the modern world economy, they have any special obligation to take notice of the vast disparities of wealth and misery which exist within the single physically-united world. Are any principles of Christian compassion and distributive justice involved? Is there any social obligation or moral imperative?

The answer which comes most easily to modern lips is that group obligations do not extend beyond national frontiers. The state is the absolute, and while sharing of national income within the national community is now one of the bases of Western democracy, there is no suggestion that the obligations go any further. In theory, at least, for British Samaritans, the man in the ditch must be British, for Americans, he must be American, for the French, a Frenchman. The good Samaritan asks to see a passport before he sets to work.

Yet such a limitation of compassion is not Christian and nothing can make it so. It is, in fact, a part of the idolatry of the nation-state which, in the modern world, is the mark of both democracies and dictatorships. A faith in which there is "neither Jew nor Gentile," a faith founded upon the common Fatherhood of God and upon mankind's sonship in Christ, must be based on the concept of mankind as a family — and a family in which fraternal charity is not limited by frontiers or race. To Catholics, whose claim to universality is most insistent, the counter-claim of the nation-state to exclusive loyalities and obligations should be especially repugnant. It is no coincidence that the Pope, in proclaiming during World War II the principles of a just peace,[1] included among them a fair distribution of the earth's resources among the peoples of the world.

The Christian answer

The important point is the point of principle. Are we or are we not in the West under a moral obligation to assist in the material advancement of hungry, shelterless, disease-ridden peoples in other less fortunate lands ? For the Christian, there is only one answer. We are. Once that decision is taken, the mechanics of putting distributive justice into effect are not insuperably difficult.

To the United Nations Relief and Rehabilitation Administration, for instance, the participating nations contributed one per cent of their national income. It would be perfectly possible to devise a standard whereby nations enjoying more than a certain level of per capita income would contribute a proportion of their wealth to the building of wealth-producing capacity in countries which do not command them now. But the mechanics of such schemes are not the problem.

The basic difficulty is that the Christian peoples of the West do not, at present, recognize the advancement of the world's poverty-stricken peoples as their duty in strict justice, as an obligation for which they will one day be called to give account. That whole peoples can be alert to the misfortunes of others is proved by the magnificent generosity of American policy after World War II. But such great gestures as the Marshall Plan are held to be exceptional and entirely voluntary and to carry no trace of obligation.

That consciences are still stirring is shown by the proliferation of small-scale Western plans for technical assistance and economic aid, but no one can pretend that the actual principle of sustained aid to backward areas is generally accepted in the West. In particular, few Catholic voices have been raised to reassert the *Pope's Fifth Peace Point*[2] or to plead for general recognition of the fact that in strict justice and charity the Christian peoples of the West must undertake a sustained attack upon the hunger, the disease, the homelessness and the despairing misery in which so many of the world's peoples drag out their lives.

That such a program might, incidentally, save much of Asia and Africa from communism is in this argument all but irrelevant — ex-

[1] Pius XII, *Christmas Messages* 1939, 1940, 1941, and 1944.
[2] Pius XII, *Christmas Message*, 1939.

cept that communism is often the scourge bred of Western indifference. Equally the fact that it would, by expanding world production and widening markets, profit Western economies is also beside the point. The real issue here is the positive issue of principle. According to Christian teaching, humanity is a single family. According to Christian charity, we are our brother's keeper. In practical fact, the West today possesses overwhelming wealth. Can there be any escaping the conclusion, that, on pain of Our Lord's own rejection, that wealth must be set to work to bring bread and hope to the millions upon millions who, in this single world society, still lack both?

The Natural Law and Human Rights*

Jacques Maritain

Jacques Maritain was born in Paris in 1882. Author of more than fifty philosophical works, this Thomist philosopher has long been considered one of the major Christian thinkers of the century. One of his more recent books, Reflections On America, *a nontechnical work, received warm praise from American critics for its remarkably acute and sympathetic insights into American life. He is currently working on a major two-volume study in moral philosophy. Among his major works are* La Philosophie Bergsonienne, The Degrees of Knowledge, A Preface to Metaphysics, Existence and the Existent, Science and Wisdom, Art and Scholasticism, Creative Intuition in Art and Poetry, True Humanism, The Person and the Common Good, Man and the State, *and* On the Philosophy of History. *At the Sorbonne, where he later received a Ph.D. in biology, he met his wife, Raïssa. How they then began their spiritual Odyssey together and were rescued from despair and suicide, the result of materialism rampant at the Sorbonne in those days, is poignantly told by Raïssa in two books,* We Have Been Friends Together *and* Adventures in Grace. *Henri Bergson, Charles Péguy, and their godfather Léon Bloy each played a part in their conversion to the Catholic Church. Later, after having gone for a long time from the study of biology deep into the mysteries of philosophy, Jacques Maritain, Bergson's most brilliant pupil, was invited to succeed Bergson at the Collège de France. Though loving Bergson as a friend, he felt constrained to point out certain errors and dangerous tendencies in Bergsonism, which Bergson himself (he later confided to Raïssa before he died) never knew were there. From 1945 to 1948 M. Maritain was French Ambassador to the Vatican. On his first visit to North America, he taught at the Pontifical Institute of Medieval Studies, Toronto, later at Columbia, Notre Dame, and the University of Chicago. He is professor emeritus of philosophy*

* This address which M. Maritain delivered when he received the Christian Culture Award in January, 1942, has since been treated more fully in *Man and the State* (Chicago: University of Chicago Press, 1951) and in *The Social and Political Philosophy of Jacques Maritain* (New York: Scribner's, 1955) [Ed. note].

at Princeton University. In 1958 Notre Dame University established the Jacques Maritain Institute, with an International Board of Consultants. M. Maritain seems to many "a man who really sees," who "distinguishes to unite," who is aware that our age needs men "with hard minds and meek hearts." Maritain is the most modern of philosophers. He received the Christian Culture Award in 1942.

I N ORDER to treat the problem in a philosophical manner, we should first examine the question of what is called natural law. There are people who believe that natural law is an invention of American Independence and of the French Revolution. Reactionaries of all categories have done a great deal to spread this nonsense; the unfortunate thing is that in discrediting the idea of natural law they have found allies among most of the contemporary jurists (particularly those of the positivist school) who, by the way, are really attacking a false idea of natural law, and in destroying this latter, are only destroying a phantom drawn from some bad textbooks.

The idea of natural law is a heritage of Christian thought and classical thought. It doesn't go back to the philosophy of the eighteenth century, which more or less deformed it, but to Grotius and before him to Francisco de Vitoria; and farther back to Thomas Aquinas; and still farther back to Augustine and to the Church Fathers and to Paul; and even farther back to Cicero, to the Stoics, to the great moralists of antiquity and to its great poets, to Sophocles in particular. Antigone is the eternal heroine of natural law, which the ancients called *the unwritten law*, and this is the name which best suits it.

Since I haven't the time to discuss nonsense (you can always find very intelligent philosophers to defend it most brilliantly) I am taking it for granted that you admit that there is a human nature, and that this human nature is the same in all men. I am taking it for granted that you also admit that man is a being gifted with the intelligence and who, as such, acts with a knowledge of what he is doing, resolving freely upon the aims which he is pursuing. On the other hand, possessing a nature, being constituted in such a set manner, man obviously possesses aims which correspond to his natural constitution and which are the same for all — as all pianos, for instance, whatever their particular type and in whatever spot they may be, have as their aim the production of correct sounds. If they do not produce true notes they must be tuned or discarded as having no value. But since man is gifted with intelligence and resolves upon his own aims, it is up to him to put himself in harmony with aims which are of necessity demanded by his nature. This means that there is, by very virtue of human nature, an order or a disposition which human reason more or less knows through our essential inclinations and according to which the human will must act in order to be in harmony with the necessary aims of the human being. Unwritten law or natural law is nothing more than that.

The great philosophers of antiquity knew, Christian thinkers know even better, that nature comes from God and that the unwritten law comes from the eternal law which is Creative Wisdom itself. That is why the idea of natural law or unwritten law was linked for them to a sentiment of natural piety, to that profound and sacred respect unforgettably expressed by Antigone. Understanding the real principle of this law, the belief in this law is firmer and more unshakable in those who believe in God than in the others. In itself, however, it suffices to believe in human nature and in the liberty of the human being, in order to believe in the unwritten law, in order to know that natural law is something as real in the moral realm as the laws of growth and of growing old are in the physical realm.

Now the law and the knowledge of the law are two different things. The man who does not know the law (if this ignorance itself does not arise from some fault) is not responsible before the law. And knowing that there is a law does not necessarily mean knowing what that law is. It is because this very simple distinction is forgotten that many perplexities have arisen concerning the unwritten law. It is written, they say, in the heart of man. True, but in the hidden depths, as hidden from us as our own heart. This metaphor itself has been the cause of a great deal of damage, causing natural law to be represented as a ready-made code rolled up within the conscience of each one of us and which each one of us has only to unroll, and of which all men should naturally have an equal knowledge.

Natural law is not written law. Men know it with greater or lesser difficulty, and to different degrees, running the risk of error here as elsewhere. The only practical knowledge that all men have naturally and infallibly in common is that we must do good and avoid evil. That is the preamble and the principle of natural law, it is not the law itself. Natural law is the ensemble of things to do and things not to do which follow from it *in a necessary manner* and from the simple fact that man is man, in the absence of every other consideration. That all errors and deviations are possible in the determination of these things proves only that our sight is weak and that innumerable accidents can corrupt our judgment. Montaigne remarked slyly that incest and larceny were considered by certain people as virtuous actions. Pascal was scandalized by this; we are scandalized by the fact that cruelty, denunciation of parents, the lie for the service of the party, the murder of "useless" old people should be considered as virtuous by the young people educated according to certain totalitarian methods. All this does not prove anything against natural law, any more than a mistake in addition proves something against mathematics, or that the mistakes of the primitive peoples, for whom the stars were holes in the tent which covered the world, prove something against astronomy.

Natural law is an unwritten law. Man's knowledge of it increases little by little with the progress of moral conscience. This latter was at first in a twilight state. Ethnologists have taught us in what structures of tribal life and in the bosom of what half-awakened magic it was primitively formed. That proves merely that the idea of natural law, which was at first immersed in religious rites and mythology, emerged as something separate only slowly, as slowly as the very idea of nature; and that the knowledge that men have of unwritten law has passed through more diverse forms and stages than certain philosophers or theologians believed. The knowledge that our own moral conscience has of this law is itself doubtless still imperfect, and it is probable that it will continue to develop and to become finer as long as humanity exists. When the Gospel has penetrated to the very depth of human substance, then will it be that natural law will appear in its flower and its perfection.

We must consider now the fact that natural law and the light of moral conscience within us do not prescribe merely the things that are to be done and that are not to be done; they also recognize rights, in particular, rights linked to the very nature of man. The human person possesses rights because of the very fact that he is a person, a whole master of himself and of his acts, and which consequently is not merely a means to an end, but an end, an end which must be treated as such. The expression, the dignity of the human person, means nothing if it does not signify that by virtue of natural law the human person has the right to be respected, is a retainer of rights, possesses rights. There are things which are owed to man because of the very fact that he is man. The notion of right and the notion of moral obligation are correlative; they are both founded on the freedom proper to spiritual agents; if man is morally bound to the things which are necessary to the fulfillment of his destiny, it is that he has the right to fulfill his destiny; and if he has the right to fulfill his destiny he has the right to those things which are necessary for this purpose. The notion of right is even more profound than that of moral obligation, for God has sovereign right over creatures and He has no moral obligations towards them (although He owes it to Himself to give them that which is required by their nature).

The consciousness of the dignity of the person and of the rights of the person remained implicit in the pagan antiquity over which the law of bondage cast its shadow. It is the evangelical message which, suddenly, awakened this consciousness, in a divine and transcendent form, revealing to men that they are called to be sons and inheritors of God in the Kingdom of God. Under the evangelical impulse, this same awakening was to be diffused by degrees, with regard to the exigencies of natural law itself, in the realm of man's life here on earth and in the terrestrial city.

It is fitting to recall here the classic distinction — a principal one for civilized tradition — between natural law, common law (or *jus gentium*), and statute or positive law. As I pointed out a few moments ago, natural law deals with the rights and the duties which follow from the first principle: do good and avoid evil, in a *necessary* manner and *from the simple fact that man is man*, in the absence of every other consideration. This is why the precepts of unwritten law are in themselves or in the nature of things (I am not saying in the knowledge that man has of it) universal and invariable.

Common law is difficult to define exactly, at least for the jurists, because it is intermediary between natural law and positive or statute law. The notion of common law developed in England in about the same manner that the notion of *jus gentium*, the law of nations, had developed in Rome. Though these two notions are very different for the historian and for the jurist, nevertheless, the philosopher is allowed to bring them together in order to disengage them from the notion of natural or unwritten law itself as going beyond the mere sphere of nature and particularized by the conditions of social life. This definition once stated, I shall use, in order to designate it, both the term common law (deprived of its specific English meaning) and the term *jus gentium* (deprived of its specific Roman meaning), these two terms being thus made synonymous.

Like natural law in the strictest sense of the term, *jus gentium* or common law also deals with the rights and the duties which follow from the first principle in a *necessary* manner, but this time supposing certain conditions of fact, as, for instance, the state of civil society or the relationship between peoples.

Positive or statute law deals with the rights and the duties which follow from the first principle, but in a *contingent* manner, by reason of the determinations set down by the reason and the will of man when they institute the laws or when they give birth to the customs of a particular community.

But it is by virtue of natural law that common law and positive law take on the force of law and impose themselves upon the conscience. They are a prolongation or an extension of natural law passing into objective zones which are less and less determined by the simple intrinsic constitution of human nature. For it is natural law itself which requires that whatever it leaves undetermined shall subsequently be determined, either as a right or a duty existing for all men by reason of a given state of fact, or as a right or a duty existing for certain men by reason of the human regulations proper to the community of which they are a part. Thus there are imperceptible transitions between natural law, common law, and positive law. There is a dynamism which impels unwritten law to expand within human law and to render the latter ever more perfect and more just in the very field of its contingent determinations. It is according to this dynamism that the rights of the human person take political and social form within the community.

For instance, man's right to life, to personal freedom and to the pursuit of his moral fulfillment, pertain, strictly speaking, to natural law. The right to the private possession of material goods, rooted in natural law, arises also from common law or *jus gentium* insofar as the right of private ownership of the means of production supposes the conditions, in fact, especially required for human work and for its normal management (which varies, moreover, according to the forms of society). Freedom from want, and freedom from fear, as President Roosevelt defined them in his Four Freedom Plan,[1] correspond to the demands of *jus gentium*, which are to be fulfilled by statute law and world political organization. The right of suffrage

[1] Reference is made here to the famous *Four Freedoms Address* given to the United States Congress in January, 1940 [Ed. note].

granted to each one of us for the election of the officers of the state arises from positive or statute law.

After these philosophical explanations dealing with the natural law, I should like to lay stress on the rights of the human person. It was first in the religious order, and by means of the sudden upsurge of the evangelical message that this transcendent dignity of the human person was revealed in human history. But from that point the consciousness of this dignity took over, by degrees, the sphere of the natural order itself, by penetrating and renewing our consciousness of the law of nature and of natural law.

When the Apostles replied to the Sanhedrin, which wanted to prevent them from preaching the word of Jesus: "It is better for us to obey God than man," [2] they were affirming at one and the same time the freedom of the word of God and the transcendence of the human person summoned and ransomed by it, raised up by grace to divine adoption; but implicitly they were affirming by the same stroke the transcendence of the human person in the natural order, insofar as spiritual totality created for the absolute.

The transcendence of the person, which appears most manifest in the perspectives of faith and redemption, manifests itself thus in the philosophical perspectives and affects first and foremost the order of nature. That is, moreover, in complete accord with Christian theology which teaches that grace perfects nature and does not destroy it. It is important to stress this fact that even in the natural order itself the human person transcends the state to the extent that man is ordered to things which are superior to time.

This appears in the first place in the natural aspirations of man towards spiritual life. Aristotle and the wise men of antiquity knew that moral virtues are ordered to a contemplation of truth which exceeds political intercommunication. It follows that if humanity were in what theologians call the state of pure nature, a kingdom of the spirits akin to that of which Leibnitz liked to speak, it would normally have had its place above the world of political life. We may look upon the spiritual network which joins together artists, scholars, poets, philosophers, and true humanists, all those who cherish the works of the spirit, as the vague lineaments of such a natural kingdom of the spirits; such a network is like the rough draft of a single family above the national frontiers. This is only a rough draft, and

---

[2] *Acts of the Apostles*, 4:19.

the Leibnitzian kingdom of the spirits is only a hypothesis for a possible world, for in reality it was by the Grace of God that there was established above the realm of emperors, kings and parliaments, a better kingdom, the Kingdom of God, the great city of the coming century, of which in the eyes of the Christian, the Church is already the beginning on earth. It remains true that this kingdom of eternal life corresponds, by virtue of a gift which surpasses all measures of nature, to a natural aspiration of the spirit in us.

The fact that the human person naturally transcends the state, to the extent that the former is ordered to supratemporal values, may be verified in many other ways.

The universe of truths — of science, wisdom and poetry — towards which intelligence tends by itself, arises, by nature, from a plane higher than the political community. The power of the state and of social interests cannot exercise itself upon this universe. The state can ask a mathematician to teach mathematics, a philosopher to teach philosophy, for these are functions of the social body. But the state cannot force a philosopher or a mathematician to adopt a philosophical doctrine or a mathematical doctrine, for these things depend solely and exclusively upon truth.

The secret of the heart and the free act as such, the universe of moral laws, the right of conscience to listen to God and to make its way to Him — all these things, in the natural as in the supernatural order, cannot be affected by the state. Doubtless, law has the force of conscience, but it is only law if it is just and promulgated by legitimate authority, not because the majority and the state are the standard of conscience. Doubtless, the state has a moral and not merely a material function; law has a pedagogical function and tends to develop moral virtues; the state has the right to punish me if, because of a blinded conscience I follow my conscience and commit an act in itself criminal or unlawful. But, under these circumstances, the state has not the authority to make me reform the judgment of my conscience, nor to define good and evil, nor to legislate on divine matters, nor to impose any religious faith whatsoever. The state knows this well. And that is why, whenever it goes beyond its natural limits to enter the sanctuary of the conscience, it strives to violate this sanctum by monstrous means of psychological poisoning, organized lies and terror.

Every human person has the right to make his own decisions with regard to his personal destiny, whether it be a question of choosing his work, or marrying the woman of his choice, or of pursuing a religious vocation. In the case of extreme peril, and for the safety of the community, the state can require by force the service of each one of us and demand that each one of us endanger his life in a just war; it can also deprive certain men of their rights, criminal individuals — for example, men judged unworthy of exercising paternal authority. But it becomes iniquitous and tyrannical if it claims to base the functioning of civil life on compulsory labor, or if it tries to violate the rights of family society in order to become master of men's souls. For just as man is constituted a person, made for God and for a life superior to time, before being constituted a part of the political community, so man is constituted a part of family society before being constituted a part of political society. The end for which the family exists is to produce and bring up human persons and prepare them to fulfill their total destiny. And if the state, too, has an educative function, if education is not out of its sphere, it is to aid the family in fulfilling its missions, not to efface in the child his vocation as a human person and replace it by that of a living tool and material of the state.

To sum up, the fundamental rights like the right to existence and life; to personal freedom or to conducting one's own life as master of oneself; to the pursuit of one's human, moral and rational fulfillment (in other words, to the pursuit of happiness, which is above all the pursuit, not of material accommodations, but of moral righteousness, internal strength and completion, with the material and social conditions involved); the right to the pursuit of one's eternal fulfillment; the right to corporeal integrity; to private ownership of material goods, which is a safeguard to the liberties of the individual; the right of assembly; the respect of human dignity in each one of us, whether or not it represents an economic value for society; all these rights spring, after all, from supratemporal values naturally contained in the human person.

The first of these rights is that of the human person to make his way towards his eternal destiny along the path which his conscience has recognized as the path indicated by God. With respect to God and truth, he has not the right to choose according to his own pleasure any path whatsoever; he must choose the true path insofar as it is in his power to recognize it. But with respect to the state, with the temporal community and with the temporal power, he is free to choose his religious path at his own risk; his liberty of conscience is a natural, inviolable right. This is the right which President Roosevelt has designated as the "Freedom of every person to worship God in his own way everywhere in the world." [3]

The same must be said of the rights and the liberties of spiritual families, which are at the same time the rights and liberties of the person in the spiritual and religious realm. These rights and liberties spring from natural law, not to mention the superior right which the Church invokes by reason of its divine foundation.

I have emphasized in this essay the rights of the human person insofar as he is human. A complete examination of the question would also involve a discussion of the rights of the civic person, in other words, political rights, and a discussion of the rights of the social person, more particularly of the working person. Thus we could outline the features of a true and integral democracy.

Amidst the difficulties, conflicts and distress of a still primitive state of humanity, the political work must realize of *what it is able*, its essential and primordial exigencies. And even that is possible only if it recognizes these exigencies, and if it is attached to a noble and difficult historical ideal, capable of raising up and drawing forth all the energies of goodness and progress hidden in the depths of man and which are today abominably repressed or perverted. The political work in which human persons may truly find communion, and to whose realization, for the sake of the centuries to come, the earthly hope of our race and the energy of human history must normally apply themselves, this work is the establishment of a fraternal city and the liberation of humanity. *Liberty and fraternity* describe the historical ideal for which we have the right to ask men to work, fight, and die. Contrary to the myth of the twentieth century as the totalitarian groups conceive it, contrary to the millenium of brutal domination which the prophets of these groups promise their people, a vaster and greater hope must surge up, a more fearless promise must be made to the human race. Libery and fraternity are not dead. If our civilization is struggling with death, it is neither because it has ventured too much, nor because it has proposed too much to men. It is rather because it has not ventured enough, and because it has not proposed enough. It will revive, a new civilization will come to life, on condition that it hope, on condition that it desire, on condition that it love heroically, liberty and fraternity.

[3] *Four Freedoms Address, op. cit.*

Jacques Maritain: A Prophet for Our Time

Sir Robert Falconer

Sir Robert Falconer was born in Charlottetown, Prince Edward Island, in Canada. He was educated at Royal College in Trinidad and was graduated from the University of London (England) with honors in classics and philosophy. From Edinburgh University he received an M.A., a B.D., and later a Litt.D.; then he studied at the Universities of Leipzig, Berlin, and Marburg. He was ordained to the Ministry of the Presbyterian Church of Canada in 1892. In 1907 he became president of the University of Toronto, and for the next twenty-five years the university became the largest in student attendance of all universities of the British Empire. Ill health forced him to relinquish the presidency in 1932 but also provided him with an opportunity for more quiet study and contemplation. Amongst his published works are The German Tragedy and Its Meaning for Canada, Idea of Immortality and Western Civilization, *and* The Pastoral Epistles. *Always the great scholar, he became interested in Jacques Maritain, especially when Maritain came to the Pontifical Institute of Medieval Studies, near the University of Toronto and close to Sir Robert's home. A friend, a churchman, and later a university president, Dr. James S. Thomson wrote in the* Dalhousie Review *(Vol. XXX) about Sir Robert Falconer after the latter's death: "(I found him in retirement) . . . still eager and alert — reading, writing, comparing the new with the old, and weighing the merits of both with the gathered wisdom of years . . . abreast of all that was coming from the publishers, but with the mature judgement of a man who had seen much, had tasted deeply of life and found it very good . . . the mingling of the scholar with the statesman, the intellectual with the practical . . . an exemplar of genuine greatness." About a year before his death, which took place in 1943, Sir Robert Falconer read the address on Jacques Maritain in the Christian Culture Series.*

Jacques Maritain is a many-sided man. He is a Christian philosopher, a social reformer, a critic of the principles of the arts of painting and poetry, and an expert in the theories and fundamentals of the modern sciences. But all these phases of his activity are aspects of a powerfully religious personality. My purpose is to speak of him as a prophet of the Christian faith. More and more he is being listened to by those of all shades of opinion who are in sympathy with a spiritual interpretation of life. I have called him a prophet, for, as an eminent scholar has said, "the final mission of Old Testament prophecy was to liberate the eternal truths of religion from their temporal national embodiment and disclose their true foundation in the immutable character of God and the essential nature of man." Social righteousness is a central theme of the prophets. That Maritain is in the true succession of those prophets is evident to anyone who is even casually acquainted with his more popular writings. In fact it is their religious interpretation of problems of the social order that has given them such a wide and varied circle of readers. He is, however, in the succession not only of the prophets of Israel, but also of the prophets and saints of the Christian Church. Like the apostle Paul he entered by a marvelous transition into a fulness of spiritual light; like St. Augustine, he passed from the brilliant humanistic society into a new hope for a city of God; like Pascal, who abandoned the sceptical libertines of seventeenth-century Paris, he consecrated his scientific understanding and literary gifts, when the light flooded his soul, to the integration of mankind in a humanism complete and entire.

Out of the most brilliant literary circle of Paris he entered, through travail, into a small company intellectually more humble but spiritually more exalted. An indication of his sense of the change, and of the isolation that he then felt, may possibly be detected in a sentence written many years later in *True Humanism*:[1] "The philosopher (who seeks to rescue the truths that have been distorted by the modern world) attempts in vain to arm himself with the perfect instruments of purification, and runs the risk of having everyone against him." In the France into which he was born in 1882, politics were interwoven with both anti-clerical and religious strands. On the right, at varying distances from the center were royalists and moderate republicans who were for the most part professing Catholics; on the left, radicals, socialists, differing in degree, and communists, many of whom were anti-clerical. The non-Catholic intellectual circles were saturated with the spirit of rationalism. Nowhere else did the power of the written word sway such an influential society. Humanism reigned in all its glory. The center of this rationalistic humanism was

[1] *True Humanism* (New York: Scribner's, 1938) p. IX.

the Sorbonne, and in that ancient body the pulse of the religious motive had grown very faint. Of the men of letters who spoke to the world from Paris, perhaps the one who received the widest attention, was Ernest Renan. He was an exponent of liberalism in religious, social and political thought. Historical criticism, in his view, had shattered Christianity as a system of supernatural beliefs, and, as an eminent French scholar says, "he radically destroyed what Voltaire had shaken." As Maritain was only ten years old when Renan died, he could not have come under his personal influence, but Renan's grandson, Ernest Psichari, who had absorbed his ideas, was one of Maritain's most intimate friends in his young manhood.

Maritain's own grandfather was Jules Favre, who died in 1880. A man of brilliant gifts, a moderate republican and a convinced democrat — associated for a short time with Victor Hugo in the middle of the century, he led the parliamentary opposition against Louis Napoleon first as President and then as Emperor of France. He joined Thiers in resisting a declaration of war against Prussia in 1870, and after the fall of Paris he became Minister of Foreign Affairs in the Government of National Defence, and as such had the thankless task of negotiating a peace with Bismarck and of signing a most disappointing treaty. While not anti-clerical, he opposed the royalists and the clericals in their policy of defending Rome for the Pope with French troops against the national Italian government, and in 1871 he resigned office, though he continued as a deputy and was made senator in 1876, supporting the government against reactionary opposition. A great orator of beautiful style, mystical, emotional and sentimental, he was also for a long time a member of the French Academy. He became a Protestant, and in this action he was joined by his daughter, Maritain's mother, who had her son baptized in this faith, though she does not seem to have implanted strong religious convictions in him. "In the family traditions of Jacques Maritain," writes his wife, "it was the idealist love of the people, the republican spirit, and political combats for liberty" [2] that were dominant.

When he entered the Sorbonne its sceptical atmosphere infected him with depression, and from no professor did he hear a voice of confident belief to dissipate the thickening gloom. Here, however, he found a great treasure, for he met the Jewish lady who became his wife. Her book, *We Have Been Friends Together*, giving the story

[2] Raïssa Maritain, *We Have Been Friends Together* (New York: Longman, Green, 1940), p. 48.

of their joint conversion is a delicately beautiful memoir of their remarkable religious pilgrimage from darkness into light. In her words,
"Every intelligible reality vanished like a mirage when one thought
of approaching and seizing it, and the sacrosanct 'facts' resolved themselves into the dust of purely empirical disputes, because what was
generally denied by the ruling philosophy was the objectivity of our
knowledge, our capacity to seize the real." This scepticism as to the
attainment of truth and the accessibility of reality plunged them into
such despair that even the thought of suicide flitted before them.
But they were saved from utter hopelessness when they crossed the
street from the Sorbonne to the Collège de France and entered the
classroom of Professor Henri Bergson. He was then the most widely
read philosopher in Europe, and he delivered his prelections with a
personality and a grace of style which filled his classroom. A ray of
light broke in upon Maritain as Bergson insisted that the methods of
pure rationalism had been a failure, and that by intuition and spiritual
sympathy we grasp "*Durée*, living time, a reality." This was a luminous life-buoy flung to him on a darkling ocean. He became Bergson's
most brilliant student, and indeed when Bergson retired was offered
his chair, but by that time he had found Bergson's philosophy unsatisfactory and had written against it. "Metaphysics," said Bergson, "consists in seeing in time a progressive increment of the Absolute."
"But," replied Maritain, if this were so, "time (would become) a
creator and metaphysics a dream." Maritain retained a strong affection for his old master until the end, though he continued to reject
his doctrine of time and change, involving, as he thought it did, a
practical negation of Being. In one of his recent essays Maritain
writes: "Bergson's stroke of genius had been to see that if phenomenal
science itself enfolds and hides, on its own level and in its formal
object, a metaphysical stuff, that stuff can only be true. . . . His
metaphysics is one of the most profound, most penetrating, and most
audacious of our time." Bergson in later life drew nearer to the fundamental beliefs of Maritain, as is shown in his *Two Sources of
Morality and Religion*, which Maritain reviewed with deep appreciation in 1941 in *Ransoming the Time*:[3] "What pure philosopher has
ever studied all these things (of mystical life) with greater good
faith, with a more humble and generous love than Henri Bergson?"
After many years, in his will, dated four years before his death in
January, 1941, Bergson placed on record that he would have become

[3] (New York: Scribner's, 1941), p. 103.

a convert to Catholicism, in which he saw the complete fulfilment of Judaism, had he not wanted to remain loyally by the side of his co-religionists, against whom a formidable wave of anti-Semitism was about to break.

Feeling their way in a twilight winter world the Maritains were, to their joy, thrown by the chance reading of an essay into contact with a powerful personality who came to them from a new universe. This was Léon Bloy. Mme. Maritain writes, "Life brought him to our shores like a treasure, legendary, immense, mysterious." This old man lived with his family in poverty; and his writings, full of indignation against injustice and oppression stirred some to call him merely a pamphleteer. But he had tender pity for all who suffered, and was widely read for his insight into the mystical, religious life. A prophet "who had lived for long years united to his God by an indestructible love which he knew to be eternal in its essence," he bore unceasing witness by words, both burning and compassionate, to his faith in the Gospel. To meet this man was a revelation to M. Maritain. Here was "a pilgrim of the Absolute" who evidently was in possession of something profoundly real to himself. Could it be the truth? Among others whom he met at Léon Bloy's was his close friend Professor Pierre Termier, a geologist of the highest rank and a devout Christian. It was an impressive combination. Slowly there deepened in the Maritains the conviction of the beauty of holiness. Could they perhaps by an act of the soul attain unto the truth of the love of God? His dawning faith led him to test this in prayer: "My God if you exist and are the truth, make me know it." Day by day the dark winter of the soul gave way to spring, and supported by their new friends they took the momentous step of being baptized into the Catholic faith. So in 1906 Jacques Maritain entered the ancestral Church which his more immediate forbears had left. Their relatives and former friends were confounded by their conversion. It was to them as though a withering frost had blighted the abundant blossoms of a spring of extraordinary promise. The step cost the Maritains much, though they were not astonished at the solitude which enveloped them. As time passed others followed them, the most notable being Ernest Psichari, who, having pondered deeply during years of soldiering in Africa, professed the Christian faith before he was killed after the opening of World War I.

Having experienced the reality of faith in and love for God, Maritain had to work out for himself a philosophy and system of beliefs which could harmonize with his changed outlook on life. For months he pursued this end obscurely, as he narrates in *La Philosophie Bergsonienne*.[4] He regarded it as a mortal error to abandon the concept to rationalism as its normal vehicle, and, unlike Bergson, he could not invalidate the concept as a medium for transmitting the real to our mind. Up until then he had been unfamiliar with the philosophy of Thomas Aquinas. But he was already a Thomist without knowing it, in that he believed in the authentic value of our human instruments of knowledge. His greatest book, *Degrees of Knowledge*,[5] contains, according to those qualified to judge, one of the most original interpretations and developments of Thomist philosophy. There we have Maritain's thought interfused with faith glowing through the intellectual transmission lines, along which the current flows. It is a difficult book, partly because of the profundity and subtlety of the thought, partly because the author has created a copious language to clothe it with the most exact possible expression. Professor H. F. Stewart's words about Descartes and Pascal are peculiarly appropriate to the style of Maritain: Descartes "wields an elaborate and highly complicated phrase, full of parentheses and charged with subordinate clauses. So does Pascal on occasion, but the prose of Descartes for all its dignity is lit with cold light, that of Pascal is shot through with warmth and passion which renders it quick and powerful." In Maritain also we have the style of a dominant personality. "He wields an elaborate and highly complicated phrase, full of parentheses and charged with subordinate clauses," but "shot through with warmth and passion"; his imagery, truthful and original, often soars into poetic beauty.

It is not my purpose, nor have I the competence, to discuss Maritain as a philosopher: suffice it to say that the Thomist philosophy which he and others have revived is receiving serious attention in widely different circles of modern thought. I will venture, however, a few words on the *Degrees of Knowledge* because the principles of his religious philosophy underlie all his proposals for the reconstructed society. He accepts the fundamental Thomist noetic: "the assumption of the existence of things apart from the mind, and the possibility of the mind's awareness of things and of its power to construct, by its own rightful activity rising from the sense, a true knowledge in con-

---

[4] (2nd ed., Paris: M. Riviere, 1930).

[5] (2nd ed., London: Geoffrey Bles, 1937). The most recent edition is: (4th ed., New York: Scribner's, 1959) [Ed. note].

formity with reality."[6] Human knowledge is only possible as a knowledge gained through the senses. We must start from the axiom that truth is "conformity between the intelligence and the thing. . . . The apprehension of Being is absolutely primary, and is implied in all our other intellectual apprehensions. . . . The natural sciences presuppose the existence in the interior world of hidden ontological structures. . . . Through the knowledge of the world of human beings our intelligence arrives at man and the soul, and by reflective and practical philosophy it soars upwards to perceive the things which are of God, passing into metaphysics. . . . Metaphysics is directed towards a world of truths above time which are realized in temporal existence and towards a supreme super-temporal reality pre-eminent above all things. . . . Being, the human soul with its transcendental properties, constitutes the rightful object of metaphysics. . . . It grasps a world of eternal truths; the intellect thirsts for things that are Divine. . . . The process by which reason demonstrates that God *Is* puts the reason itself in an attitude of natural adoration and intellectual admiration. . . . 'He who is' is pre-eminently God's name. But the Divine nature is hidden from our metaphysical gaze. . . . Personality is necessary for God, the very seal of transcendence, infinite personality, transcendent in His essence, yet immanent in all things, in order ceaselessly to give them movement. . . . He knows and really loves created things. God is love. . . . Thus we rise to the super-rational though this knowledge remains conceptual and human."

Higher than metaphysical knowledge is the experimental knowledge of the deep things of God when mystically the soul "feels the life of God." The supreme form of wisdom, an order infinitely above the other degrees of knowledge, is given by supernatural grace, which grafts a new spiritual nature into the soul through the indwelling of God, rising in the saints to rapt contemplation of the Divine, a foretaste on earth of the experience of our homeland in heaven. "There must be in the soul in a state of grace filaments delicately sensitive to the breath of heaven. . . . We are like children who have been endowed with a supernatural art, a pencil wherewith to write on the sky. It is necessary that God should put his hand over ours to guide our trembling lines." This practical science of contemplation and union with God, "a loving attention to God," engenders in the saints the present experience even through suffering, of Divine love, to be fulfilled hereafter in the eternal beatific vision. The delectation — it

---

[6] *Degrees of Knowledge, op. cit.*, p. 28.

is not too strong a word— with which Maritain describes this contemplative life of wisdom suggests that here he is giving us a tran-
script of his own experience. Now and then in the concluding
chapters of *Degrees of Knowledge*, we catch prevenient tones in an
intellectual prelude, as it were, to the heavenly world, while for their
supreme poetic expression we must listen to Dante as in the last cantos
of the *Paradiso*:[7]

> Forth from the last corporeal are we come
> Into the heav'n that is unbodied light,
> Light intellectual replete with love,
> Love of true happiness replete with joy,
> Joy that transcends all sweetness of delight. . . .
> There is in heav'n a light, whose goodly shine
> Makes the Creator visible to all
> Created, that in seeing Him alone
> Have peace.

Can the beatific vision, the supreme knowledge of Divine love, as
fully experienced by the saints hereafter in joy, be symbolized in a
more beautiful emblem than the Heavenly Rose of the saints who
celebrate His glory whom they love?

> Faces had they of flame, and wings of gold;
> The rest was whiter than the driven snow.

A great deal of Maritain's work in recent years is concerned with
the application of his Thomist thought to modern social and political
problems; to mention only such writings as *Freedom in the Modern
World*,[8] *True Humanism*,[9] *Ransoming the Time*,[10] and "*The End of
Machiavellianism.*" [11] We may recall the world of which he was writing. The brilliant and gay culture of Paris was disintegrating morally,
socially and politically. In Western civilization there was little conviction as to the reality of spiritual truth. Such humanism as existed was
a mass of implicated and tangled ideas, uprooted from any superhuman source, living on themselves or decaying, mere patches of

[7] Dante Alighieri, *Divine Comedy* (New York: Everymans Library, E. P. Dutton,
1908), xxx: 39–43; 100–104.
[8] (New York: Scribner's, 1936).
[9] *Op. cit.*
[10] *Op. cit.*
[11] *Review of Politics*, January, 1942.

floating islands torn by storms of unbelief from the mainland and drifting hither and thither as the gusts changed. In Descartes, Rousseau, and Kant, rationalism had set up a proud and splendid image of the personality of man, and condemned any intervention from outside in this perfect and sacred universe. Yet in little more than a century this proud anthropocentric personality had perished; first with the triumph of the Darwinian ideas, while the *coup de grâce* was given by Freud. In the nineteenth century man sought security through the accumulation of material wealth, and in the twentieth came a reversal of all values. A secular doctrine of progress motivated by absolute atheism had scorched the European scene. Christianity had passed into eclipse. The failure of the Christian people to effect a real humanism was followed by the rise of what were practically new religions, or rather substitutes for religion. The spirit of Nietzsche ruled the German world with its blood nationalism; that of Marx ruled Russia with its cult of atheism. Communism is an earthly religion of the most imperious quality. It seeks to provide its adherents with a new hope of a far better human society when the final triumph over all that oppresses mankind's material life shall have been achieved. Here I would interject the remark that the incredible sacrifices now being made for their homeland by the Russians prove that their hopes, whatever their roots, have welded them into an unbreakable unity. Will this suffering release powerful spiritual elements which we know are embedded in the Russian character?

German national socialism is the result of "the intensely and morbidly industrialized German civilization deeply penetrated by the spirit of modern capitalism, which, after a crushing military defeat, arrived at general bankruptcy together with frightful material misery of the poorer classes." Grounding their effort on a ridiculous biological theory of race and blood, the Nazis set forth to wipe out other civilizations and to dominate the world. To begin with they tried to drive the Jews out of Germany, and to annihilate them, using myth, illusion, prestige of race, as fabricated reasons for their cruelties. Never anywhere had the Jews been so assimilated to any people as in Germany. Devoted to earthly business, money having for them a mystical attraction, they had there become thoroughly reconciled to the Prince of this world. But the national hatred of the Germans towards them springs also from another source: the Jewish people bear witness to the Divine in history; they cling to a belief in the justice of God to be revealed in time. Their passion for the Absolute exasperated tyrants

57

who are mere clods without a spark of the Divine. Israel is a scapegoat against which the impure sufferings of the world strike back. Nobly has Maritain repaid the debt to his wife and Henri Bergson by his repeated appeals for a place for the Jews in a pluralistic civilization.

A further factor in the distress into which the modern world has fallen is the capitalistic system which hides a radical disorder. The objective spirit of capitalism is the "exaltation of man's active and inventive powers." In it the poor man exists only as an instrument of production, a "hand," not a person. This social system has worsened until it is on the point of becoming intolerable. To counteract the evils of capitalism, however, socialism is no sufficient antidote. "In socialism also the very idea of freedom and autonomy is in danger. A proletariat in part plutocratized, in part a proletarianized swarm, may range itself under the banners of a demagogic, fanatical and sectarian communism."

Now we are in this horrible catastrophe into which an anthropocentric humanism, one in which man's ideals and hopes have been set entirely on an earthly existence, has plunged us. This description has brought Browning's lines to my mind:

> Grey plain all around:
> Nothing but plain to the horizon's bound.
> I might go on; nought else remained to do,
> So, on I went; I think I never saw
> Such starved ignoble nature; nothing throve.[12]

The outbreak of World War II saw ranged in its serried might the forces of the god of this world against all that is Christian; Christianity was to be wiped out. We have lived to behold the final fruit of Machiavellianism. Maritain traces the growth of this system through four centuries from the moderate type to the complete development in our day. Moderate Machiavellianism is the practice of those who hold in *theory* to the concept of the common good as the end in politics, but frankly use Machiavellian means to procure their ends. Now we are confronted with open and unabashed Machiavellianism. It

---

[12] "Childe Roland to the Dark Tower Came," *The Poems of Robert Browning*, (New York: Everyman's Library: E. P. Dutton, 1921), XI, p. 52. Maritain in *Reflections On America*, (Marpers 1958) is pleased at the U.S.A.'s attempt to achieve a society freed from the evils of both raw capitalism and naked socialism; so is R. L. Bruckberger, O.P., in *Image of America* (Viking, 1959). Even the so-called socialist parties of Western Europe drew praise from Mortimer J. Adler, speaking in the Christian Culture Series in Detroit on April 10, 1960, in that they recently by their statements seemed to be approaching a quasi-democratic capitalism [Ed. note].

means the accepting of nonmorality in practical politics, the worship of the state, "an impetuous, irrational, revolutionary, wild and demoniacal Machiavellianism, for which boundless injustice, boundless violence, boundless lying and immorality are normal political means, and which draws from this very boundlessness of evil an abominable strength."[13] A nation will only be saved if it will stand and fight the Machiavellian monster. Only if what remains of Christian civilization opposes it will absolute Machiavellianism be crushed. Besides, Maritain holds that "there is a natural justice of God in human history. . . . The sanctions of historical justice fail much more rarely than our short-sighted experience might induce us to believe."

The aim of the United Nations, as proclaimed by its adherents from the beginning, was to promote freedom for all. President Roosevelt promised that our victory would mean a victory for freedom: freedom of speech and religion, freedom from fear and want throughout the world.[14] Maritain would doubtless accept this program; for he too is a prophet of freedom, but of a full and complete freedom. Free choice is not an end in itself. "French liberalism and indeed the ruling liberalism of the 19th century, assumed that freedom of choice was an end in itself. But the absolute right of each part to realize its choices tends naturally to dissolve the whole in anarchy."[15] Free choice is given in order that man may reach the freedom of personal autonomy. The more complete a man, the freer he becomes. While "freedom is an inalienable property of every intellectual and spiritual nature it is because the will has by nature a capacity for the infinite, and tends necessarily to an infinite good." Nowhere more fully than in the beatitude of love is there freedom of autonomy. . . . It is with the liberty of God himself that the man of perfect soul is free."

We hope that, in the final analysis, the twilight that precedes our dawn will usher in a better civilization; but Maritain would say that if the result is to be worth the endurance of the evils of the black night, it must issue in a *theocentric* humanism, "a spiritual resurrection instinct with a love whose center is fixed infinitely above the world and temporal history. . . . It must be the blossoming, the earthly fructification of human life — material, moral and intellectual — in justice, nobility of heart, wisdom, science and art — the work of the spirit of liberty. . . . The common good in the temporal order is an inter-

[13] J. W. Evans and Leo R. Ward, editors. *The Social and Political Philosophy of Jacques Maritain* (New York: Scribner's, 1955), p. 304.

[14] *Four Freedoms Address*, United States Congress, January, 1940.

[15] *Freedom in the Modern World*, op. cit., p. 40.

mediate end, which gives the state its character, to the establishment of social conditions which will secure for the mass of men such a standard of material, intellectual and moral life as will conduce to the well-being of the whole community; so that every citizen will find in it a positive help in the progressive achievement of his freedom of autonomy."[16] In the new Christian society there will be pluralism; and, as is not the case in totalitarian societies, religious uniformity will not be imposed. Medieval Christianity will not be restored, nor will there be a new theocracy. "The end of freedom, insofar as it concerns the community of men, constitutes the only city which imposes on human personality neither constraint nor privation for the common good of this city will be the good also of humanity." In the new commonweal there will be embodied a greater variety of personal liberties for the individual, for the family, for the group. While it will be vitally Christian, unbelievers will share with believers for its secular and temporal ends, and in it the dignity of human personality and its spiritual vocation will be promoted. Modern civilization, though a worn-out garment, is not to be thrown away, but the imperishable strands of its past must be re-woven into a new garment. The true, theocentric humanism "re-habilitates the life of the profane city, the social and political order, the movement of the temporal progression of humanity — a temporal regime conformable to human dignity.... It is only in a new Christendom, in the future, that the ethical and affective value of the word democracy, which corresponds to what may be called a popular civic consciousness, will be really achieved. . . . The realization of this hope none of us may see, for the liquidation of four or five centuries of history does not take place in a day."

How is the ideal to be inaugurated? How are democracies to discover their vital principle of justice and love, the source of which is divine? We must begin to realize this integral humanism by each Christian thinking, acting and living in a Christian way in all phases of common life. We must not shun political effort, though there should be no strictly Christian political party. Believers should infuse the Christian spirit into their activities in the terrestrial city. Honorable citizens, working in groups authentically Christian in spirit, will carry on temporal activities in the present with the remote object at long range of renewing society on a theocratic basis. They will be a minority acting like a leaven of truth, justice and love. A Christian Diaspora, spread in groups over the whole surface of the globe, they

[16] *Ibid*, pp. 42–3.

will disseminate among the nations a new Christendom. The terrestrial city will be irradiated by gifts from the celestial. The grace of God will perfect, not destroy, human nature, and will help it to discover greater truths in the natural order, while the individual will, through Divine wisdom, develop his personality for the future beatific vision of the love of God.

Maritain writes, of course, primarily for members of his own communion. What has he for us outsiders? To the Scottish Presbyterian puritanism in which I was born and bred, he would probably be antipathetic; my church he holds to be non-apostolic, its worship jejune, its doctrine perilously defective. But he is willing to have us co-operate in establishing a new humanism, in promoting a new Christendom. While he would not allow that we have explicit faith, he believes that we may have implicit faith in Christ. "The basis of fellowship with non-Catholics is not of the order of the intellect and of ideas, but of the heart and of love. It is friendship, natural friendship, but first and foremost mutual love in God and for God. Not a fellowship of beliefs but a fellowship of men who believe. What each one is before God neither the one nor the other knows. . . . Only through love can peace and union come to men. . . . This mutual comprehension cannot in any way involve any less intangible, more definite, more visible communion, expressed in the order of the speculative and practical intellect by some community of symbol or sacred ritual. But on the level of the temporal and profane life it is proper that the effort towards union should express itself."

We non-Catholics welcome Maritain as an authentic prophet for our time. His passion for sanctification, without which no one shall see the Lord, his insight into Divine love and wisdom, his transfer of the fruits of this contemplation for the healing of our disordered society, his interpretation of the meaning of personality and freedom in their reality and fullness — all this is enriching our Christian heritage. Moreover, his conviction that a living God of wisdom and justice moves through history supports us in the demonic struggle of our days, and encourages us to hope for the gradual realization in time to come of a humanity more integral, victorious and at peace.

Intellectual Curiosity in Catholic Schools

Lawrence E. Lynch

Dr. L. E. Lynch, the President of the Catholic Philosophical Association of America for 1958, received most of his education at the University of St. Michaels, the University of Toronto, and at the Pontifical Institute of Medieval Studies. He was born in Toronto in 1915, and he lives there now with his wife and children. He teaches at the Pontifical Institute of Medieval Studies. Like Marshall McLuhan (another contributor to this volume) he has often appeared on the Canadian Broadcasting Company programs. He has translated into English, from the German, Justice *by Joseph Pieper. From the French he has translated* Introduction to the Study of St. Augustine *by Etienne Gilson, and he has collaborated in the new translation of* The Degrees of Knowledge *by Jacques Maritain. He has contributed to several scholarly journals, such as* Medieval Studies *and the* New Scholasticism. *He was chairman of the Administration Committee of the World University Service of Canada, 1949–52. He was a member of the World University Service Canadian Seminar in Holland in 1949, and he was Chairman of the Canadian Institute of Public Affairs at the Lake Couchiching Conference in 1957. The following essay was given as part of the Christian Culture Series in 1958.*

In an article entitled "American Catholics and the Intellectual Life."[1] Monsignor John Tracy Ellis, Professor of Church History at the Catholic University of America, called attention to a condition of the Church in America that had often been mentioned but never seriously investigated — namely, the contribution Catholics are presently making to the intellectual life of their community.

Monsignor Ellis' remarks were prompted by reading a comment made several years ago by Professor Dennis W. Brogan of Cambridge University: "In no Western society is the intellectual prestige of Ca-

---

[1] *Thought* (New York: Fordham University, Autumn, 1955), 351–388. Published as a book under the same title (Chicago: Heritage Foundation, 1956).

tholicism lower than in the country where, in such respects as wealth, numbers and strength of organization, it is so powerful."[2] Monsignor Ellis' conclusion constitutes a confirmation of that judgment. His findings were subsequently reprinted in various forms and given wide circulation in both the Catholic and secular press. Further corroboration of his opinion soon came to him in the many newspaper editorials and personal letters his work occasioned[3] — letters from bishops, college and university professors, editors, lawyers, parish priests and seminary professors. Many Catholic organizations such as the National Catholic Educational Association, the National Newman Club Federation, and a conference of the deans of Catholic graduate schools made his work the basis of serious and lengthy discussions. Monsignor Ellis has summarized these comments in the following words: "On the whole, therefore, the reactions summarized in the present report reveal a substantial agreement with the principal conclusions reached last Fall in *Thought*. That so large a segment of Catholic opinion should have been roused to express its ideas on this theme is itself immensely encouraging. It does, however, logically suggest a further question: What is going to be done about the situation?"[4]

Sometime later, John Wright, then Bishop of Worcester, Massachusetts, now Bishop of Pittsburg, commented on the same theme: "What a tragic irony it would be, if, after centuries of battling for the natural law and the rights and function of reason, as well as for the primacy of the intellect over passion and emotion, instinct and even will, the Church should find herself represented in the world of the college, the press or the forum by persons contemptuous of that 'wild, living intellect of man' of which Newman spoke, and cynical about the slow, sometimes faltering, but patient, perservering process by which intellectuals seek to wrest some measure of order from chaos. . . ."[5]

Constructive suggestions to remedy the situation have not been wanting, but they very largely follow the line of causes Monsignor Ellis laid bare:

1) The spirit of our times: when money is used as a measure of

[2] *U.S.A., An Outline of the Country. Its People and Institutions* (London, 1941, p. 65.

[3] "No Complacency," *America* (April 7, 1956).

[4] *Ibid*, p. 25.

[5] *Jubilee* (February, 1956). Also in *American Catholics and the Intellectual Life*, *op. cit.*, p. 8.

success, scholarship must surely come off a very bad second or third choice.[6]

2) Conformity: Catholics, as a minority group, have tried to conform and prove how "American" they are by adopting the common American judgment concerning intellectual achievement.[7]

3) The absence of an intellectual tradition among American Catholics: a condition which results from many causes but mainly from the demands made on the Church by so huge a country, a large population and constant immigration.[8]

4) A failure in leadership: Catholics in positions of authority, both clerical and lay, have largely failed to appreciate and encourage intellectual work.[9]

The following are some of the remedies suggested by Monsignor Ellis and his correspondents:

1) A deliberate effort to create a living intellectual tradition in as many Catholic families as possible.[10]

2) Joint planning by and cooperation among Catholic school authorities with a view to overcoming needless duplication of effort in Catholic colleges and graduate schools, a duplication which has often resulted in fruitless competition and lower standards.[11]

3) Greater recognition of the problem and more vigorous leadership in solving it on the part of bishops and heads of religious communities.[12]

4) Better relations in matters of education between the clergy and laity.[13]

5) More contact between Catholic and non-Catholic scholars in their own professional fields.[14]

The present paper is undertaken with the hope of making some small contribution to the "great debate" as Bishop Wright terms it. The main point of the remarks that follow will be to suggest that the causes indicated above are secondary causes, operating as they do within the order of sociology, programs of school administration and techniques of learning. Our question will be, rather, this one: Are

---

[6] "American Catholics," *op. cit., Thought*, 364; Heritage, p. 29.
[7] *Ibid, Thought*, 356; Heritage, p. 20.
[8] *Ibid, Thought*, 357; Heritage, p. 21.
[9] *Ibid, Thought*, 365; Heritage, p. 31.
[10] *Ibid, Thought*, 358; Heritage, p. 21.
[11] "No Complacency," *op. cit.*, p. 15.
[12] *Ibid*, 15–16.
[13] *Ibid*, 17.
[14] *Ibid*, 20.

there more primary causes at work? If we are in a period of anti-intellectualism, may not our analysis of the causes of that frame of mind tend to neglect or underestimate causes proper to the *intellect* itself? May not very serious restraints upon intellectual curiosity and troublesome obstacles to intellectual achievement lie hidden within the *interpretation*, often given to fundamental Catholic ideas concerning education? In short, would it not seem proper to be somewhat *intellectual* about the reasons for the anti-intellectualism? Perhaps a small beginning, at least, will be made if we turn our attention to the following concepts: Christian *education*, Catholic *schools*, faith, "knowing one's faith," and truth. These will, indeed, be the themes of the sections that follow.

Christian education and Catholic schools

Perhaps the easiest way to introduce the problems I see stemming from the concepts "Christian education" and "Catholic schools" is to point to a common identification of terms in the secular order. Today it is current usage to call a teacher an "educator." Certain overtones would perhaps be reserved for the word "educator" — he must be older, more experienced, perhaps in an administrative rather than an active teaching post — but the difference is one of degree only. The work of education is a task allotted to teachers. It is accomplished in schools. Now influenced by the terminology and ideas of our contemporaries, Christian education has come to be considered the proper task of Christian, or in the present context, Catholic schools. As a direct consequence of a growing dereliction of duty, the whole task of educating — a responsibility usually divided among the family, Church and political society — is becoming more and more the responsibility of the school. Etiquette, hygiene, basic moral training, prayers, missionary activities, civics, military training — all of these are foisted upon the teacher and the school. They are made the responsibility of classroom study. Moreover, in the case of the Catholic school, the aims and purposes of Christian education tend to become the end which determines the curriculum and daily routine of the Catholic school.

The document to which all present-day discussions of Christian education — at least, discussions engaged in by Catholics — eventually revert is the Encyclical of Pius XI entitled *Christian Education of Youth*. In that document Pius XI says at the very outset: "From these same principles, the excellence, we may well call it the unsurpassed excellence, of the work of Christian education becomes manifest and clear; for after all it aims at securing the Supreme Good, that is, God, for the souls of those who are being educated, and the maximum of well-being possible here below for human society."[15] Now by transferring the work of Christian education to the Catholic school, this becomes the purpose of the Catholic school. And yet through some strange oddity of textual interpretation, we seem to concern ourselves only with the first "aim" mentioned by the Pope: "The Supreme Good, that is, God." If the second part of his statement — "the maximum of well-being possible here below for human society" — is considered at all, it seems to be given a purely moralistic interpretation. "The maximum well-being" would consist in lives of moral excellence, in spite of the Holy Father's clearly stated phrase "for human society." Following this line of thought, moral virtue (or, as will be pointed out separately in a later section, preserving the Faith or teaching "Catholic truth") becomes the prime, although certainly not the only, objective of Catholic schools. Students' sanctity and piety transcend learning and intellectual habits as the school's purpose. In short, while claiming to educate man "for what he must be and for what he must do here below, in order to attain the sublime end for which he was created,"[16] the Catholic school seems more intent upon disciplining the human will and — by a strange Jansenism — human passions, rather than upon learning. Development of the intellect, with which man is to know God in the next life, seems by some odd quirk of "charity" left to merest chance. Intellectual virtues, in which a school might well be interested, are placed in a position of inferiority; intellectual curiosity is oftentimes deprecated as a possible danger to piety!

If, however, the Encyclical of Pius XI is more closely scrutinized, such an interpretation will be found to be a dangerous and tragic travesty on the doctrine the Holy Father is promulgating. A few very well-known "principles" (or, if you prefer, deeply rooted conclusions) command his whole treatment of Christian education.

1) Education, being a practical activity, must be considered in view of a principle that determines everything in the practical order, the end. Hence, one of the Pope's first statements: "It is therefore as important to make no mistake in education as it is to make no mistake

[15] *Five Great Encyclicals* (New York: Paulist Press, 1945), p. 39.
[16] *Ibid*, p. 39.

in the pursuit of the last end, with which the whole work of education is intimately and necessarily connected."[17]

2) In all practical matters there is a due and fitting ordering of ends: means being determined by non-ultimate or intermediary ends, these in turn by more ultimate ends and, finally, by the ultimate end. Hence, the three societies concerned with education are carefully distinguished by Pius XI[18] on the basis of the end peculiar to each: the family, civil society, the Church; the rights and duties to educate enjoyed by those three societies are carefully harmonized by the subordination of their ends.

3) A proper order exists between nature and grace. The Holy Father says: "Consequently, education, which is concerned with man as a whole, individually and socially, in the order of nature and in the order of grace, necessarily belongs to all these three societies, in due proportion, corresponding, according to the disposition of Divine Providence, to the coordination of their respective ends."[19] And again "The fundamental reason for this harmony is that the supernatural order, to which the Church owes her rights, not only does not in the least destroy the natural order, to which pertain the other rights mentioned, but elevates the natural and perfects it."[20]

The Pope proceeds to examine the coordination that should prevail among the various agents at work in Christian education in accordance with these principles. To the Church belongs the pre-eminent right to educate "by reason of a double title in the supernatural order"[21]: to wit, the direct command of Her Founder to teach all nations, and her supernatural motherhood in virtue of which she "generates, nurtures and educates souls in the divine life of grace, with her Sacraments and her doctrine."[22] To the family belongs the inalienable right to educate in virtue of its fecundity in the natural order, a fecundity which is the principle of life, and hence also the principle of education to life, together with authority, the principle of order."[23] And to the political society belong "true and just rights . . . in regard to the education of its citizens,"[24] rights that "have

[17] *Ibid*, p. 38.
[18] *Ibid*, p. 40.
[19] *Ibid*, p. 40.
[20] *Ibid*, p. 44.
[21] *Ibid*, p. 40.
[22] *Ibid*, p. 41.
[23] *Ibid*, p. 45.
[24] *Ibid*, p. 28.

been conferred upon civil society by the Author of Nature Himself, not by title of fatherhood, as in the case of the Church and of the family, but in virtue of the authority which it possesses to promote the common temporal welfare, which is the purpose of its existence."[25]

It should be noted that all of these declarations of right (based on the duty to attain a certain end) are made with reference to education. The Pope speaks of schools only within that broader context. Thus, in a very early passage of the encyclical, he says: "Therefore, with full right the Church promotes letters, science, art, insofar as necessary or helpful to Christian education, in addition to her work for the salvation of souls; founding and maintaining schools and institutions adapted to every branch of learning and degree of culture. Nor may even physical culture, as it is called, be considered outside the range of her maternal supervision, for the reason that it also is a means which may harm or help Christian education."[26] Notice the clear ordering of ends: schools (physical training, arts, letter and science), Christian education, the salvation of souls, the vision of God.

This explains, I think, why the Holy Father only turns to the question of Catholic schools towards the end of the encyclical, and why he prefaces his words about Catholic schools with a brief statement about schools as such: "Since however the younger generations must be trained in the arts and sciences for the advantage and prosperity of civil society, and since the family is unequal to the task, it was necessary to create that social institution, the school. But let it be borne in mind that this institution owes its existence to the initiative of the family and of the Church, long before it was undertaken by the state. Hence, considered in its historical origin, the school is by its very nature an institution subsidiary and complementary to the family and to the Church."[27] The school, then, trains men in the arts and sciences for the advantage and prosperity of civil society.

In the Catholic school — and here Pius XI quotes Leo XIII — "It is necessary not only that religious instruction be given to the young at certain fixed times, but also that every other subject taught be permeated with Christian piety."[28] In virtue of the order existing between grace and nature, this can only mean that the arts and sciences, as well as religious instruction, are to be taught in an atmosphere "permeated with Christian piety." On the other hand, inasmuch as

[25] *Ibid*, p. 48.
[26] *Ibid*, p. 42.
[27] *Ibid*, p. 59.
[28] *Ibid*, p. 60.

nature is never replaced or destroyed by grace, this requires that the Catholic school achieve the proper end of a school before it means anything for it to function in a Christian atmosphere. But in achieving that end in a Christian atmosphere, it is better as a school. It is, thereby, "for the advantage and prosperity of civil society" — as well as being of service to Christian education and the sanctification of man. But, note, it must be a school, in all that implies, before it can be a Catholic school and in any way serve Christian education.

At this point I am reminded of a thought-provoking passage from St. Augustine :

Frequently some question may arise about earth, or sky, or other elements of nature, movement, orbits, or even the size and distance of the stars, the regular eclipses of sun and moon, the succession of the seasons; the nature of animals, vegetables, minerals, and kindred things, about which a non-Christian may have knowledge derived from most accurate observation and reasoning. It is most deplorable, mischievous, and a thing to be avoided, that any Christian should ever deign to speak on such matters only from an acquaintance with previous Christian writings and thereby utter nonsense, as far from the mark, to quote the common saying, as is East from West. In such a case the unbeliever would only be moved to unrestrained laughter.[29]

To sum up: there is no question that sanctity is the aim of Christian education; but learning is the end of the Catholic school. On this score, we should remember that Thomas Aquinas has been given to us as the doctor of the schools, and we have done much to guide our thinking by his. But have we learned the lesson of his sanctity? In a recent article,[30] Thomas Deman, O.P., has pointed out quite clearly how the life of grace, the operations of the gifts and virtues, sustained St. Thomas in the life of the intellect. It prompts one to ask: are we not indulging in a form of Christian pragmatism, when we interpret sanctity in terms of the practical, active life only when we emphasize the role of the moral virtues in strengthening our wills and appetites to make ordinate and proper use of material things in our daily lives? May not fortitude be sought in the interest of truth? May not temperance be cultivated so as to discipline the sensible pleasures we seek —

[29] *De genesi ad litteram*, xix. 39, p. 261.
[30] "Knowledge and Sanctity according to St. Thomas," *The Life of the Spirit* (London: Blackfriars), XI, 129, pp. 394–406.

that our intellect's work may not be impeded? Is not prudence required for proper study? Is not justice, exercised towards our neighbor as scholar, as precious a discipline of the will as justice exercised towards our neighbor as merchant or workman?

The Catholic school must, indeed, be permeated with Christian piety. But piety is reverence. And is it not more fitting for the Christian teacher as teacher to show reverence for his students' intellects even more than for their physical persons or human susceptibilities? What greater reverence can be shown the human intellect than to help it know truth? This, it would seem, is one way in which learning can be pursued in our Catholic schools without divorcing it from or rendering it antithetical to moral virtue and personal sanctity. And in an age in which citizens are more and more subject to intellectual temptations, particularly temptations of a philosophical and political kind, who is to say that a moral discipline and sanctity which safeguard the intellect — although cultivated with a view to the ultimate vision of God — may not be, indeed, "for the advantage and prosperity of civil society?"

Faith and "knowing one's faith"

We now turn to the next set of concepts we proposed to examine: faith and knowing one's faith. Monsignor Ellis has described [31] the Church in America as preoccupied with the gigantic task of absorbing well over ten million Catholic immigrants in the period 1820–1920, a task that absorbed all of the Church's energies and resources and left precious little leisure and few means for intellectual pursuits. We must agree, I believe, that such a historical fact is responsible for the situation we are now going to investigate. Circumstances dictated that the great work was to preserve the faith — preserve it in the sense of defending its dogma or of perpetuating the faith as a way of life. Catholic schools were called upon to play a major role in this work — and in view of our present preoccupation in this paper, it is with the effect that it had on the school that we are solely concerned. To safeguard the faith as a way of life, practical religious training became more and more a concern of the school; to preserve the faith as a body of belief, a knowledge of catechism and apologetics became a prime objective of teaching in Catholic schools.

Let us now ask these questions: What intellectual challenge is there in faith conceived in a moralistic or legalistic manner as primarily a

[31] "American Catholics," *op. cit., Thought,* 353; *Heritage,* p. 180.

way of life? What intellectual curiosity is aroused by faith viewed as a set of dogmatic formulas to be learned in catechism or as a set of arguments devised to defend the faith — usually against the charge that it is opposed to reason? As Thomas Donlon, O.P., has pointed out so clearly,[32] where students are urged to lead good lives, it is rhetoric (the art of persuading) rather than science (the knowledge of truth) that dominates the classroom — preaching rather than teaching! Where the objective is to have students know their faith (in the sense of being acquainted with doctrinal formulas and their compatibility with reason), what mystery is to be found in God to challenge one's intellect? And if there is no mystery about God, what mystery will attend His works? We should never forget a very apt comment of St. Thomas: "If the teacher should determine a question solely by authorities, the pupil will be made certain that it is so, but he acquires nothing of science or understanding and departs empty-headed (*vacuus*)."[33]

Here we must return to fundamentals if we would restore what historical circumstance has deformed. The first of these is the concept of faith. For St. Thomas faith is first and foremost a knowledge. He compares its role in the order of supernatural knowledge to *intellectus*, the understanding of principles, from which all natural knowledge originates. And he issues a very important warning: "The act of the believer does not terminate in the statement (*ad enuntiabile*) but in the object (*sed ad rem*)."[34] Faith, then, is not an act of the intellect whereby men cling to propositions or formulas; it is an act of the intellect whereby men know the first truth, God.

Secondly, what is meant by "knowing one's faith"? Not merely a knowledge of arguments designed to show the faith is reasonable; not simply a knowledge of factual data related to the Church's history, practice or liturgy. *Fides quaerens intellectum* remains the best description of the intellect's search when, informed and challenged by faith, it seeks to understand what God has revealed to it of His own divine life. Such knowledge is the product of the effort man makes to penetrate the deposit of truth God has graciously given his intellect. But why is it challenged to do so?

According to St. Thomas the act of believing, while it is an act of the intellect, is commanded by the will. In faith the intellect finds

[32] *Theology and Education* (Dubuque, Iowa: Wm. C. Brown, 1952), pp. 71–80.
[33] *Quaest. quod.*, 4, q. 9, a. 17.
[34] *Sum. th.*, 2–2, q. 1, a. 2.

itself admitting the certitude of a truth without being able to point to reasons for its conviction. It is secure in its knowledge, but perplexed by the reasons for it; it is fastened by its own proper object, truth, but not by the evidence of its object. So, St. Thomas remarks, the intellect remains dissatisfied; it still feels compelled to think about and delve into (*sed adhuc habet cogitationem et inquisitionem de his quae credit*) the things it believes.[35] From the intellectual curiosity thus aroused emerges what we now speak of as "theology."

That curiosity may issue into an effort to achieve an exact knowledge of the *revelata* through a careful examination of the language in which divine science was communicated to man or through psychological or anthropological investigations of the peoples to whom it was revealed. Or, pursuing a different tack, it may follow the logical pattern of scientific knowledge Aristotle has bequeathed the Western world. In this latter sense, the meaning of St. Thomas' analogy between faith and the understanding of principles (*intellectus*) takes on a clearer meaning. For just as natural intellectual principles may cast their light upon moving bodies and provide us with a scientific knowledge of those bodies, so, too, may the truths of faith, revealed by God, act as a supernatural light to give us a scientific knowledge of things as seen with the eyes of God. As science is an understanding of principles, so, too, is theology an understanding of faith. Knowing one's faith, then, does not lead to a factual knowledge of formulas or data, but to a scientific knowledge of God and the things of nature seen through revelation. Starting with the stage of participating in God's knowledge (in the certitude the intellect has of the truth God reveals to it), the intellect is moved by native curiosity to understand more and more fully all that is implied in the truth it thus possesses. But its whole activity is centered on the divine nature which it seeks to see more completely. Viewed in this way, understanding constitutes a true habit, the intellect is concerned more with knowing than it is with clinging to formulas. In a word, faith challenges the intellect to real intellectual work — the grace of faith perfects the nature of the intellect.

Now activity of that kind is most proper to the school, dedicated as it is to learning. Faith as a mere clinging to God through an effort of will, faith as the voluntary acceptance of truths which are merely accepted and deemed impervious to intellectual penetration, faith which is an act of the will and which remains secure from the attacks

[35] *De ver.*, q. 14, a. 1.

72

of reason because it is of things not seen, may be a temptation to the overly zealous apologist. But it is the faith of a Descartes, not an Aquinas; a sincere faith, no doubt, in Descartes' case but fraught with deadly dangers to the Catholic faith.

Truth and truths

Finally, let us look at the last notion we propose to examine: truth. In this case our question is this: What dangers does a moralistic interpretation of truth set in the path of the Catholic school? What does such a view of truth do to the spirit of learning?

Nowhere, I think, is the "arid land of American Catholic complacency" [36] so evident as in the commonly expressed remark: "Well, we Catholics have the truth!" It is the sign of a mental attitude utterly disastrous to intellectual stimulation. It would be bad enough if it were simply taken to refer to truth concerning faith and morals — as though by merely being a Catholic we as individuals were brought into possession of a vast treasure of moral truth. The Church possesses such truth: we may possess it, but only as a result of an effort of slow and disciplined intellectual effort. Even the Church has not come to possess it by a merely passive acceptance from her Founder: papal infallibility does not by any means do away with hard study and much learning. It is, indeed, a source of great strength to a Catholic to know that the Holy Ghost preserves from error doctrinal definitions made by the Popes; it is no reason for intellectual complacency.

But there are far more damaging overtones in such an attitude. First, it implies that the only truth in which we show any real interest is "moral truth." Second, it suggests that truth is a kind of completed whole, uniform throughout, and to be approached as ? Catholic approaches revealed truth, in faith. Such an attitude merits, I believe, the name "theological positivism." Technically speaking, such a view considers truth univocal — concerned with objects of faith and morals, and learned primarily by authority. But then the question at once arises: does any truth (which does not have to do with man's last end immediately) exist in natural science, art, poetry, literature? If the answer is: "No," then the further question follows: "Why, then, bother with schools?"

Considered from a somewhat different point of view, such an approach to truth makes it extremely difficult for a Catholic student

[36] John A. O'Brien, *Catholics and Scholarship*, (Huntington, Indiana: Our Sunday Visitor Press, 1938), p. 51. Also see James M. O'Neill, *Catholicism and American Freedom*, (New York: Scribner's, 1952), p. 113.

to undertake and profit by the study of any matter that does not immediately concern salvation. We have all heard or read the feeble efforts of Catholic students struggling to appreciate a play or story: the hero did the right thing, the heroine acted immorally. Moral judgments do have their place; didactic intent may be justified in art. But what of the truth of the artifact? Are we not to seek truth in the artistic structure of a novel? In the visible pattern or rhythmic sound of words? In the events of history? In the efforts men make to achieve justice in law? In the test tube? An overly developed preoccupation with moral judgments is, I fear, the basic reason for the depressingly naïve answers Catholics often give to the most complex political and economic problems. It is also the reason for that distressing habit of many Catholics of seeking the Catholic view of, or solution to, practical contemporary problems.

Truth is not an exclusive prerogative of the Church, even though it is her obligation to protect and foster truth wherever it may be found. Pius XI quotes approvingly the following words of Manzini: "The Church does not say that morality belongs purely, in the sense of exclusively, to her; but that it belongs wholly to her. She has never maintained that outside her fold and apart from her teaching, man cannot arrive at any moral truth; she has on the contrary more than once condemned this opinion because it has appeared under more forms than one."[37]

Moreover, truth is not univocal but, rather, analogical. The true is a transcendental property of all things, and the evidence with which it declares itself is as varied as the things themselves. Only an intellect capable of being tuned to many wave lengths will catch it in all its variety. Sometimes truth is the property of a naturally stable and unchangeable reality (God, for example), and "being true" has, correspondingly, an air of permanence about it. At other times it is the property of a naturally changeable and changing reality (a tree, for example), and then "being true" is less enduring—but nonetheless true. Hence, quite different techniques are needed to grasp it. Once recognize that there are various kinds of truth, and you must admit (if truth is good at all!) that there are various sciences of it, and that each science must be left free to discover truth for itself. Thus, the Holy Father says: "The Church, therefore, far from hindering the pursuit of the arts and sciences, fosters and promotes them in many ways. For she is neither ignorant nor unappreciative of the many

[37] *Five Great Encyclicals, op. cit.*, p. 42.

advantages which flow from them to mankind. On the contrary, she admits that just as they came from God, Lord of all knowledge, so too if rightly used, with the help of His grace they lead to God. Nor does she prevent sciences, each in its sphere, from making use of principles and methods of their own." [38] Then Pius XI adds a few words that point to the roots of academic freedom in Catholic schools: "This norm of a just freedom in things scientific, serves also as an inviolable norm of a just freedom in things didactic, or for rightly understood liberty in teaching; it should be observed therefore in whatever instruction is imparted to others. Its obligation is all the more binding in justice where there is question of instructing youth." [39]

There is, then, a truth to be found in art, literature, science. It is not, note well, a moral truth, a truth concerning man's actions in view of his last end, but a truth found in the order and beauty God has placed in things in creating them. It might also be added, too, that there is truth in the social artifacts (cities, states, guilds, unions, welfare organizations) man has constructed with his reason in completing the social order God left him to fashion. A Catholic should be on the watch for truth everywhere, if he has a "Catholic" mind, and not just in the manuals of moral philosophy and theology!

Our point might well be illustrated with a historical example. It was once the fashion to think of scholasticism as a single theological or philosophical doctrine that was supposed to have held the minds of European scholars until the 15th century. Such a view was in great measure the result of the conviction that "Catholic" truth is a monolithic, unchanging, body of truth. It is now clear, however, that even in questions involving moral and theological speculation, the positions held and taught in the great universities of France, England, Italy and Germany during the 13th and 14th centuries were so varied that classification into a manageable number of "schools" is extremely arbitrary. It is just one historical phenomenon which attests in a very practical way to the varied forms of truth.

Aristotle tells this instructive story: strangers often came to visit the famous philosopher Heraclitus, but finding him warming himself at his kitchen-fire, they hesitated to enter. Seeing them, Heraclitus bade them enter, adding the comment that they should not be afraid to do so because there were gods in the place. In that spirit,

[38] *Ibid*, p. 53.
[39] *Ibid*, p. 54.

says Aristotle, we should undertake the study of all phases of nature: not just the beauty of the heavens and the pleasing qualities of animals attractive to the senses, but even those that appear ignoble, "For each and all will reveal to us something natural and beautiful,[40] since "every realm of nature is marvelous."[41]

The challenge of wonder, according to Aristotle,[42] has led men to philosophize. St. Thomas [43] has described it as the *desiderium sciendi*, the longing for knowledge. Can there be any less wonder in the works of God's hand for a Catholic than for a pagan? Is it not our job, as Catholic teachers, to devote every talent we possess to arousing in our students a restless sense of intellectual curiosity that will make them discontent until they have seen the wonders of God's work, until they have begun to yearn for the vision of His face?

[40] *On the Parts of Animals*, 654a, 23.
[41] *Ibid*, 17.
[42] *Metaphysics*, 1, 3, 982b, 12ff.
[43] *Sum. the.*, 1–2, q. 32, a. 8. Also see Aristotle, *Rhetoric*, 1, 2, 1371a, 32.

The Indispensable Foundation
Of Intellectual Culture

Friedrich Wilhelm Foerster

*Dr. F. W. Foerster, once Professor of Philosophy at the University
of Vienna and also Professor of Philosophy and Pedagogy at the University of Munich, was born in 1869 in Berlin, Germany, son of the
Director of the Berlin Observatory. A brilliant university career had
to be sacrificed for many years of exile at various periods; right from
the beginning, in 1895, when he was imprisoned for three months
after being tried for allegedly criticizing the Kaiser and condemning
materialistic militarism. He foresaw clearly, and courageously tried
to head off, each World War, as he pleaded for metapolitics: the
application of sound ethics to public as well as private morality. He
has been called "one of the most highly respected, as well as one of
the most bitterly attacked, figures of Europe"; "the educator of nations"; "the conscience of two generations"; "a leader in three fields:
ethics, character education, and the philosophy of culture." This
splendid Christian humanist, like Maritain, Dawson, and Chesterton,
whom he so greatly admired, holds that "the soul of culture is the culture of the soul." He sees no solution to the deepest problems of philosophy and life apart from the Cross of the crucified God-Man. Both
Pius XI and Pius XII commended his fruitful writings. The Protestan Faculty of Theology at the University of Leipzig gave him an honorary Doctorate in Theology. The Nazis burned his books in 1935, but
since 1955 several of his books have been reprinted in a "Germany
reconciled with Europe," because "reconciled with truth," with the
aid of the Foerster Society there. A new edition of Foerster's* Christ
and the Human Life *in 1953 came out in the United States, Italy, and
Japan. Seventeen years before, in 1936, his* Marriage and the Sex Problem *was published in the United States and bore a laudatory preface
by Fulton J. Sheen. Foerster has written over thirty books and is still
writing at the age of ninety-one. Recently his extraordinary memoirs
were published in Germany, and a book on* Political Ethics *by Foer-*

*ster appeared in Turkey. He received the 1955 Christian Culture
Award and wrote this essay, which was broadcast at the time. He still
resides in New York City.*

Certain considerations will show that genuine intellectual culture
involves not only moral but religious bases and guarantees. Obvious
today, to even the slightly aware, is this ominous fact: *the catas-
trophic abuse by man of man's scientific and technical progress.*

History yields for our contemplation eras of vast unification, and
co-operation between nations and between powers in man's soul. It
also reveals eras of disintegration, secession, and obstinate self-concen-
tration. Sometimes the immediate cause of this abandonment of all
co-operation and community has been the overtension of unity
coupled with the determination to express, and live out untrammeled,
certain personal talents and functions. Today, at the end of a pro-
longed period of disintegration, we are almost ready to admit that
the continuation of man's existence on this planet largely depends
on a new complement of all nations and of the warring elements in
the human soul. But isolation and disintegration have already gone
so far that the suprahuman help of Divine Providence is desperately
needed to inspire mankind and to heal the sorely divided modern
soul.

Wars of principles and ideologies preceded both recent World
Wars, and it was the disease of spiritual chaos that boiled over into
political and social chaos, tension and explosion. Principles born to
be complementary to each other are still, however, locked in conflict,
emphasizing pseudo self-sufficiency: authority and liberty, democracy
and leadership, self-determination and tradition, religion and intelligence, individualism and socialism. How can the synthesis that again
may provide tranquility be arrived at?

Faith and intelligence should walk hand in hand. The contemporary war between them is really unnecessary and out of date. There
is an inscription on the great portal of the University of Cairo which
reads: "Chemistry is important; God is more important." This admo-
nition is as timely in our nuclear age as it ever was, because human
intelligence, so successful in discovering and applying the mysterious
potential in natural forces, has also procured the key for opening and
unleashing incredible powers capable of annihilating all that lives on
earth. Who is supposed to exercise control of the key? Intelligence,
the discoverer of the key, is of itself devoid of the moral power of

control and incapable of restraining the diabolic potentialities in human nature from misusing science and mobilizing discoveries for hellish intents. It is very unfortunate that man's triumphal mastery of external nature had to coincide with his alarming defeat in mastering the untamed forces in his own nature. Richard Wagner's *Rheingold* is an image of the tragedy of scientific success divorced from moral maturity. Wagner has called Wotan the incarnation of modern intelligence, drunken in pursuit of conquest of nature's treasures and highly successful until he is himself overcome and reduced to slavery by the unharnessed powers of his own nature. The contemplation of this tragedy of the isolated human intelligence may help contemporaries to search for a solution.

There is no doubt among serious thinkers about the urgent need of a sufficient spiritual and moral counterweight in every person, so that the fruits of the domination of external nature can be controlled for the benefit of mankind. Self-control, however, is resultant of proper spiritual orientation and motivation, not merely by an appeal to crass self-interest. Alas, modern intelligence is alarmingly undernourished spiritually. Plato's words of wisdom to persons in an earlier age of mental confusion are quite pertinent today: "Without the science of the highest good, all other science has no value at all."[1]

Intellectual culture not only a function of intelligence

Religious groups throughout the world today lament the religious void in the curriculum of the public schools; however, they sometimes direct their appeal only to the section of the populace that is already interested in the salvation of human souls and seem to forget that the typical men of our technical civilization, devoted chiefly to the development of human intelligence, are usually left cold by impressive moral absolutes. We must go beyond showing that the intellectual development of modern youth requires spiritual influence to complement that development; we must show that, without spiritual influence, the development of the intellect itself, even in its technical functions, may be paralyzed. In certain warships armed by steel plates and other metals, magnetic currents are produced which dangerously deflect the needle of the compass from its direction toward the pole, unless special protective, isolating material is used. In a like manner, man's intellectual compass, more than moderns tend to realize, needs efficient protection against the upsurge of bodily influences that tend

[1] *Republic*, VI, 505.

to deflect the needle from its inflexible orientation towards objective truth. Without religion, the aforementioned necessary protection is absent. Logic is no exclusively intellectual function; it is the function of a moral human being, one who preserves the intelligence against the temptation to dodge or deny objective truth because of possible unpleasantness to himself or others. Galileo possessed a superior character in addition to a superior intelligence when he dared to risk all in telling the truth about the movement of the earth : "E pui si muove." A modern chemist once said to this author that he had to warn students, more and more, against being victorious at any price in the race for success; e.g., against the temptation to forgo the repetition of a certain experiment under different temperatures because the adherence to the moral conditions of scientific research might prevent the scientist from being first in publishing his discovery. In his autobiography, Liebig, the great chemist, stated that a really conscientious piece of research is so thwarted by obstacles that only an extraordinary devotion to truth is able to preserve a man against the temptations to flout the laws that lead to an honest and valid conclusion.

Intelligence is misused and corrupted by collective passion

Both Gustave Le Bon [2] and José Ortega y Gassett,[3] of France and Spain respectively, had already been commenting on the new emerging weapon of social magnetism and of collective madness; but it was an Armenian writer, Sergel Chakhotin,[4] who, between World War I and II, further revealed the tremendous dynamism of newly aroused public opinion, often emotional, on the unprotected intelligence of the individual person. Schopenhauer, had he lived in our century, would certainly have added an analysis of the dangers resultant from subtle propaganda to the serious challenges to intellectual probity. The evidence of the propaganda of both recent World Wars, as well as the mass propaganda of mass media when misdirected today, should convince us of the need to safeguard the intelligence, with renewed religious and moral strength.

Theology and anthropology

In a long lifetime I have had many opportunities to impress on an uprooted, young academic generation the overwhelming importance of religious culture in the achieving of any real intellectual progress.

[2] *World in Revolt*, (New York: Macmillan, 1921).
[3] *Revolt of the Masses,* (New York: Norton, 1932).
[4] *Rape of the Masses*, (New York: Longmans, Green, 1940).

Invariably, the most effective method was to introduce the students to the deepest psychology underlying their own human nature : a recognition of all the tendencies and potentialities in our character which might enslave intelligence, or seductively swerve it towards the wrong direction in the service of evil. To illustrate these tendencies, I frequently found the philosopher Schopenhauer [5] of invaluable service, for he was an exceedingly keen observer of the game of instincts and their power to usurp the direction and control of our inner life.

Men under the degrading tutelage of mere natural impulse, whose intellects are bereft of the power to comprehend the nature of the activities that enslave, who even glorify their bondage as a mark of freedom, constitute, according to Schopenhauer, the vast undiscriminating mass of all classes. How difficult to achieve real objectivity wherever the force of vital natural impulse is involved! Like a body, with a lead weight attached, being drawn back to the position required by the center of gravity, the intellect is constantly being drawn to the center of gravity of self-interest; will usurps reason. Entirely dominated by egoistic considerations, their thinking and character enfeebled, how many argue, talk, and act as if their minds were merely extensions of animal feeling, and their brains only the anatomic elongation of the backbone. Schopenhauer used for illustration the famed statue of Apollo Belvedere, stressing the manner of the head enthroned on the body, as a symbol of complete spiritual domination over the body and its impulses.

From the glaring contrast between those liberated from vital impulse and its slaves arises the inevitable loneliness and suffering of genius. The people enchained by the enchantments of immediate interests are intolerant of the horizons beheld by genius. They strew palm-branches before the latter when they feel their self-interest served; but let genius bring light that seems to unmask dark desire, and the cry rings out: "Crucify Him!"

Schopenhauer was no man of religion, although he always pays the highest respect to the Saints. He is an Ecclesiastes without faith. His profoundly stimulating statements about human nature and his insights, like those of many a sincere contemporary, help modern man to understand the misery of his mental condition; and can issue in man's glimpsing the mystery, as well as the obvious necessity, of man's intellectual and spiritual redemption.

[5] *The World as Will and Idea.* This book was first printed in 1818; according to Foerster this book of "earthy realism" had a tremendous effect on both Wagner and Nietzsche [Ed. note].

There is indeed a certain anthropology that can serve as the hand-maid of theology: the study of divine reality, because it illumines natural reality so honestly that it destroys complacent illusions. Thus contemporary man is prepared to understand that human reality innately craves for divine reality and is unable to master itself alone.

The conversion of a French radical

Almost on the eve of World War I a serious French educator, M. Dufresne, at the end of a long life, after decades of experience as an enthusiastic devotee of "Ecole laique," was led through pedagogical and psychological observation, to the conviction that nothing could be more inimical to the development of real intellectual culture than the superstitious divinization of reason propagated by the French Revolution:

"When Robespierre had the brazen crucifix on the altar of 'Notre Dame' replaced by a famous actress, to represent the goddess 'Reason,' he had the exalted illusion that an abstract mystery was being replaced by a living creature. But it was really a mere abstraction, a foggy nothing, which the actress embodied, whereas the brazen crucifix represented that real being of flesh and blood to which all human generations bowed and will always bow, because it is filled with our life and has suffered our death; Man and God together — *Ecce homo.*"[6]

Psychoanalysis reveals the power of the unconscious

Modern psychoanalysis, like Schopenhauer, casts light on the intellectual bondage that is the enemy of man's freedom. It would be a grave error to discount the tremendous contribution that contemporary psychoanalysis has made to the understanding of man's nature, because of the errors, exaggerations and confusion of some of its proponents. Freud, in his essay on the psychology of "Forgetting," draws on a discussion between Memory and Pride, as thought out by Nietzsche: "'I have done that,' says my Memory. 'I could not have done that,' says my Pride, remaining inexorable. Finally my Memory yields."[7] Thus is the needle of our intellectual compass deflected from its inflexible loyalty to objective truth, as our memory succumbs to the deep-rooted need for self-esteem. Intellectual servitude is con-

[6] *Le Gaulois*, January 10, 1914.
[7] *Basic Writings of Sigmund Freud* (New York: Random House, 1938, Modern Library ed.) 1, 7.

stantly being entrenched through our complacent passivity before vital personal needs and impulses. Surely the educator is remiss who does not encourage his students to increase in this kind of self-knowledge and also to become aware of the ethical and religious compensations ever at our disposal if we are sincere in striving for intellectual probity and progress.

In Dante's *Divine Comedy* [8] after the poet reaches the river Lethe he learns that, though the drinking of its water will bring about forgetfulness of past guilt, one may not imbibe this water of oblivion unless one first repents for one's sins. How valuable and wise this insight both for individual persons, and for nations. An incorruptible conscience paves the way for the correct functioning of an otherwise unreliable memory. Sometimes, too, the incessant violence of our memory needs sedation; there are cases of severe suffering and mad revolt where personal excitement must yield to a loftier, nobler view of life; apparently tragic events of fate must recede into the right context.

The importance of ethical and religious control over memory and the senses ought to be evident to every intelligent observer. Woe to the nation that turns its back on the intellect. Yet the intellect is not self-sufficient. Ethics alone is not enough. There must be for personal, national, and international sanity a moral and religious foundation, the guarantee of true intellectual culture.

[8] Canto XXIX and XXX, Purgatory.

Obstacles to Life of Mind and Spirit

Frank O'Malley

Frank O'Malley, professor of English at University of Notre Dame, was born at Clinton, Mass. in 1911. He received his B.A. and M.A. at the University of Notre Dame, and he has been a member of the English department there since 1933. For the past twenty-two years he has been Managing-Editor of the Review of Politics, *and he was a close associate of the late Waldemar Gurian. This review, partly due to Professor O'Malley's brilliant assistance, has won immense intellectual prestige for Notre Dame. He has written, too, for other prominent magazines. Recently St. Benedict's College, Atchison, Kansas, awarded him an honorary degree of Doctor of Letters. The following essay was given in the Christian culture Series in 1943.*

OUR AMERICAN civilization is undeniably one of the most potent of world civilizations. And it is a culture of freedom in which the life of the mind and the spirit should flourish. Yet some aspects of contemporary American civilization definitely interfere with and obstruct the life of the spirit. These same features surely taint the spirit of Catholics in this country and make them, in many important respects, indistinguishable from non-worshippers.[1]

Sentimentalism

We can all become very tender about some poor child who must die before Christmas. But since our tenderness is not authentic good-

---

[1] The achievements, in the face of enormous odds, of Catholics in this country have been noted by Dawson — and we would not deny them. Here we suggest only the dangers and perils to what has been accomplished. The problems of the Catholic minority in American Culture have been pointedly and understandingly described by Father Thomas McAvoy, C.S.C., in a series of articles: "The Formation of the Catholic Minority in the United States, 1820–1860," *Review of Politics*, X (January, 1948), "Bishop John Lancaster Spalding and the Catholic Minority (1877–1908)," *ibid.*, XII (January, 1950), 3–19; and "The American Catholic Minority in the Later Nineteenth Century," *ibid.*, XV (July, 1953), 275–302. A great virtue of Father McAvoy's studies — of unusual importance in the writing of the history of the Church in the United States — is their placing of the situation of Catholics within the total picture of American cultural and social development.

ness, a real principle of action and obligation in charity, a responsibility deriving from our need to recognize our right relations as individuals to the whole community, we are almost apathetic about the hunting and maiming of the Negro, the mark set upon the Jew, the poverty and disease that still afflict considerable numbers of our population. We like to have reality (the true nature and civilization of which the liturgy reveals to us) and the firm obligations of reality concealed from us. We prefer to feel good rather than to be good; we prefer to be deluded into static complacency by the soothing voices of orators, preachers and publicists who assure us that we are beyond censure, beyond judgment. For the true form and strength of our magnificent act of worship we substitute the more pallid and more feeble formulas of minor pieties. In all this we retard the dynamics of the living Church. Today, against the formidable and perversely "religious" drive of Soviet metaphysical materialism and atheism conjoined with brutish physical power, we fortify ourselves, as John Courtney Murray has observed, with a practical materialism compounded with a sentimental moral idealism which equals for us the "American way of life." As Catholics we have in truth a firmer fortification — yet we do not seem to realize it. If we had a better sense of our life in the Church, we would have at this hour a better courage and a better power to confront the terrors of history and to resist the pressure of the age — upon leaving the consecrated precincts of the Church.

Commercialism

It is not necessary to cry this up, so obvious is it. Our lack of reverence for personality and communities of personalities is revealed in the instinct to exploit, often with high pressure methods, people or values or institutions for profit or fame or power or success of any kind — and what can be more horrible than the commercial exploitation of spiritual realities? Certain endeavors labeled Catholic seem to have dangers in this regard. They would force, through commercial techniques and means and even by commercial standards for achievement, the entrance of the Church — or the Church as their sponsors understand it — into society at large. But these movements merely force the note outrageously. For the Catholic Dale Carnegies are not likely, in the end anyway, to be distinguishable from their prototype, notorious for his commercial, exploitative approaches to human relationships. A Catholic Dale Carnegie-ism is not expected to be the salvation of the nation or the world. It is too much like, disconcertingly like, the world it imitates too much. It does not really distinguish its cause from the world that is not holy. When and if an organic Catholic or Christian culture develops in our country, it will not come from the rush and rampage of any ape-ing "how to win friends and influence people" evangel. Moreover, our resources as Catholics are infinitely greater — and decidedly more interesting and less tarnished — than those of the New York or Hollywood wits. With respect to any kind of commercial exploiter of the spirit, these words from Psalm 42 apply: "From the unjust and deceitful man, deliver me: for Thou art my God and my strength."

Sectarianism or Provincialism

Americans are often accused of not having enough appreciation of the ways and problems of other peoples and cultures, of lacking, on the spiritual and human level, universalization of point of view. There is considerable truth in this charge. And American Catholics share in this provincialism and display it in various disturbing ways. Consider, for instance, the current state of Catholic journalism, especially in the general run of Catholic newspapers. Nothing could possibly be more provincial or sectarian than the sadly unenlightening accounts of "Catholic" personages and "Catholic" doings, ironically summarized in the legendary but representative headline from a Catholic journal: "Catholic Plane Crashes on Catholic Meadow." Our newspapers by and large may be, in the narrowest possible sense, Catholic by denomination but they are hardly Catholic by inspiration or spirit.

Here, too, we may note the common attitude of Catholics toward a Catholic literature. They see it as something hopelessly sectarian, as the product of highly-denominationalized mentalities and movements. But the truly great and serious Catholic poets and novelists of our civilization (Bloy, Bernanos, Mauriac, Undset, Claudel, Péguy, Hopkins, to mention only a few) show that a Catholic literature is in no way narrow or sectarian but rather fully and universally Christian (embracing "the whole world spiritually as a vast kingdom of realities"[2]), that the significance of the Catholic writer is not to be found finally in his moralism or even in his esthetic character or in his intellectual power. Instead it is to be seen that his way is essentially liturgical: his life and his meaning rest at the heart of the world of

[2] Romano Guardini, *The Church and the Catholic and the Spirit of the Liturgy*, (New York: Sheed and Ward, 1953), p. 26.

86

the Church, the world of worship; his own world of intellect and art moves vitally within this world of worship. As Guardini writes, "A religious process of incalculable importance has begun."[3] In this process a powerful Catholic literature has been created. And Catholics should understand this process more fully and vitally themselves. Then they may arrive at and acquire a genuinely Catholic worldview. Without it they shall be — and ought to feel — segregated, sullen and arbitrary.

Catholics everywhere, speaking in the main, have too determined a tendency to restrict the limits of their activity or influence in constructively spiritual and intellectual directions. Of course, in this country, some Catholic persons and organizations, uninhibited as well as of exceedingly limited outlook (that of a primitivism combining sometimes a pseudo-Americanism with a pseudo-Catholicism) have never hesitated to rush onto the streets, practically with club and gun, to uphold, in ways unspiritual and rude and dubiously Catholic, the name and dignity of the Church. The profound point is: we say, as Conrad Bonacina declares, that Catholic Christianity is the universal religion of humanity. But then the question comes: what good is our saying it, "if we show by the whole tenor of our apologetic that we really believe no such thing, that when it comes to the point we are not equal to the logic of such a tremendous conception?"[4] Actually, if we as Catholics in America do believe in Catholicism as the universal Kingdom, as the Church of all mankind, a requirement of faith, "then it behooves us to think out the implications and see to it that our *Weltanschauung* as Catholics accords with them."[5] Our Church has a historical mission which it must gravely regard and we must ourselves gravely regard its demands upon us. Jean Daniélou now acquaints us with our true vocation: since Christianity must become incarnate among and transfigure different civilizations and cultures, it unavoidably becomes our vocation to circulate or disseminate through the alien world and never to seclude or enclave ourselves. Going out among others, "we must become one of them, but we must without question avoid being contaminated by our contact with them. All is lost if, when we go out among them, we become like them, instead of their becoming like us."[6] In such an event, we

[3] *Ibid.*, p. 11.
[4] Conrad Bonacina, "Catholicism and the Latin Culture Heresy," *The Wind and the Rain*, vol. VI, no. 2 (Autumn, 1949), p. 88.
[5] *Ibid.*
[6] Jean Danielou, *The Salvation of the Nations* (London, Sheed and Ward, 1949), p. 65.

have failed utterly to distinguish our cause from the nation that is not holy.

Externalization

In our civilization, too much stress is laid upon external and artificial devices, upon techniques, practices, processes, analyses and activities. We do not realize sufficiently the importance of development, of growth, of synthesis, of creation. We are great believers in efficiency, in the mechanical and industrial manipulation of all our resources. And in a culture which understands machines and formulas rather than spiritual form, there cannot be too much chance for religion and spiritual regeneration, for those creators of culture who see existence under the aspect of eternity, eternal form.

Nowhere does the barbarism of externalization more unpleasantly show itself than in our universities and colleges .What is the formula by which we conduct our schools ? It seems to be : bureaucratic organization and oppressiveness plus busyness plus competitiveness sometimes amounting to murderous connivance. Contrarily, what should the form for the Christian school be ? This: respect, reverence for the personalities of both teachers and students plus development (for "what ultimately matters is not activity, but development," [7] a sentence which should be the sign-manual for Christian education) plus a real sense of community. The grievous question is: in how many of our schools does this form shine ? Or, in how many Catholic schools and colleges is any serious effort made to achieve a Christian community and a Christian culture ? There are, naturally, here and there the valiant efforts and programs of those who struggle away to reveal the relationship between religion and culture and to establish the synthesis to which the decent mind aspires. But on the whole there are only opportunities for parochial pieties on one side and the academy on the other — and nothing or no one to join the two. We have, in too many of our colleges, either religion without culture or culture without religion and, broadly reflecting, our intellectual works are indistinguishable from those accomplished in the schools normally stigmatized as secular or "unholy." Routine is preferred to revelation. That sense of *mystery* which characterized early Christian education is lost or ignored. Our effort now is chiefly distinguished by our almost passionate desire for the tangible and an extravagant confidence in machinery as if it were itself an absolute, a confidence which Matthew

[7] Guardini, *op. cit.*, p. 208.

88

Arnold long ago called the besetting danger of our civilization. And having removed practically all traces of our real form, our real aim and meaning, we have, in the mood of fanaticism and even frenzy, accelerated our operations.

We should, however, come back to our Christian senses, and to a new realization of that impetus which would release us from the traps of routine. Christian education, as Dawson envisages it, was once "a process of catharsis, an illumination which centered in the sacred mysteries, and which was embodied in a cycle of symbolism and liturgical action." [8] In such a process, "Christian education was not only an initiation into a Christian community, it was also an initiation into another world: the unveiling of spiritual realities of which the natural man was unaware and which changed the meaning of existence." [9] We shall have to agree with Dawson when he specifies that modern education has failed to provide this extraordinary kind of initiation. We shall have to agree, further, when he affirms that in our modern education there is "no sense of revelation." [10] Modern education, in the Catholic colleges no less than in the others, "is accepted as instruction — sometimes as useful knowledge, often as tiresome task work in preparation for some examination, but nowhere do we find that joyful sense of the discovery of a new and wonderful reality that inspired true Christian culture." [11] With Dawson's stimulation, we shall have to remind ourselves that "all true religious education leads up to the contemplation of Divine Mysteries, and where this is lacking the whole culture becomes weakened and divided." [12] Dawson realizes that some may protest that there is here involved the world of worship rather than the world of education. But he points out firmly that "it is impossible to separate the two, since it was largely in the sphere of worship that the Christian tradition of education and culture arose and developed. The first Christian education was the initiation into the Divine Mysteries in the liturgical sense, and it brought with it a development of religious poetry and music and art which were the first fruits of Christian culture." [13]

Now those of us who are Catholic teachers or scholars or students today are faced with the grave problem of how, in our various realms

[8] Christopher Dawson, *Education and the Crisis of Christian Culture* (Chicago, Regnery, 1949), p. 10.
[9] *Ibid.*
[10] *Ibid.*
[11] *Ibid.*
[12] *Ibid.*
[13] *Ibid.*, pp. 10-11.

of science and art, to discover and display that "wonderful reality" informing Christian culture, of how to provide at least the minimum means for education towards Christian culture,[14] of how to draw the works of the mind within the world of worship. Etienne Gilson is right when he insists that piety — or religion — does not dispense with technique. But it may be added that technique does not dispense with transfiguration. And Gilson poses the problem for all of us: "To serve God by science and art, it is necessary to begin by practicing them *as if* these disciplines were in themselves their own ends; and it is difficult to make such an effort without being taken in. So much the more difficult is it when we are surrounded by savants and artists who treat them effectively as ends. Their attitude is a spontaneous expression of naturalism, or to give it its old name, which is the name for all time, of paganism, into which society ceaselessly tends to fall back because it has never completely left it. It is important, however, to free ourselves from it. It is impossible to place the intelligence at the service of God without respecting integrally the rights of the intelligence; otherwise it would not be the intelligence that is put at His service; but still more is it impossible to do so without respecting the rights of God: otherwise it is no longer at His service that the intelligence is placed. What has to be done in order to observe this second condition?"[15] This is indeed the question — *what has to be done in order to observe this second condition?* — on which all of us, in any way responsible for the education of Christians, must constantly meditate. Otherwise we do not justify our reason for existence or justify the existence of our schools.

[14] Here reference must be made to the concern shown in a number of very recently published, or republished, essays by Christopher Dawson, Dietrich von Hildebrand, and Father Leo R. Ward, C.S.C. Dawson: "The Study of Christian Culture as a Means of Education" (*Lumen Vitae*, Vol. I—1950—No. I); "Education and Christian Culture" (*Commonweal*, Dec. 4, 1953); "Future of Christian Culture," (*ibid.*, March 19, 1954). Von Hildebrand: "Catholicism and Unprejudiced Knowledge," "The Role of Reverence in Education," in *The New Tower of Babel* (New York, P. J. Kenedy, 1953). Ward: "Is there a Christian Learning?" (*Commonweal*, September 25, 1953); see also Father Ward's *Blueprint for a Catholic University* (St. Louis, B. Herder, 1949). Perhaps the whole hope of the redirection of life and studies in the Catholic universities and colleges of America can be reduced to the teachers, to their absolute importance: the power of the living presences of their Christian minds, their vital possession of the realities of Christian culture, will give form not only to their own works and utterances but also — and this is the heart of the matter — to the lives and minds and works of the students coming under them. Our paramount problem today is how to develop these Christian teachers, these true "creators of culture who see existence under the aspect of eternity, eternal form."

[15] Etienne Gilson, *Christianity and Philosophy* (New York, London, Sheed and Ward, 1939), pp. 116–117.

Surely one of the terrible obstacles to the work of synthesis so absolutely necessary is the sense of inferiority with respect to, the lack of pride in their faith, which has led Catholics, as Newman once chided, to surrender their sacred life and tradition so as to get on better with the world: "In proportion as you put off the yoke of Christ, so does the world by a sort of instinct recognise you, and think well of you accordingly. Its highest compliment is to tell you that you disbelieve." [16] Gilson has made a precisely similar observation: "What is the greatest praise that many among us may hope for ? The greatest the world can give them: he is a Catholic, but he is really very nice; you would never think that he was one." [17] But this sense of inferiority is also, oddly, accompanied by a partisan optimism and complacency about Catholic affairs. What Gilson regrets and what we all must regret — is "that instead of confessing in all simplicity what we owe to our Church and to our faith, instead of showing what they bring to us and what we would not have without them, we believe it good politics or good tactics, in the interests of the Church itself, to act as if, after all, we distinguish ourselves in no way from others." [18]

Perhaps all the weaknesses of modern culture, ours and those of other countries, can be caught up into the one great vice of spiritual mediocrity, described by Georges Bernanos as "a colorless and odorless gas; allow it to accumulate undisturbed and suddenly it explodes with a force beyond all belief. . . . The dire omen for all of us . . . is not that Christians should be less numerous but that the number of mediocre Christians should increase. Smile, if you like, at mediocre Christians, the power they still can wield is vast." [19] This is the strange power of those who are spiritually powerless. They are the ones who fear truth and reality and the voices of truth and reality in any field of action. Their dead or dying hands seize and do not release until they have crushed the life of the soul, of the mind, of culture.

[16] John Henry Newman, *Discourses Addressed to Mixed Congregations* (New York, 1950), pp. 181–182. In the same discourse (VII: "Nature and Grace") Newman also cites an opinion of divines and holy men "that the number of Catholics that are to be saved will on the whole be small. Multitudes of those who never knew the Gospel will rise up in judgment against the children of the Church and will be shown to have done more with scantier opportunities."

[17] Gilson, *op. cit.*, p. 117.

[18] *Ibid.* Still we must remark here upon the proper pride of faith characterizing and inspiriting the minds of some of the greatest Catholic intellectuals of the modern world: men like Gilson himself, Maritain, Dawson, Guardini, Karl Adam, de Lubac, Daniélou, Sturzo, Pieper, von Hildebrand, among others.

[19] Georges Bernanos, *Plea for Liberty* (New York, Pantheon Books, 1944), pp. 165–166.

There is the danger that, in the sight of all this spiritual mediocrity, of the frailties of Catholics themselves, some of us — who know better — might become perfectionists, inclined, without warrant, to withdraw from or reject the world. Since we do not find it as we want it, we shall have none of it. The perfectionist, in Waldemar Gurian's evaluation, "professes to be exclusively interested in the absolute good, and therefore, he regards everything that is not perfect as bad . . . [he] observes that the ideal is not realized in his environment; therefore, he emphasizes the weaknesses of his surroundings and is a defeatist by his very readiness to admire and understand far-distant worlds," [20] and no other than utopian worlds. But his abandonment of the world to the devil is not perfection — just perfectionism. To be exact, there is in the Church a legitimate perfectionist way of life, the higher life of the pure contemplative. Yet the great men and women drawn, with justification, to this life have not disesteemed the importance — and perplexity — of worldly existence; nor have they felt that it was somehow unnatural and out-of-joint with true Christian living. They have realized, in the perspective of the Incarnation-Redemption, that it is necessary for men to move through and with matter to the fulfillment of the spirit. Most of us cannot and will not be anchorites. We shall have to live as Christians in civilization; and in this solution civilization will be accepted in all its density and regarded as capable of Christian transfiguration. Actually, all the claims of our secular state-in-life, of our *natural* life, are in themselves good, can be the basis of spiritual development and can serve to bring us towards the highest perfection of supernatural life.[21]

The Christian man knows that his achievement of intellectual and moral virtue ought not to set him at severe odds with the society in which he finds himself. It is not a question of his compromising with the too frequently false standards of modern civilization or of submitting all the high and treasured quality of his meaning as a man and as a mind to what may seem to him the lower character of workaday existence. The necessity for the Christian man, exercised in the Christian understanding of life and of the movements of history and contemporary events, is to comprehend the world in all its weaknesses and terrors no less than in its glories and wonders. With

[20] Waldemar Gurian, "The Mask of the Devil," *Scrip*, The University of Notre Dame Quarterly, vol. 14, no. 1 (August, 1942), pp. 5–6.

[21] On this matter in general, see J. M. Cameron, *Scrutiny of Marxism* (London, SCM Press, 1948), pp. 102–111 and H. A. Reinhold, "The Christian in the World," *Orate Fratres*, vol. XXV, no. 9 (August, 1951), pp. 405–411.

his Christian understanding of and sympathy for the plight of people in a difficult and dangerous civilization, the Christian man must try to illuminate, for himself and for others, the difficulty and the danger. Because of the human deficiencies inevitable in the Church itself on earth, the deficiencies which are Christ's very Cross, he knows that he cannot expect perfection from ordinary humanity, that he cannot isolate himself from men and the real world, that he must live in the face of all sorts of exigencies and evils and strive to alleviate them. The Christian knows that he must live as a Christian in the more or less un-Christian world. Having this knowledge he will show himself courageous and hopeful in the darkest moments; and his Christian courage and Christian hope will help him to make sense today.

Modern Phychology and Moral Values

Noël Mailloux, O.P.

Father Mailloux, the well-known Canadian priest and psychologist, was born in the province of Quebec in 1909. He received his Ph.D., and studied philosophy and psychology, at the Angelicum in Rome, and later became a Research Fellow at the University of Cincinnati. He is the founder and director of the Institute of Psychology at the University of Montreal and a professor of experimental psychology at the same university. Previously he was professor of psychology at the College of Philosophy and Theology of the Dominican Fathers at Ottawa. He has been a director of the Center of Research on Human Relations at Montreal. Presently he lectures part time in psychology at the University of Montreal, and also directs the Orientation Center in Montreal where disturbed youngsters live and study and where many others are helped, too. He was President of the Canadian Psychological Association in 1954–1955. Mailloux has written many scientific papers for scholarly journals, has lectured at the famous Menninger clinic, and has produced five volumes on "Scientific Methods in Education." He has been a pioneer in Canada and also in the United States in urging, long ago, the proper reconciliation of the truths of experimental psychology with the truths of faith.

I AM GOING to write about the struggle of a conscience trying to assert itself in the growing man, and to describe the way it functions in the mature man. But before I do that I would like to clear away some misconceptions about modern psychology and moral values.

Being born in a so-called age of science, modern psychology was confronted with a distorted picture of moral values — distorted by minds confused by decades of materialistic thinking. It was then impossible for modern psychology to approach the study of good and evil as affecting human behavior without being biased by current prejudices. However, it is most comforting to observe how these prejudices are crumbling one after the other as more adequate and precise knowledge about the motivation of conduct is accumulated.

It has now become possible, on a strictly empirical basis, to straighten out those distortions which still prevail and which still disturb the peace of those who are sincerely convinced that Christian belief can be reconciled with scientific conclusions.

Undoubtedly empirical science has recently made a brilliant contribution to the understanding of how a moral conscience is born in the individual and how the individual progressively acquires genuine moral values. Because of this new understanding, psychology has been able to liberate itself from the fetters of biologico-physical frames of reference, which did not apply in this specific realm, and which hampered for far too long the correct understanding of mature moral behavior. Let me here mention just a few of these which are now being confined to their proper share of application.

First, the principle of determinism. Usually this was formulated in mechanistic terms — it was the theory that everything that one does is determined by forces which are independent of the will. But it has been modified by contemporary psychologists, to the point of embracing self-determination — that is, free-will. It has finally been understood that the alternative to psychic determinism is not freedom but its opposite, namely indeterminacy, chaos, and unpredictability in human behavior. Now it is widely recognized that when it is affirmed that human acts are determined, this means precisely, not that these acts have a necessary cause, but that they necessarily have a cause which may well be a deliberate, free, autonomous decision.

Another distortion which can now be straightened out, is that moral laws can be formulated in the same way as physical laws. We know now that this is not so. Even if the curve of normal distribution, let us say, offers a reasonably satisfactory frame for arriving at a physical law, it is no sufficient basis for the establishment of moral law. Statistical frequencies can no more be regarded as normative principles of conduct than statistical correlations can replace a dynamic or causal interpretation of it. There will be less confusion in the modern approach to the study of values when it becomes quite clear that what men generally do is not a valid criterion to determine what they should do or what it would be most reasonable for them to do. Then, also, scientists will not continue to encourage parents to rear their children in conformity with transient social standards entirely devoid of compelling obligation, and to be satisfied with this so-called adaptation or adjustment to reality as a substitute for moral virtues.

Finally, we were confronted with the amazing assumption that the categories of right and wrong were to be replaced by the categories of rational and irrational. This led again to the old confusion between "being normal" and "being moral." A few centuries ago it was all too common for people to regard insanity as a sign of diabolical depravity. In the same way, in our period of enlightenment, scientific authorities did not hestitate to proclaim that right and honest behavior as well as human happiness derived immediately from mental equilibrium and emotional maturity.

To understand the proper functioning of moral conscience, instead of relying on the centuries-old experience of spiritual life and sanctity, they unhesitatingly resorted to the naïve use of the newly elaborated models of psychopathology. From then on, the asceticism of the virtuous man, the remorse of the regretful sinner, and the mystical love of the saint were regarded as disguised manifestations of grossly pathological conditions. The ascetic was a masochist; the remorse of the sinner was nothing but delusional guilt feelings, and the saint suffered from misplaced and distorted eroticism. Finally, religious dogmas were equated with the magical superstitions of the obsessive-compulsive neurotic. Of course, such speculations have nothing to do with science. Finally, in recent times, several scientists have restricted the use of psychopathological frames of reference to the interpretation of pathological phenomena. They have stressed the reality of genuine moral values and the highly integrated functioning of a fully developed moral conscience as distinct from the distorted and rigid claims of an infantile super ego.

These considerations lead us to deal with what is the deepest conflict in the moral conscience. We are well aware that in the moral sphere maturity implies the capacity to recognize the Good as absolute value, and to see in it the sufficient and principal motivation of conduct. Man can show himself to be reasonable only in the measure that he achieves in himself the triumph of the rational over the irrational, and is capable of basing his conduct on judgments of value truly independent yet sustained by this absolute principle. Hence there arises in him a state of continuous conflict. He is pulled by primitive fixations back to the state of the infantile conscience — this so-called super ego. The imperative demands of this imaginary conscience in the unconscious are ever seeking to re-establish their dominance in conduct. Indeed, in the normal individual, rational conscience but slowly arrives at affirming itself, and at purifying the moral judgment so as to liberate it from the concrete, subjective, and selfish considerations which controlled it in childhood.

In this typically human conflict between the infantile and the mature, the reason of the normal individual triumphs only by virtue of lucidity and determination. But the conscience of the neurotic allows itself to be overcome by fantasies in the pursuit of infantile aims. For the sake of clarity let us get back to the child who is just beginning to learn to be master of his own acts. He is beginning to learn to deliberate — to choose — without as yet being able to base his conduct on an idea of good or evil which still remains beyond the grasp of his imagination.

First of all it is evident that good and evil for the child bear the aspect of pleasure or pain, and he esteems as good whatever gives him satisfaction, evil whatever causes him suffering. His educators, aware of this state of mind, attach reward to good conduct, punishment to bad. Later the child has to learn that certain actions pleasant in themselves must be avoided, whereas others disagreeable in nature must be done. Take the case of the youngster who persists in sucking his thumb, or who is careless about habits of normal hygiene. In these cases recourse is had to praise or blame to overcome resistance and to aid the child in this new phase of self-conquest. Finally a time comes when his conduct can no longer be the object of our constant vigilance. At this point we induce him to act in accordance with our demands by emphasizing the possibility of his losing our affection or of keeping it.

It is but natural that these primitive motivations, which gave to our emotional life its first orientations and dominated for so long our behavior, by no means lose their power when the notion of the good in itself, arises in conscience and renders it autonomous. At this moment we are at the threshold of a new stage, the most difficult of all, which leads us to the full development of moral maturity, of a virtuous life. Yet, paradoxical though it may seem, the criteria of value of our infantile conscience frequently continue to exercise sufficient attraction to arrest our progress or even cause us to retrace our steps. Moreover, if in spite of everything we persevere in our forward march, we may be haunted by an excruciating sense of inferiority in which one must finally recognize the feeling of guilt peculiar to the infantile conscience. Think of the terrible crisis which must

normally and inevitably be encountered by all those who devote themselves to scientific, artistic, social or moral pursuits. As is well known,
it is precisely at the moment when these men of "values" turn to
the end to be realized, in a spirit of greatest disinterestedness, that
discouragement attacks them, and the temptation to doubt their own
capacity paralyzes their creative effort. Their intense and assiduous
meditation imposes on them many sacrifices. Their career, far from
immediately exciting the admiration and love of those around them,
often subjects them to a certain contempt and isolation. At this point
the infantile conscience which still survives in them makes itself
heard by disapproving a conduct too far removed from the norms
which it upholds. It is only by the exercise of great firmness and
strength that the rational adult conscience succeeds in pointing out
the path to be followed. It is with no little difficulty that it succeeds
in dominating the primitive feeling of guilt, if it does not succumb
to its urgings.

It is little wonder then, that for the average man, who in many
respects remains a child, gain, human respect, and fear of abandonment by friends, should continue to appear as the determining motivations in conduct. At the critical time of temptation, the rational
conscience, ever-hesitant and weak, all too easily capitulates to the
infantile conscience. The individual has recourse to a petty compromise, and becomes the prey of remorse to escape the feeling of
inferiority.

In the case of the neurotic, the possibility of envisaging such a compromise does not even exist. The conflict in which he finds himself
implies but two alternatives: the toleration of his inferiority or the
escape from it by self-destruction. In fact, incapable of self-satisfaction,
of maintaining his self-respect, of establishing a genuine love relationship with others, he feels himself to be utterly worthless, without
value, and sees no other solution to his situation than self-destruction.
By enlightening us upon this issue, psychopathology has rendered one
of the greatest services we would have expected from it. The moralist
can now with greater clarity understand the fearful and insidious
obstacle which the individual has to overcome in his upward path. He
can use this penetrating intuition to formulate more precise directives
for the education of human personality.

These few illustrations of the functioning and characteristics of
the neurotic conscience also enable us the better to understand the
deformations of the religious attitude of the neurotic. It is not our

intention here to make a study of these peculiarities. It is enough to say that the neurotic is often a believer who endeavors to be religious according to his capacity. Unfortunately in the exercise of his religion he encounters what seem insurmountable obstacles, which inevitably lead him to an impasse, or to discouragement. His religiosity becomes the unconscious vehicle of his infantile longings and a source of uncontrollable anxiety. Against this he mobilizes his habitual mechanisms of defence, denial of reality, compensation, rationalization, etc. But all this is too widely known to be insisted upon. It is more to the point to retrace the origin of these deviations and to show how they all derive from the ever stronger interference of the infantile conscience with the functioning of the rational conscience.

The first characteristic of the rational conscience is that it is a faithful witness to conduct. It maintains an adequate contact with reality, and all the actions which it dictates are, we may say, but the response to its demands. From this fact the motivation of these acts possesses an objectivity that cannot be ignored. Not so with the infantile or neurotic conscience. Dominated by a strong primitive sensualism, it attains to God as to all other realities, under the veil of an imagery extremely unprecise and subject to the arbitrariness of instinctual influences. Thus we can understand the obsessions and the exalted "mysticism" of certain neurotics as well as the myths and magic rites of uncivilized peoples. Unfortunately, certain thinkers have been so naïve as to believe that true religion is reducible to these primitive and delirious fantasies. In my opinion, it is as far removed from them as a musical symphony is from the clatter and noise of the street, as a perfect work of art is from a vulgar rigmarole, or as inspired poetry is from an incoherent reverie.

In the second place, judgments of conscience appear to us as imperative, commanding a particular form of action. In other words, conscience commands obedience. Here again a profound difference separates the rational from the neurotic conscience. Like the infantile conscience, the neurotic conscience continues to feel itself dependent and heteronomous. But the rational conscience chooses with deliberation; is in independent, autonomous. In face of the demands of the Creator, of the demands of the natural and of the positive law, the only alternatives for the neurotic conscience are passivity or revolt. On the contrary, the rational conscience discovers a relation of justice, and freely assumes all the obligations deriving therefrom. Acts external and internal, corporal gestures and intimate sentiments of the soul are ordained by this virtue of justice, with a view to rendering complete homage to Him who is recognized as the supreme Excellence.

Finally every deliberate action merits the approval or disapproval of conscience, which performs, as it were, the function of a judge. From conscience we derive the immense satisfaction of being able to love ourselves rightly, the reason being, that we know ouselves to be better after submitting voluntarily to the Deity our poverty as creatures, and after serving duly Him whom we reverence. On the other hand, if we fail, conscience arouses in us a reasonable feeling of guilt, remorse. But far from crushing us, this sorrowful regret for error committed contains already in itself the desire for resurrection and for aspiration to a love more intense and more stable. Remorse prepares the way for hope. Such is not the case with the neurotic conscience. Here we can experience only the narcissistic and illusory satisfaction of being able to love ourselves, because, blind to our indigence as creatures, we exalt ourselves to the point of equating our human selves with the Creator. When however this narcissistic identification fails, we inevitably feel our personality attacked by an irrational feeling of guilt leading to a complete break-down. The feeling of guilt experienced as an irremediable inferiority, paralyzes every effort at resurgence and leads to the dread and rage of despair.

It will be clear that we cannot be charged with not entertaining for science a due respect. Indeed, in our opinion, neglect even of the smallest scientific discovery would be tantamount to sinning against the light. Yet even when he has explored the domain of psychology to the best of his ability, the priest who is endowed with a profound faith and some experience of human unrest, will be acutely aware that he has need of an added illumination if he is to understand those who suffer. Moreover, he cannot ignore the supernatural dynamism of grace, which intervenes unconsciously to lead us to actions which neither the motivations of irrational unconscious, nor those of deliberate reason are sufficient to explain. The priest will be grateful to psychology for what he can learn from it. Nevertheless, since as a matter of fact a certain aspect of life transcends the range of psychological techniques, and being unable to remain satisfied with an exclusively naturalistic interpretation, he will look to theology for light on the nature of moral and religious conflicts.

We know indeed from the experience of the ages, that the pressure of grace in hours of purification is infinitely more to be reckoned with than the most violent pressure of temporal reality. The supernatural world has demands, exigencies, more arduous, more imperious than the natural. Beholding it, even the individual who has attained the limit of human perfection and the level of greatest personal maturity, begins to fear. The average man is afraid to be free: the superior personality, also, is afraid — afraid to be free as God wills him to be free, that is to say, afraid to go beyond to surpass his human liberty, so as to will what God wills, to will the good and the end that God wills he should pursue. At this level the individual is inevitably caught in a terrifying inner conflict, in which it is the Divine intention that he be humanly aided. Here a knowledge of dynamic psychology will be useful. The same mechanisms of defence will operate here as elsewhere. Nevertheless if dynamic psychology be separated from the data of empirical theology it will afford a purely *material* understanding of the phenomena. One will have an illusion, and only an illusion, of solving the problems.

Just as the psychologist learns to efface himself before the human reason he has helped to liberate, so the spiritual leader learns to efface himself before the spirit whose ways he has prepared. To both one can recommend a passivity respectful to the inner forces of organization. On the one hand the data on which they labor are the same. Yet beyond a certain limit their respective contributions appear complementary, one to the other.

The Nature of Science and the Nature of Man

Ruth Nanda Anshen

Ruth Nanda Anshen ranks among the most scholarly editors of our day, and she is likewise a philosopher and author of considerable distinction. She is a former member of the Faculty of Letters and the École Libre des Hautes Études. She has lectured at the universities of Heidelberg, Frankfurt, Freiberg, Munich, Athens, Ankara, Teheran, Istanbul, the American University of Lebanon, and the Hebrew University of Israel, and she was also invited to give lectures in Moscow. She planned and edited the renowned World Perspective Series *of volumes "dedicated to an encyclopedia of modern thought that would tend to reconcile the creative forces of West and East in a universe of discourse." Currently Dr. Anshen plans and edits the learned* Science of Culture Series *of volumes on such topics as* Freedom: Its Meaning, Science and Man, Language, *and* Moral Principles of Action. *After brilliantly presiding over the editing of these two eminently successful ventures of publishing, she has planned and is editing a* Religious Perspective Series, *assisted by a board of consultants that number some of the greatest names of East and West. Christopher Dawson wrote* The Historic Reality of Christian Culture *as Volume No. 1 in this series. Dr. Anshen is a member of the American Philosophical Association, the American Oriental Society, the International Philosophical Society (History of Science section), and the American Metaphysical Society.*

Studies of man are made in all institutions of research and higher learning. There is hardly a section of the total scholarly enterprise which does not contribute directly or indirectly to our knowledge of man's nature. Not only philosophy and theology, not only history and the other humanities, not only psychology, sociology, biology and medicine investigate man's nature and existence, but also the natural sciences do so, at least indirectly, and even directly, whenever they reflect upon their own methods, limits and purposes.

In view of this vast endeavor which goes on in the whole civilized world, one asks: Is there any need for a special concern for the study of man? Is this not at best a reduplication of studies done anyway and at worst a premature attempt to produce a synthesis of the present results of the other studies on a level of diminished scientific strictness?

It is the conviction of the author of this essay that there is such a need, even an urgent need.

The first conviction is a negative one: It is the belief that man has lost himself as the living center in a world produced by himself. He has been divided into the different levels which are the subject matter of the different scientific approaches to reality. He has become a physical object among physical objects, a chemical object among chemical objects, a biological object among biological objects, a psychological object among psychological objects, a sociological object among sociological objects. He has become a conglomeration of pieces of reality, of spheres of objects. And the subjectivity left to him has been either driven into the cognitively irrelevant corner of the emotions (of which poetry, religion, metaphysics, etc., are supposed to be expressions), or his self has been formalized into the logical subject of scientific analysis. But man as the experiencing, deciding, responsible self has become lost. And with the loss of the center, the different spheres of the scholarly approach to man in himself and in his world have become falsified. Man's self-interpretation has become distorted. He has become an object among objects. This is the negative presupposition, however it is expressed, which has produced the quest for a doctrine of man as man.

The positive presupposition is that in all realms of scholarly work there is an awareness of this situation and a desire to overcome it. Most impressive has been the reaction of many scientists to the problems of the "atomic age" created by the technical application of their own theories. The question of the human meaning of scientific research cannot be repressed any longer in view of the immensity of these problems.

In biology and medicine the qualitative uniqueness of every life process, and especially the uniqueness of that process which is called human, has come into the foreground of investigation. And, above all, biology, psychology and medicine have made parallel efforts to overcome the traditional split between the psychological and the physiological sides of human nature. Man has tried and is trying to find a body-mind unity which does not reduce the one side to the other. One very important contributing factor in this development is therapeutic psychology which has already drastically changed our picture of man.

Matter itself is receiving an interpretation as to its nature within a wider frame of reference than ever before. It is increasingly recognized among some natural scientists, who for some time have experienced the anguish of mind following the implications of their researches, that the forces, "the effective units which determine material events, the events in spatial matter, are all of trans-spatial nature; that experience clearly indicates another form of causality than the one fitting the frame of the 'field theory'; namely, that if the 'field' is left to itself, it remains in a homogeneous state of quiescence and becomes 'excited' only through something else, the 'spirit of unrest.' In other words, natural science itself begins to recognize that matter is the agent which excites the field. And although the material particle is hidden in a spatial environment, from which its field effects originate, it actually exists beyond time and space." [1]

Historical studies in all directions, including political, social, economic, cultural and religious history have begun to ask the question of the characteristics of man as they are manifest in history. The exclusively factual and causal approach to history generally, and its special divisions like history of the arts, of literature, of societal forms, of religion, has been broken down in many places. The question of meaning has not replaced the question of fact but has given research another dimension and a direct relevance for man's self-interpretation.

Important developments in philosophy and theology point in the same direction: The so-called existentialist movement from Pascal to Heidegger is largely a revolt against the ruling philosophy which neglected the existing man and turned exclusively to the structures of his world and himself as a part of his world. Recent theology, in partial collaboration with philosophy and reviving some of its classical traditions, has emphasized the doctrine of man as introductory to its other doctrinal statements.

This is the situation, both in its negative and its positive aspects: No convincing picture of man has arisen in spite of the many ways in which human thought has tried to reach it. But one thing has been achieved: The problem has made itself felt with great force in many places in spite of considerable resistance.

[1] Hermann Weyl, *Philosophy of Mathematics and Natural Science*, (Munich, 1927), (translated for Princeton University Press, 1949).

There is, however, another rather serious reason for the study of man, man, in his ontological substance and reality. It is the fact that under the impact of these developments, a linguistic confusion in all important matters of man's existence has taken place in the Western world, a confusion which makes cooperation extremely difficult. Most concepts used in scholarly attempts to draw a picture of man are ambiguous, or obsolete, or fashionable cliches. It is impossible *not* to use them, but they mislead if they are used. This is not a recent development, although the methods of contemporary publicity have supported it and are one of the greatest impediments for healing it, but it is a result of the intellectual and social history of the last centuries. A change is possible only if this history in all its ramifications is studied from the point of view of the disintegration of language concerning man which has taken place in the last centuries.

Such an analysis may lead to the synthesis man seeks, not that synthesis, that eclectic conglomeration without a center, which is represented by the gathering together of the fragmented parts, but that synthesis which is the symbol of the unmediated wholeness of feeling and thought, preserving the original and organic unity and constituting the core of reality.

The historical approach must be done in interdependence with a systematic approach. Concepts, developed in one sphere must show their relevance for other spheres. This also is being done in a casual way in contemporary literature. It must be done methodologically. The departmental boundaries must be trespassed continuously. It is ultimately impossible to make a true statement about the physiological dynamics of the human body; and vice versa, it is ultimately impossible to describe the self-destructive tendencies in a neurotic patient without describing the structures of estrangement in man's social existence. These examples could be increased indefinitely. They show that the departmentalization of our knowledge of man, although it was and is a matter of expediency, is at the same time a cause for distortion.

Scholars in various fields of learning begin to agree that such an analysis as is herewith advocated has hardly as yet been made. They also agree that the plan for such a study should be devoted not to teaching or research as such, in the pragmatic sense, but in the main to the application of abstract thought to the ever-expanding body of knowledge at our disposal, to the end that wholly novel principles and theories on the main problems of civilization should be brought into existence. They further agree that the basic necessity is to attempt to correlate the great accretion of facts in relation to the nature of man and the nature of nature.

It is the thesis of the present writer that in spite of the difference and diversity of the disciplines represented in the world of the mind, there exists a strong, common agreement among many concerning the overwhelming need for counterbalancing the multitude of compelling scientific activities and investigations of objective phenomena from physics to history and psychology. To provide this balance, it is necessary to stimulate an awareness of the basic fact that ultimately the individual human personality must unite all the loose ends in a whole. To anchor this spirit, and to impress it on the intellectual life of humanity, on thinkers and doers alike, is indeed an enormous challenge which obviously cannot be left entirely either to natural science, on the one hand, or to organized religion, on the other. We are confronted with the necessity of discovering the principle (or principles) of differentiation and yet relatedness and making it clear enough to justify and to purify scientific, philosophic and other knowledge while accepting their mutual interdependence.

In a statement by Lewis L. Strauss concerning "the great challenge of our times" which arises out of man's natural science and his inventions, the need for such a study of man was implied in the following words: "the philosophers, historians, sociologists, theologians, and all the leaders of thought (would be invited) whose concern is with man rather than the physical universe which man is in." [2]

The whole history of physical science has indeed taught us how the exploration of ever wider fields of experience reveals unsuspected limitations in accepted ideas and points to a freer attitude necessary for the recovery of order and harmony.

Modern man is faced with an unfortunate condition: research outruns the organization of knowledge; knowledge outruns his understanding; reductionist dogmatism, as the result of quantitative, scientific methods of analysis, determines his thinking; mutations in thought which could be engendered not only through the cross-fertilization, but, more important, depth-fertilization of ideas and disciplines, are impeded by the atomization and isolation of those very ideas and disciplines.

At one time in man's history an idea could be suppressed by showing that it was hostile to religion. In this way theology was sometimes the chief source of fallacies. Today, when a concept can be discredited

[2] *The New York Times,"* June 21, 1957.

by branding it as unscientific, the power previously exercised by theology has been bestowed on science. Hence science is in danger of becoming in its turn the greatest single source of error.

A study of man does not oppose the significant influence science has had on modern thought and action. On the contrary, it supports it. But it is convinced that the limitations of the scientific method must be recognized and its scope modified. This is in the interest of other human ideals which are threatened and in the interest of science itself. Natural science is menaced by self-diminution unless it can harmonize with the wider and deeper range of human thought and human experience. The very tendency in natural science to accept the results of its method as the ultimate reality rather than as the product of the method itself, is indeed cause for profound concern.

The unique achievement of scientific method is *detachment.* Yet, we must concede that there are a great number of things our knowledge of which dissolves if we look at them in a thoroughly detached manner. The meaning of a word is obliterated if we cease to mean anything by it; the proof of a mathematical hypothesis disappears if we cease to trust it; and a moral ideal evaporates if we stop respecting it.

In fact, a process of moral inversion sets in as a result of the false ideal of detachment. When once the direct expressions of our moral passions are discredited by a detached scientific approach, they will seek some other outlet which is protected against our scientific self-doubt. The various forms of scientifically denatured morality which have emerged during the past two centuries are but different outlets for subverted and frustrated moral passions.

Men will not pursue moral ideals indefinitely when their science tells them that morals have no reality. This is so, not because men become indifferent to morality but because they slip into the more logical state of complete moral inversion. A great upsurge of moral passions is likely to bring about explosion and catastrophe. This is what happened under the impact of the modern dynamism and political demonologies in the totalitarian revolutions of our time over immense areas of Europe and Asia.

Teachers and men of action in business and government, as well as the people at large, are making known their unformulated but deeply felt wish for a "body" to consider the ethical problems that they see as critical both for world survival and for individual happiness. And now in our time, scholars from many fields see in a study of man an answer to the fragmentation of knowledge that threatens to vitiate the advance of science through sheer lack of central and meaningful focus.

It is important to recognize another fundamental deficiency of natural science (including the behavioral sciences, deterministic psychology and psychiatry) as it is interpreted today. There are those learned and ingenious natural scientists who maintain that every higher type of organization is understandable in terms of the units and the relations out of which it is built, and that if we fail to predict their properties from those of their units, this is due to a lack of information which we shall some day obtain. What does this mean? Of course, if the "relations" of the units from which an organization is built include their relations *within* the organism, then the statement says no more than that the organism is composed of parts. If, on the other hand, as it would seem, the relations which explain the organism are thought to be those which the parts are known to manifest outside the organism, then the statement is certainly untrue. Electrons and neutrons are not thought to be sentient, while the higher animals are known to be. If an animal laps up a saccharine solution, the rational explanation of this lies in the fact that the solution tastes sweet and that the animal likes it. The tasting and the liking are facts that physics and chemistry neither explain nor can yet explain on the basis of their *present* postulates. This is applicable as well to man.

And this conclusion demonstrates the ineptitude of the method, because it acknowledges a conscious desire by an individual capable of such desire. It leads further to the recognition of deliberate actions by individuals and the possibilities of error on their part. Thus a whole series of conceptions emerges that are absent from physics and chemistry as known today. Indeed, nothing is relevant to biology, even at the lowest level of life, unless it bears on the achievements of living beings: achievements such as their perfection of form, their morphogenesis, or the proper functioning of their organs; and the very conception of such achievements implies a distinction between success and failure, a distinction unknown to physics and chemistry.

For example, the distinction between success and failure is present in, and is indeed essential to, mechanistic science; and the logic of engineering, for instance, does substantiate in fact what is here submitted in biology. No physical or chemical investigation of an object can tell us whether it is a machine and, if so, how it works. Only if we have *previously* discovered that it *is* a machine, and found out also approximately how it works, can the physical and chemical examination of the machine tell us anything useful about it, as a machine. Similarly, physical and chemical investigations can form part of biology only by bearing on *previously established* biological achievements, such as shapeliness, morphogenesis, or physiological functions.

A complete physical and chemical topography of an animal (or man) would tell us nothing about it as an animal, unless we knew it previously *as an animal*, and if the rules of scientific detachment required that we limit ourselves exclusively to physical and chemical observations, we would remain forever unaware of animals or of any other living beings, just as we would remain ignorant also by such observations of all machines and other human contrivances.

The achievements which form the subject matter of biology can be identified only by a kind of appraisal which requires a higher degree of participation by the observer in his subject matter than can be mediated by the tests of physics and chemistry. The current ideal of *scientificality* which would refuse such participation would indeed destroy biology but for the wise neglect of consistency on the part of its supporters. For there can be no dichotomy between the physical and biological sciences, since there can be no break between living and non-living substances.

The faith in the mechanistic concept of behavior and mind is taken almost universally for granted among some neurologists and psychologists, who regard its acceptance as basic to their claim to be scientists. But the present writer submits that this belief is incomplete; for this belief assumes, for example, that Sophocles' conscious thoughts had no effect on the writing of his plays, that the plays have been performed ever since by actors whose thoughts had no effect on what they were doing, while successive generations of audiences applauded without being in the least affected by the fact that they enjoy the plays. In other words, it is submitted that the character of the mind-body relationship still remains unresolved since Aristotle.

The foregoing has attempted to point to the misleading compulsion exercised today by the erroneous ideal of scientific detachment. If this ideal could be re-evaluated by a revised conception of scientific merit, the relation between mind and body might perhaps be reviewed in the following direction: conceding that no process is presently known to be accompanied by consciousness, we might suppose that a future enlargement of physics and chemistry might account for the sentience of certain material structures. It would then seem unwarranted to retain for such structures the conception of automatic functioning, which is derived from our *present* physics and chemistry. Action and reaction usually arise together in nature. Hence it would seem reasonable to expect that the new physics and chemistry, which would account for the production of consciousness by material processes, would also allow for the *reverse* action, that is, of conscious processes acting on their material substrate. We need new definitions of mind and consciousness. It is not the independence of mind that is the object of our search but a fuller and yet unimagined relationship. The problem is one of *nexus*.

Only such a conception of the human mind can acknowledge our claim to mature and responsible personality and individuality and account for the obligation to treat each other as responsible persons. It alone makes it possible to acknowledge the independence of mental growth which, though conditioned by circumstances, is only partly determined by circumstances. It confirms, therefore, man's capacity and right to serve the growth of thought and to seek the truth, aiming at universal validity. It permits us to hope that the ideals from which we seek guidance for our judgments and actions may reflect to some extent the proper meaning of existence. Thus it makes it possible to conceive of a free society in which these independent strivings will co-exist and cooperate with mutual enrichment and mutual enlightenment. For it is of the very essence of a scientific theory that it commits man to an indeterminate range of yet undreamed of consequences that may flow from it. We commit ourselves to these, because we believe that by our theory we are making contact with a reality of which scientific theory up to the present has revealed only one aspect. It is this commitment that lends universal intent to a scientist's most original, solitary thoughts. Through the acceptance of this we shall restore science to the great community of human aspirations by which men hope to fulfill the purpose of their existence. We may thus show that the pilgrimage from potentiality to actuality can be made only on the staff of intuitive as well as discursive knowledge. And by recognizing the trans-spatial and trans-temporal nature of man and reality, we shall be able to point again to the abiding truth that the rediscovery of man implies the rediscovery of God.

Religious Wisdom and Scientific Knowledge

Etienne Gilson

Dr. Etienne Henri Gilson of the Academie Française and co-founder and professor for close to three decades of the Pontifical Institute of Medieval Studies of Toronto, Canada, was born in 1884 in Paris. It was at the Sorbonne that Lévy-Bruhl taught him historical method and suggested that he examine the borrowing of Descartes from the work of the scholastics. This led him to the discovery of Thomas Aquinas and the Middle Ages. He was also a pupil of Bergson at the Collège de France; later a professor there. As a captain of a machine-gun division in World War I, he was taken prisoner and learned English from a fellow prisoner; after the war he administered relief-operations in Russia. He has taught at both Lille and Strasbourg. Amongst the distinguished lectureships held by Gilson have been: Gifford Lectures at the University of Aberdeen; William James Lectures at Harvard University; Richards Lectures at the University of Virginia; Mahlon Powell Lectures at the University of Indiana. He is a member of the French Academy, the Royal Academy of Holland, the British Academy, the American Academy of Arts and Sciences, and the Pontifical Academy of St. Thomas Aquinas in Rome. He was a Member of the Conseil de la Rèpublique, 1946–48; technical advisor to the French delegation to the United Nations Conference in San Francisco, and French delegate to UNESCO. Gilson is author of over forty outstanding books, such as The Unity of Philosophical Experience, God and Philosophy, Dante the Philosopher, Reason and Revelation in the Middle Ages, Being and Some Philosophers *and the* Philosophy of St. Thomas Aquinas. *Recently the Pontifical Institute of Medieval Studies, Toronto, Canada, produced a L.P. recording of a lecture titled "Philosophy and Science." A new book dealing with the future of science and philosophy will appear in the Fall of 1960. The recipient of many honorary degrees from universities in many countries, Dr. Gilson received the Christian Culture Award in 1949.*

CHRISTIANITY AND CULTURE

THE PERSONAL reflections I am about to submit are not those of a scientist, but of a Christian philosopher fully aware of his shortcomings in the field of positive science. After assimilating the content of a score of books, a Greek philosopher could rightly boast of knowing the science of his own times. Nor were these books particularly hard to understand. Things began to change in the seventeenth century, which Whitehead [1] has called the century of genius, when mathematics began to be considered as the true language of science. Yet, even Descartes, who was largely responsible for this evolution, did not hesitate to write a complete system of physics in one volume, after which he felt confident that with time, he could dispose of the whole of biology in the same way. At the beginning of the nineteenth century, the existence of a scientist able to master the whole field of scientific knowledge had already become highly improbable. Such a man would have had to be a Newton and a Darwin rolled into one; a rather unlikely combination indeed. In our own times, the very progress of science has been attended by a still more acute specialization. A modern academy of sciences is a body of scientists, each of whom, although competent in some branches of his own field, lays no claim to have mastered contemporary science as a whole. Everyone knows this from bitter experience. When we seek medical advice, we are often advised to consult a specialist. Naturally, this specialist will have a general knowledge of medicine, just as any scientist has a general knowledge of science, but there are many fields where neither one would venture to risk an opinion. Physicists who deal with physical theories often have to seek mathematical advice, and mathematicians themselves are constantly doing it within their own circle. Modern science has become much too big to lodge entirely in the brains of any single man.

Yet we cannot help worrying about what it says, not only because science is present in every one of the many gadgets we constantly use at home, but also, and still more, because it tells us what kind of world we are living in. From this point of view, it would be interesting to know, among those of us who are at least sixty years old, how many realize that they are living in their third universe? Any man who is fifty-five was born in the good old universe of Newton, ruled by a force of attraction causing absolute motions in an absolute space. In 1905, while asleep or thinking about something else, the same

[1] *Science and the Modern World*, Lowell Lectures of 1925, Harvard University, (New York: Macmillan, 1925).

man entered the universe of Einstein, which was that of relativity. This new scientific world was much more different from the world of Newton than the world of Newton was from the world of Ptolemy. From 1905 up to 1927, we were living in space-time, that is in a universe where what each of us considers as past, present or future is all given at one time, and where each observer determines in space-time his own space and his own time, and does it in his own way. Despite its revolutionary nature, the world of Einstein still retained an important feature of the Newtonian universe, namely, its unqualified recognition of scientific previsibility owing to the complete determination of physical phenomena. Now, this is precisely the reason why, today, other physicists find it natural to speak of the "old universe of Newton and Einstein," as though they were one and the same universe. For indeed, when in 1927 Heisenberg published for the first time his "relations of uncertitude," he was making possible the completion of what is now called "undulatory mechanics," that is of a physical universe so astoundingly new, even in comparison with that of relativity, that Einstein himself up to the end refused unreservedly to accept it. And no wonder. In this particular world of science, where the structure of matter is discontinuous, each element is a corpuscle associated with a wave, but their relation is such that, if we know the one, our knowledge of the other is affected by a certain co-efficient of uncertitude. As a consequence, it is now considered impossible to situate with complete precision, in space and time, the elementary physical transformations which take place in the world. Now, for a phenomenon to escape the determinations of space and time, is also to escape the determination of causality. In point of fact, the very identity of a material particle becomes questionable if we cannot know for sure where it is when we know when it is, and vice versa. In such a universe, there still are laws and, practically speaking, they remain just as safe as the classical ones, but their nature is no longer the same. Instead of resulting from strictly determined elementary phenomena, the laws of the new physics express a statistical average. There passes the dividing line between the ancient physics of Einstein and Newton on the one hand, and the new physics of Bohr, Heisenberg and de Broglie on the other hand;[2] up to 1927, scientific previsibility was supposed to

---

[2] Niels H. D. Bohr of Denmark, W. K. Heisenberg of Germany, and Prince Louis-Victor de Broglie of France: three Nobel Prize Winners; almost the parents of the new Quantum physics.

rest upon strict physical determinism; today, scientific previsibility results from the global probability arising from innumerable elementary indeterminations. Incidentally, this means that the strictly determined mechanical world of dialectical materialism, which Marxists still mistake for the world of science, died 32 years ago. They don't seem to know it yet.

This elementary survey of the history of science in the recent past was necessary to give a concrete meaning to the words "scientific knowledge." It is nothing like the exhaustive and self-satisfied knowledge of all things which some people imagine. On the contrary, we find ourselves, right now, in the very middle of another century of genius, probably far greater than the seventeenth century ever was, but, for this very reason, the universes of science now succeed one another with a curiously accelerated speed. Like the patriarchs of the Old Testament, they seem to obey a law of diminishing longevity. The system of Ptolemy died fourteen centuries old, which was a ripe old age; that of Copernicus, which replaced it, lasted almost three centuries; that of Einstein, twenty-two years, that is, supposing that his world is dead, which Einstein himself stoutly refused to concede. Naturally, these revolutions do not break up the continuity of the progress of physical science; each universe paves the way to its own successor which, in turn, is bound to maintain all that was true in the preceding one; yet, when all is said and done, the fact remains that, by reason of its accelerated progress, modern science is exhibiting an always decreasing stability.

This should not induce us into believing that these repeated scientific revolutions are due to a sort of restlessness innate in the minds of modern scientists. The reverse is true. Inertia is not only a property of matter, it is also found in minds. We call it intellectual conservatism, routine, or simply prejudice. When old intellectual positions ultimately surrender, there are cogent reasons. A scientific system endures, in the minds of scientists, as long as one or several irreducible facts do not constrain them to change it. Even then scientists regularly begin by overhauling the old system in order to adapt it to the these facts rather than to give up the old explanation for a new one. All these incredibly new notions, whose full philosophical impact we philosophers are still far from having grasped, are as many answers of the human understanding to the challenge of observable facts. Now what is most remarkable about this, is another fact, namely, that the human undertstanding did find the answers. I am not here expressing a personal impression which, not being a scientist, I am not qualified to express; I am merely reporting the personal experience of the greatest scientists of our own times. Confronted with their own amazing discoveries, they entertain no doubt about their truth, but are beginning to wonder about their possibility. "What is most incomprehensible about nature," Einstein says, "is its incomprehensibility." As to Louis de Broglie, in one of the most remarkable chapters of his book, *Physics and Microphysics*,[3] he makes this almost identical remark: "What is most marvelous about the progress of science, is that it has revealed to us a certain concordance between our thought and things, a certain possibility for us to grasp, through the resources of our intelligence and the rules of our reason, the deep-seated relations that obtain between phenomena. We do not wonder enough about the fact that some scientific knowledge is possible."

This remarkable statement clearly shows that nothing equals the ignorance of modern philosophers in matters of science, except the ignorance of modern scientists in matters of philosophy. For indeed, if the problem at stake is that of the possibility of science, it can truly be said that ever since the times of Plato and Aristotle, philosophers have never ceased to worry about it. What must the nature of the world be, in order that matter itself be intelligible? And, if it is, what must the nature of the mind be, in order that the world be intelligible to it? Last, not least, how account for this reciprocal harmony which obtains between nature and reality, and without which science itself would not be possible, or rather, of which science is the most perfect expression?

One may well wonder, since scientists themselves are asking these questions, why they do not attempt to answer them; and still more why, when philosophers try to solve the problem, scientists do not pay much attention to their answers. The reason for this is simple. It is that the question of the possibility of science is not itself a scientific question. Any attempt to answer it in a scientific way results in a vicious circle, since a scientific demonstration of the possibility of science implies the existence of science, whose possibility it tries to demonstrate. We must therefore choose between two possible attitudes; either to content ourselves with accepting the intelligibility of the world as unintelligible, or else resorting to philosophical reasoning which, since it has to explain why scientific demonstration is possible, cannot itself be a scientific demonstration.

[3] London: (Hutchinson, 1951), translated by M. Davidson, (Michel Cie), with Foreword by Albert Einstein.

There might be a further reason for the reluctance of so many excellent minds to accept philosophical explanations in this matter. Since the problem is about the intelligibility of nature, its answer has to be sought beyond the order of nature. Now, according to the very etymology of the world, the *philosophical* knowledge of what lies beyond nature (in Greek, *phusis*) is metaphysical by definition. Moreover, since the only way for us to account for the intelligibility of the world is to resort to a cause whose nature and operation made it to be, and to be intelligible, the answer to the problem must need be found in the crowning part of metaphysics, that is in that part of it which deals with the first principle and the highest cause. If there is such a cause, its name is God. In short, the only discipline that can answer this question is divinity, or theology. Now I quite agree that, to many scientists, philosophical or theological answers do not sound serious. But this is beside the point; for indeed it would not be serious to give metaphysical or theological answers to scientific questions; but the question asked by these scientists is not a scientific one; science never worries about its own possibility: were science not possible, it would not exist; that is all. What is now happening is that, on the basis of their scientific knowledge, some scientists are beginning to ask metaphysical and theological questions. And they are welcome to do it, but if they do, they will have to look for metaphysical and theological answers.

This is the kind of answer which philosophers have been trying to find for more than twenty centuries in the West, and, in the East, for more than twenty centuries. But if we go back far enough into the past, we shall observe another curious fact, namely, that when philosophers found answers to such questions as the origin and nature of the physical world, they did not create them out of nothing. They merely elaborated in a rational way solutions of the problem which had come to them through another channel than those of either science or philosophy, namely religion. Religious knowledge is neither science, nor philosophy, because it does not rest upon any kind of demonstrations but upon faith; it shines from on high, as a light that has nothing else to do than just to be in order to be seen and to impart visibility to many other things. On account of its primitive evidence, it is called a revelation, and because, in its light, we understand the rest, we call it wisdom. I know of no better description of this type of knowledge than a simple sentence of the Vedanta, which dates from about the fifth century before Christ: "That doctrine is not to be obtained by argument, but when it is declared by another, then, O dearest, it is easy to understand." Religious wisdom is that doctrine which is not to be obtained by argument, but which is easy to understand when it is declared by another, who is God.

Here again, I am not offering any scientific argument, nor even a philosophical one, but I am quoting a fact, or if you prefer, a human experience that is as old, if not as mankind, at least as that part of mankind which has left us a written expression of its beliefs. Not to lose ourselves in the endless field of past centuries, let us single out what has always appeared to me as the most striking exemplification of this experience, namely the spreading of the Gospel among the peoples of Greco-Latin culture in the second century after Christ. Thomas Aquinas calls it the greatest of all miracles. It was, and, insofar as I can see, it still remains an extraordinary phenomenon. Here was a civilized society which found at its disposal at least four or five scientific and philosophical interpretations of the universe; I am not now talking of mythologies, but of doctrines as purely rational as those of Plato, Aristotle, Democritus, Lucretius, Zeno or Epictetus. Of the men who were living in those times, it can be said that they had the pick of the best, since they could freely draw from any one of the systems which, still today, are considered in our universities a necessary introduction to the study of philosophy. Yet, many of these men became Christians, and if we ask them why, they unanimously give the same answer. They all had read the Bible, a book written in a rather barbaric language, whose crude statements were not supported by a single philosophical argument, and yet to their deep surprise, they had found its doctrine infinitely more intelligent than that of any one of the philosophies they knew. Scripture was giving to philosophical problems non-philosophical answers that were deeper and more true than those given by philosophy itself. And it was all so simple. "In the beginning, God created heaven and earth." He created them out of nothing; and He could do it because, His name being "He Who Is," or "He Is," [4] He was being itself; consequently, He could cause beings. But God was not only power, He was also wisdom. So He ordered His creation according to number, weight and measure, and just as he had put wisdom in things, He likewise put it in the mind of man, when He created him to His own image. In my own turn, and after so many centuries, I feel like apologizing in concluding: this is why the world of nature

---

[4] *Exodus* 3:14.

is intelligible, and this is also the reason why the human mind is able to understand it. As Scripture says: God has poured wisdom out "upon all his works, upon every living thing according to his bounty."[5]

Is this philosophy? Not a bit, but I beg to submit that no philosopher ever said anything half as satisfactory on the question.

If there is any truth in what has just been said, the endlessly controverted problem of the relations between science and religion should not even arise. If they do not ask religious questions, scientists will never be offered religious answers. Nor will these religious answers ever pretend to be scientific ones. Religious wisdom tells us that in the beginning God created heaven and earth, but it does not pretend to give us any scientific account of the progressive formation of the world. As Thomas Aquinas aptly says, precisely about this very text, there were things which Moses could not express to an ignorant people without using images which they could understand.[6] Likewise, Scripture says that God has created all things in number, weight and measure;[7] and this again is a purely religious statement, but it is up to science, not to religion, to calculate these numbers, to weigh these weights and to measure these measures. Science deals with nature *qua* nature, religious wisdom deals with nature *qua* work of God.

Such is the true reason why, far from keeping away from science, a truly religious mind should do its utmost to follow it in its progress, as the most perfect homage rendered by nature to its creator. "The heavens show forth the glory of God, and the firmament declares the work of his hands."[8] This has never been more true than in our own days, at a time when astrophysics is beginning to reveal to us the prodigious dimensions of the world we are in. But there is something else which, in their turn, scientists could usefully remember: these words of Psalm 18 were already true at a time when men knew practically nothing about the nature of things in general, and when they were entirely wrong about what the Scripture calls the firmament; they still are true, and much more evidently so, in our own century of scientific genius; and the same will become still more manifestly true when our own science of nature, an object of

[5] *Ecclesiasticus* 1:10.
[6] *Sum. th.*, 1, q. 66, a. 1, pd 1m.
[7] *Wisdom* 11:21.
[8] *Psalms*, 18:1.

amazement to its creators themselves, will have been superseded by a more perfect one. This fact exemplifies more clearly than all I could say the difference there is between these two orders of knowledge: the words of science pass away; the words of wisdom do not pass away.

The Grounds of Peace

Charles Malik

Dr. Charles Habib Malik, the renowned philosopher, professor, and diplomat, was born in Lebanon in 1906. He received his B.A. from the American University of Beirut and his M.A. and Ph.D. from Harvard University. Later he became a professor of Mathematics and Philosophy and taught at several universities, including Harvard. Honorary degrees have been granted to him by many universities, and he is a member of over fifteen learned societies and associations. He has written several learned books such as: An Appreciation of Professor Whitehead, War and Peace, Problem of Asia, *and* The Universal Declaration of Human Rights, *and he has contributed to many learned periodicals. For many years he was the Ambassador of Lebanon to the United States and Lebanese Representative at the United Nations, and in 1958 he was elected President of the U.N. General Assembly. As Chairman of the Commission on Human Rights, Dr. Malik won the acclaim of the whole free world. In his syndicated column in a Sunday paper in 1957, Bishop Fulton J. Sheen referred to Dr. Malik as "the most brilliant mind and one of the most enlightened consciences in the U.N." In* Life *magazine on Nov. 24, 1952, it was editorially stated that the U.N. seemed to be in grave trouble but "at least it has Malik," and said that any organization that provided the sounding board for this great teacher and philosopher was indeed worthwhile. Again in an editorial on September 29, 1958,* Life *wrote in part: "The U.N. has already distinguished itself (in this 13th session) by electing Charles Malik to the presidency of the General Assembly. We welcome him as a serious philosopher and Christian teacher whose greatest service to the West . . . is in continually calling it to be faithful to its own ideals. As Socrates used his logic, so Malik uses his eloquence against sloth, pride, errors." Dr. Malik received the Christian Culture Award in 1953 and gave an address that is still timely today.*

Peace is on all minds today and many lips are pronouncing on peace: its possibility, its character, its probability. Most recently Pius XII, who has certainly earned the encomium "pope of peace," President Eisenhower, and Prime Minister Churchill have each made profound statements on peace.[1] The new leaders of Russia keep reiterating their peaceful intentions. Not only world leaders but ordinary men and women must be concerned with this vital theme.

At the outset I would like to raise a question: whether peace is the highest of goals, whether it should be sought unconditionally, or bought or achieved regardless of price. Though many would answer affirmatively, I feel that they are in grave error. Nothing could be more disastrous than peace at any price, based on the argument that war is the supreme evil. The fact is there are things higher than peace for which we would gladly die, without which life is not worth living: i.e., the defence of our children and our honor. But even more important are truth and justice. An alleged peace based on falsehood, on error, on distortion or injustice is actually stillborn and will soon disintegrate into actual warfare. Hence an inquiry into the nature and conditions of peace is of paramount necessity. Great civilizations of the past have declined into decadence when they ceased to have values higher than peace for which they were willing to die, and which could inspire them to live.

With Thomas Aquinas we can accept the teaching of Augustine that peace is the "tranquillity of order." And how much disorder, in many forms, oppresses the world today: internal disorder within the nations that ought to be cured; international, which the United Nations attempts to alleviate; personal, involving mind and emotion; moral, in the dislocation of values. We may ignore none of these aspects.

In considering further the indispensable foundations for peace, I cannot well overlook comments on the current world situation, but I shall cast aside the evasions of politics and diplomacy, conscious that these remarks are for a religious university, where unswerving loyalty to truth should be pre-eminent.

The desire for peace at present does seem especially strong. From

[1] In his Easter message of 1953 Pius XII warned against the discouragement and weariness that affect those of good will, while the enemies of peace are unwavering. On April 16, 1953, President Eisenhower in a message, "The Peace We Seek," called upon Russia to exemplify by deeds, not only by words, its peaceful intentions. On May 11, 1953, Prime Minister Churchill, to a packed House of Commons, in a "sweeping, ambitious and eloquent" address specified an approach to peace [Ed. note].

all sides we hear the hope that the powers that be can negotiate an honorable peace in Korea,[2] but I have met no one who wants a dishonorable peace, or peace at any price, notwithstanding the length of the negotiations in progress. The hunger is for an honorable peace, acceptable, enduring. It is, then, well worth while to inquire into the content and to take more time in negotiations, in order to ensure honorableness and hence durability.

But the achievement of peace in Korea will only be one step towards lasting peace for the world, for the Korean crisis has been symptomatic of something, still more universal and fundamental. We shall be confronted by imminent danger for a long time to come. When the history of our epoch comes to be written in some far-off future date, such incidents as Korea may well seem but the preliminary phase of a peculiar kind of war. A strange metaphysical paradox exists: the present, far from determining coming events, is itself remotely determined by the future. The future in its full concrete character is still open and is not fully determinable by the present; when it eventually determines itself, light will be cast back on the present; and the meaning of our present will become clearer in the context of further unravelled history.

The happy "old days" of our fathers or even of our boyhood when security seemed endless are gone, nor must their memory be replaced by the illusion that some magic or chance or external accommodation or necessity will usher in relaxation and tranquillity. Relaxation in the world's great tension will be won only through patience and hardheaded, intelligent, even perilous effort; which means recognizing the existing danger fully. War is more apt to come if we are living in a fool's paradise than if we look up and grapple with its possibility like men. Not only blinking at facts hastens war; so does inflating facts beyond their proper dimensions. Deadly things can not be effectively challenged by frantic gestures, but rather by calm and precise appreciation of the truth.

Radical differences, however, mark the situation today from that before World Wars I and II. Both 1914 and 1939 saw a mighty military machine in the heart of Europe bent on military conquest. The Soviet military machine today scarcely has the same concept of war the Germans had then. The Russians are infinitely more realistic and cautious; caution breeds reflection, which in turn breeds the possibility of modification of policy and can lead to a peaceful settlement.

[2] After months of attrition and intransigence on moral issues, like the repatriation of prisoners, the truce was signed on July 27, 1953.

In the second place, the mighty concentration of power without whose participation there can be no general war today exists largely in two nations:[3] the Soviet Union and the United States of America. But these countries need no territorial expansion; so the urge so exceedingly potent in 1914 and 1939 to expand beyond one's borders is largely absent from the causation of war today.

Thirdly, the fact America and Russia are not as critically contiguous to each other as was Germany to her neighbors is of great importance in weighing the factors of peace and war. Between these two giants there is abundant room to maneuver and trade; opportunity to reflect and devise alternatives to war. Significantly the revolutions, upheavals, and even military exploits of the recent years have somehow been localized enough that none of them has led to a general war.[4]

Fourthly, it is a fact that neither the American character nor the Russian character glorifies war, whatever may be the wishes of certain cliques or parties or governments or individuals. Since general war today must be total war, involving every citizen at every level of his existence, no war today can be really waged without the leaders being reasonably sure in advance of some positive, sustaining response on the part of the general public. But this brings into play, in the final analysis, the basic national character of the people. The aggressive character of communism is not so much military as it is social, political and ideological; which obviously leaves room for meeting the menace other than by actual war.

Finally, the growing consciousness of the immense destructiveness of modern war serves as a powerful brake upon any responsible leader's desire to resort to war as an instrument of national policy. It is therefore natural to assume that people are not going to provoke war, and that if war comes, it will be more because people have stumbled into it. And this necessarily means active and constant search for alternatives.

The quiet contemplation of all these five essential differences between the present situation and the state of affairs prior to the last two world wars should enable us to place the present danger in its proper perspective. Certainly, we are in danger of war, but there are certain powerful factors which seem to conspire to make war avoidable.

[3] Seven years after Dr. Malik's statement, in view of the swift industrialization and militarization of communist China, some observers might want to reflect on this point further [Ed. note].

[4] Dr. Malik had in mind such happenings as the collapse of Chiang Kai Shek, the Korean invasion, and even the communization of Czechoslovakia [Ed. note].

With the essential hopeful differences, between the situation now and that of 1914 and 1939, there seem to be three fundamental, less hopeful aspects to consider: no Iron Curtain in the present sense existed between 1914 and 1939, effectively splitting the world into two parts and preventing significant economic, social or intellectual intercourse. This great factor militarily creates the possibility of war, inspiring profound mutual distrust, misunderstanding, and strangeness, while stimulating the armaments race. Until the Iron Curtain is in some effective way lifted, there can be no real peace.

The second difference influencing the possibility of war is the communist ideology, which works by boring from within, undermining existing social, economic and political institutions, propagating revolutions and upheavals throughout the world. Such a revolutionary movement with an elemental universal appeal to all men did not emanate from Germany either in 1914 or 1939.

The third factor which must be weighed in relation to war and peace is the rise of Asia. Outside Japan, Asia, until recently, did not play an effective and direct part in the determination of universal war and peace. But today many peoples in Asia are being gradually sucked into the communist orbit; a process of suction, however, which cannot be allowed indefinitely to go unchecked, clearly upsetting the equilibrium of peace and increasing the danger of war. These three elements of difference are determinant factors in the evolution of war or peace today.

What must be done to strengthen peace? On the purely physical plane, peace is always a question of equilibrium of forces; literally a problem in physics. In the extremely delicate equilibrium of forces throughout the world, as soon as this equilibrium is upset, even if angels were on the side of the greater force, there would be a temptation to strike; and communists are not angels. Even apart from the fact that they seem to require (they may be forced to modify this doctrine in the future) a world revolution to make the world safe for communism, they will be tempted to strike, at least by internal subversion, wherever they confront a weaker situation.

Several such tempting situations exist today: in Asia, in the Middle East, and even in Europe, despite all the armaments of NATO. That is one reason why in these regions communism is on the march in one form or another. The problem, therefore, on the purely physical plane, is how to remove these temptations as effectively as possible.

Western rearmament, as I understand it, is designed, with well-meant intentions, to restore these equilibriums of power. This rearmament seems to be aimed precisely at helping to prevent any further loss of territory, through the temptations of power vacuums, to the communist realm, whether this loss comes about by revolution from within or by conquest from without. The Western world seems to feel that any further defection in Europe or in Asia will sooner or later spell disaster and must be prevented at all cost; a point of no return, with war already begun. Hence, clearly stating, under these circumstances, "thus far but no farther" as a policy, stabilizes the foundation of peace.

But even if the present territorial and political situations were neatly frozen, I still doubt that peace could in the long run be ensured. So long as Europe is partitioned by the Iron Curtain and China is not economically and politically independent, the balance of power in the world is dangerously upset. I believe that no work for peace is more necessary than to try urgently to restore a healthy, strong, united, self-confident, independent, and friendly, Europe and China. This requires, in my opinion, much greater boldness and imagination on the part of statesmen than thus far has been displayed. So long as the Western world is not disposed to devise ways and means for penetrating the communist realm just as effectively as communism has been trying to penetrate the West, the streaming of influence will always be one-sided, and a menace to peace. Whatever this desideratum entails, it must include mutuality of intercourse, equality of relationship, a finely-balanced system of action, reaction and interaction — the meeting of communist dynamism by a dynamism equal to theirs.

Now, this splendid balance is impossible without lasting solidarity and unity in the Western world. Hence we cannot afford the luxury of any further unseemly spectacles of apparent quarrels. The current scandalous bickering among the Western powers must cease;[5] security must take precedence over prosperity; and everything possible should be done to promote a friendly Near East. Western statesmen must take on a bolder responsibility in seeking an over-all settlement based on justice and on the agreement of all interested parties; must

[5] Apparently different conceptions of the kind of peace to be negotiated in Korea were being played up by press and radio and television, following a speech by Churchill in early May and too-bluntly critical remarks on the United States by Atlee, until Eisenhower tried to calm the tension. Even a "new Munich" had been mentioned as a danger by some journalists in the United States [Ed. note].

penetrate beneath the surface of external political arrangements and seek to provide both vision and motive power for the implementation of profound social, economic and psychological transformations.

It is customary these days to speak of the developed and undeveloped, or underdeveloped, countries. This distinction refers to the extent to which technology has exploited the resources of nature. In the last analysis this is measured by the per capita income of peoples. Development is therefore something relative, for even the most developed countries, like Canada, are still patent for further development. But so far as a minimal, decent standard of living is concerned, one can say that about two-thirds of the world are very poor. The average American or Canadian is at least twenty times as rich as the average inhabitant of these regions, and because of this problem alone there can be no peace in Asia, Africa, and Latin America. A deep sense of dissatisfaction sets in. I know, because I come from one of these regions. It is no comfort to these people to tell them that it is their fault and the fault of their ancestors that they are poor; to have them realize that the average American and Canadian has twenty times the opportunity of enjoying a rich, material existence and to some extent, consequently, a rich intellectual and cultured existence.

The high conception of the Point Four Plan is America's response to this challenge, and in the British Commonwealth of Nations the challenge is met by the celebrated Colombo Plan.[6] Point Four may eventually prove to be one of the most creative ideas of the 20th century. We are at the barest beginning of this development today, and I doubt not that the American people, when they fully comprehend the magnitude of the need and the sort of issues at stake for war or peace, will find that every effort must be exerted to increase one hundredfold the help extended to the underfed and needy until these can stand on their own feet. Point Four is certainly one of the major grounds for peace in the world today. You have only to consider President Eisenhower's speech in which he depicted an exalted vision of

[6] The Point Four Plan is President Harry S. Truman's inaugural address, Jan. 20, 1949, in which he emphasized four major courses of action for peace and freedom: continued support for the United Nations and related agencies; continuing of United States' programs for world economic recovery; strengthening of freedom-loving nations against the dangers of aggression; the application of modern technology and capital to the existing manpower and natural resources of the "have-not" areas. The *Colombo Plan*, so-called from Colombo, where the Foreign Ministers of the Commonwealth Governments met in September, 1950, is for Co-operation Economic Development of South and South-East Asia.

a world in which the money now spent on armaments will be turned to the benefit of the backward areas.

The deepest ground for peace, however, something beyond the military, political, and economic, is the spiritual. The communist assault on the world today is primarily spiritual and must be met on that plane; otherwise all else will prove of no avail. Marxian socialism is at once the outcome and the aggravation of this inner spiritual decay. There is in Karl Marx and in all that has stemmed from him a thoroughgoing economic determinism; a materialism of the most sordid type, an elemental lust for power, an absolute moral relativism; a radical cynicism concerning man's freedom and his inner personal worth; a fundamental denial of objective truth and of reason's ability to grasp it; and finally, not only radical atheism in the sense of disbelief in any personal, living God, but a violent, militant rejection of everything worthy of our love and adoration beyond the things that perish with time. One would be very ignorant to deny that materialism, sensualism, relativism, cynicism, anti-intellectualism, atheism, and the exaltation of the economic and political, have been for generations working havoc in the Western soul. No peace can be based on any compromise with Karl Marx and his main tenets, for his sect aims at nothing short of the most radical transvaluation of the deepest, positive, Western beliefs, even though known and cherished for thousands of years. Were it not for the prevalent, spiritual decay in the Western world, however, communism would never have taken root.

All great tragedies in history arise because somewhere, somehow, man misinterprets himself, takes himself to be what he is not, or not to be what he is. You and I are not only political animals, belonging to a certain collective group and feeling the strength of its solid cohesion and the venerableness of its traditions; nor are we mere creatures of desire and lust, for pleasure and power, gravitating toward one thing today another tomorrow; today perhaps a village, tomorrow a palace, today a bicycle, tomorrow an airplane. You and I are willing to walk barefooted and sleep on the floor if only our deep moral and spiritual needs are recognized and met. This, then is precisely the historic issue of our age: whether man, you and I in person, are to be dissolved without any trace into the determinations of our body and into economic and political determinations, or whether there are independent sources of truth and being which, far from being determined by politics and economics, themselves lay down the fundamental laws which govern politics and economics. The issue of our age is whether the mind and spirit of man are autonomous. Herein lies the tragedy of our epoch: incalculable energy and care is devoted to economics, politics, administration, and military arrangements; comparatively little, to the deeper levels of human existence.

We live in an age of universal rebellion: earth is storming heaven; the lower has risen against the higher; the external has overwhelmed the internal; the means has obscured and even replaced the end; the material has gotten the better of the spiritual. Therefore a profound act of repentance and re-orientation is needed if there is going to be any peace.

Man is not a mere political or economic animal, nor is he a creature of nature alone. Man lives by friendship and love; thrives upon righteousness and justice. Nor will he rest until he has embraced some kind of myth. His deepest peace is in the myth that is true. His spirit must be fed, his hope reassured. Unless man truly knows that he is a partner in the maintenance of righteousness here on earth, he will rebel, not only against a million bombers, but against the universe itself. Hence, we must look beyond the politicians and economists, statesmen and generals, with all due respect to them, right to the agencies which promote man's humanity: to the institutions which deal with his spirit and his mind.

And what are these agencies and institutions which minister to truth, love, righteousness and justice? They are principally five: the home, the school, the church, the factory, and the "word." Peace is lost or won in the home, in the school, in the church, in the factory, and in the printed or spoken word.

The family, these days, suffers from enormous strains. The solid virtues of the home have disintegrated, children are not obedient. But if peace or love thrives not in the home, there will never be peace in the world.

So long as mechanism, utilitarianism, vocationalism, and professionalism, dominate educational theory in the school, how can we produce a race of men whose souls possess peace and rest? The soul rests only in the vision of truth, and in an education that is liberal, free, unhurried, and disciplined by reason and argument, utterly "useless," taking unbounded joy in knowledge and being for their own sake.

Peace in industry can never come about with employer and employee pitted against each other, material profit their only objective.

Only as the factory becomes a sort of sacrament and communion in which the industrial process is executed for something more lofty than mere material gain, can man's turbulent desires be settled.

How can there be peace if the public is constantly fed with the cheap, the fantastic, the sordid, the mysterious, the thrilling, the sensuous? Peace resides not in the imagination and the senses, but in the heart and mind. Popular literature does not command and challenge, nor does it portray the difficult, the remote, the inaccessible, the holy. It makes everything easy, simple, and ready at hand for the listless observer. It feeds with a spoon. The "word" must be rescued from the present sacrilege to which it has fallen, and be restored as the faithful bearer of beauty and truth and goodness and a peace that is permanent, real, and eternal.

The Church is the original ground for all hope of peace. Though other grounds may fail us, this ground will never falter, because its Founder has already conquered the world. The family, the school, the economic process, the babblings of men are subject to the law of decay and death, and to live they must keep rising with Him who overcame death.

Peace is replenished in our souls every time we turn to the Prince of Peace for help and forgiveness. He gave us His peace, not indeed as the world gives, but as He alone knows how to give. And He asked us to pray incessantly, assuring us that whatever we ask in His Name shall be granted to us. Peace finally is the gift of God through the prayer of the Church.

Amid the Encircling Gloom

Sigrid Undset

*Sigrid Undset, the eminent Nobel Prize Winner in Literature for
1928 was the first recipient of the annual Christian Culture Award in
1941. She was born in Norway in 1882, the daughter of a prominent
archaeologist, who had married a Danish girl with Norwegian, Scottish and Danish blood in her veins. Sigrid Undset's experience for
some years as a clerk only helped her preparation for writing, as she
always was delving into research and reading. When she produced
her first book at the age of twenty-five, her mother inscribed an almost
prophetic wish on a favorite author's book which she presented to her:
"May you, too, as an author always be incorruptibly honest, fearlessly
seeing life as it is and truthfully reporting it." Professor A. H. Wins-
nes* called her "the Great Christian realist par excellence." With a
breadth of vision and a depth of insight, she is able to summon characters and situations from the past or present and make them pulsate
and live. "I am a person who has lived two thousand years in this
land," she playfully remarked once; but in a deep sense, it was true.
Her great trilogy* Kristian Lavransdatter, *her four-volume* The Master of Hestviken, The Wild Orchid, *and* The Burning Bush *are some
of her books best known and loved. In 1959, Four Stories, splendid
examples of the novella, were published in the United States, with
high critical acclaim. Driven from her beloved village home of Lille-
hamer during World War II by the Nazis, who slew her son, Anders,
she came via Siberia and Japan to the United States and stayed until
1945 in Brooklyn, growing to love America and being tremendously
revered and loved in return. During the almost five years she spent
back home before her death in 1949, she wrote the powerful* St. Cath-
erine of Siena. *On her sixty-fifth birthday King Haakon awarded her
the highest distinction, the Grand Cross of the Order of St. Olav, "for
eminent services to literature and to the nation." Both in her work
and in life she was a woman of indomitable integrity and loyalty;*

* *Sigrid Undset: A Study in Christian Realism,* (New York: Sheed and Ward, 1953).

loyal to her own three children, to her step-children, to her painter-husband, even when their civil union collapsed after her conversion to the Catholic Faith. Strength, dignity, tranquillity, sustained by faith in mankind faithful to God, touch her honest realism. Most Sigrid Undset friends will read the address that follows for the first time.

Unspeakable are the horrors of World War II. Who can approximate an adequate idea of them: the suffering of the wounded, the armed and the unarmed, men, women, children; the concentration camps; the Polish nation split by two totalitarian powers, the hell of bombed Rotterdam; Britain blasted from land and sea; the destruction of crops and livestock, jeopardizing the health of the citizens; the damage to the treasures of arts and crafts, the heritage of centuries of civilization; the plunder, burning and annihilation?

The memory of my own Norway is fresh. Much of our old good things and probably most of our new good things, the creation of the last three generations will have gone; that is, when the hordes of invaders will have been driven out. We Scandinavian people, like those of my mother's country, Denmark, had developed our own way of life: eager to keep abreast of the march of material and scientific progress, we were, in some realms of modern life, in the vanguard of social improvements; we had tried to preserve all that was best and had proved suitable for our natural conditions and national temper; had really succeeded fairly well being both conservative and radical.

And yet, far worse than all the horrors I have hinted at, is the evidence that men who have felt called upon to be leaders have chosen *lies* as their chief weapon. In principle, the leaders of the new totalitarian state seem to prefer to employ lies; a grotesque situation indeed.

In the so-called exact sciences: physics or medicine, the urgent demand is truthfulness without reservation or equivocation; straight thinking, an incorruptible will to make precise observations, a conscientious manipulation of every scrap of evidence; otherwise the work may be entirely in vain. With the social sciences, however, leading men of our time have placed their trust in lies. For swaying the minds of men and focusing all the strength of a nation on goals to work, fight, suffer and endure for, the new leaders of the totalitarian nations firmly believe that lies are the best food for the souls of adults and children.

Fate's most exquisite irony. For centuries the white man has prided himself on the advance of enlightenment. Scorn was expended on the superstitions of the "Dark Ages," the murky Middle Ages; overlooked was the fact that these superstitions were conditioned by erroneous interpretations of sound observations that were only defective because the later technical instruments had not yet been invented; the erroneous explanations of observed facts were given in perfectly good faith.

But we have lived to see self-constituted leaders deliberately propagate superstitions in which they themselves cynically disbelieve. All the facilities of modern propaganda and educational technique are manipulated to prevent the people thinking for themselves and to mislead them. Lies and terror are the great weapons both national socialism and national communism are using to prevent the intellect from thinking straight and to isolate it from a sense of the real.

No true society can long be sustained on such ideologies, no enduring structure where men can fully live and be at home. The battle between the totalitarian and the democratic and, professedly Christian, nations is not primarily concerning which will build a society with different ideas and ideals; it is a battle on our side to stem the tide of destruction; on theirs to dominate and march on. They *must* attempt the subjection of people after people, *must* suck out the life-blood of others to nourish their own existence, while they survey the globe for new prey. With armed force we stand against the spread of the death march of their lethal ideologies across the nations, but that is insufficient in itself.

We have the lesson of world cultures that have collapsed before now, great culture-creating peoples reduced to small vegetating tribes of fellahin or wandering nomads. The Asia Minor, where St. Paul travelled from city to prosperous city, the North Africa where St. Augustine worked and studied in an urbane, sophisticated milieu, became ruin-littered deserts. But the world of St. Paul and St. Augustine was wide, and primitive communications prevented destruction from spreading endlessly; there were people and places whence reserves could be drawn or fresh growths of civilization might arise. Our earth today is smaller; distance is abbreviated. There is nothing to prevent one type of civilization or one wave of destruction from embracing the whole earth.

Nothing, except human determination to evolve and spread another type of civilization and to stem the wave of destruction. As probably never before in history, the fate of mankind today rests on the efforts of living men; on our conscious resolutions as to the kind of future we desire; on our readiness to plan for it, and our willingness to live and die for it. Total mobilization of mind and heart and soul and bodily strength will be needed to bring an integral and humanistic world society out of the awful chaos of our time.

To us Catholics, the fundamental horror of this chaos is that it proves the tremendous power of lies, and we know from whom all lies spring ultimately. We know the name of the Father of Lies. Of course, we Christians of all, or at least most, denominations did not exactly disbelieve in the existence of the Devil. For us Catholics it was an article of Faith to believe in him. To believe, however, is one thing; to realize is another. Though all of us know that we must some day die, few but the Saints are accustomed to realize it, so long as health is good and we are enjoying the satisfactions of living. We believed in the Devil all right, fought him sometimes in our private lives when he tempted us with tricks we learned all about in the confessional. We recognized the traces of his claws or cloven feet. But how many of us were aware of the immense power of evil, working underground and breathing the very atmosphere that we breathed, the huge spiritual force of a discarnate Personality intent on exploding and destroying what God created, because he himself is denied the power to create? How many of us had an inkling of the might and the cunning of superhuman envy, despair and hate towards a Creator-God, and a Father-God, by a fallen angel, who *cannot* generate and *will not* serve? I do not mean that we ought to understand the mind of Satan, because that is completely beyond our human faculties. But we ought to understand how far the evilness of the Evil One exceeds our power to imagine and to fight. This is surely one of the instances where we can say with the Apostle: "Of myself I can do nothing," but I can do all things in Him who strengthens me."[1]

Certainly, the states that have been built on democracy are far from immaculate; they have plenty of heavy sins and stupidities to account for. Promises and treaties were broken before the world saw the rise of the totalitarian states. Politics, too, used crooked ways, deceits, lies. Yet there was always present some sort of common sense in the nations, a warning voice which said: Truth is the safest foundation to build upon, the lie is a thing one should avoid, if possible. Well, it ought not astonish us, as Catholics, that the democracies too are made up of imperfect, sinful men and women. For more than a century,

[1] St. Paul, *Epistle to the Phillipians*, 4:13.

133

the onslaught on the Church by all schools of thinkers who were optimistic about the progressive evolution of humanity was at the bottom inspired by resentment against the Christian Creed, just because it maintains that mankind does not really progress at all. Men and women will have to war forever against evil and misery, against the temptations in their own souls to sins of pride and greed and deceit, as well as against the oppression that the weak and the innocent receive from those who yield to the temptations of evil. The war against evil will go on until the Day of Judgment. This Christian philosophy of life will call upon men and women to fight in an unending battle; to be ever armed and watchful; and to be never lulled with vain hope that any good things won may not be disputed, will not need to be defended and remade forever. And even when I myself was very far from being a Christian, I was never able to understand why this Christian "sceptical" view of humanity should be called reactionary or cowardly or unnatural, by its opponents, who very often fought for the same ends: more justice, charity, understanding and brotherhood, but who wanted to stiffen the morale of their armies by a faith in the finality of every conquest made in the direction of a better, more enlightened, more just and peaceful society. The refusal to face the possibility of spiritual or social backsliding for humanity, the optimistic confidence that whatever mankind has achieved in the direction of the noble and the good will be safe until it gets transformed into something better, always seemed to me the fundamental weakness of most of those who called themselves free-thinkers, even when I called myself a free-thinker, but with several mental reservations.

It is true, however, that the democratic conception of human life will ever contain the elements necessary for a possible regeneration of society, for new adjustments and bettering of the people's conditions under leadership of the fittest individuals; namely, the men and women who have the courage and the will to respect truth, whether they seek the true laws of the nature that environs us or the truth of human nature. It is also a truth, even a commonplace, that the origins of this democratic conception of human life are older than Christianity; that it is, in essential features, our heritage from the ancient Greeks, and that this pagan people were passionate inquirers into the nature of things and seekers of Truth. Their love of liberty, their beautiful veneration of human personality, was limited only by their discrimination between more or less valuable people and nations and races. Perhaps it was limited only because they were not granted the revelation of the basic human equality, consequent on the Fatherhood of God and our common heritage of original sin.

Certainly it is also a bitter truth that Christians for almost two thousand years have been slow to realize, quick to forget, the implications of their Faith when they confessed their belief in God the Father and the fall of man; that in spite of the differences that give races and nations and every single individual their own separate personalities and make us unlike one another, all men are equal in the glory of being made in the image of God and are equally disgraced by the taint of original sin.

Yet at the core of Christian culture, I think, is the acceptance of this fact of our fundamental equality in glory and in infamy, of the brotherhood of all men. However imperfectly it may have been realized by individual Christians in all walks of life, how brutally Christians may have sinned against it, you cannot *deny* it without denying Christ. Nazis or Fascists have tried to deny it and still call themselves Christians, but they have had to distort the teachings of Our Lord's Life and His Words and His Death; they have to hide their children and young people away from His influence. You cannot deny this basis of human equality and brotherhood and try to build a democratic society on any other concept of men being each others' equals; the unlikeness of gifts and tempers that make us into separate individuals and some few men the leaders of the many, with power over their fellow men, will be aggravated a thousand times when those on top imagine that they themselves are not in the hands of some Power which will hold them responsible, whatever this Power may be. Some call it a spiritual force behind the visible world, or the ghosts of their ancestors, or dynasties of gods in earth and sky, or the one God. Any attempt to build communism, except on a spiritual communion of Faith, like the communism of the Monastic Orders for instance, must lead to an everlasting battle between unlike types of personalities and unending attempts to liquidate or suppress unwanted varieties of individuals.

The honor bestowed on me through the first Christian Culture Award I appreciate most highly; yet I am sure many workers in the different walks of life were much more worthy of the choice. I do not underrate the importance of the realm of letters in preserving and re-creating the value of our Christian culture; yet I cannot help thinking that, beyond the task of literary people in times like ours, the most important work now is theirs who achieve the closest communion with Him Who has said of Himself: "I am the Way, the Truth and the Life." [2] He is the only escape from universal destruction, the only Truth who can defend against the power of the lie, the single source of life in a world drunk with the odor of death. And who they are who have achieved this communion and are drawing most copiously from the well of living water, to quench the hell fires of the Father of Lies, is not given any of us to know. Certainly, we see sometimes the traces of their work, sparks of their vitality lightening up the world's darkness; in the ministry of God's Church, in the schools, in the homes, in the realms of science and art, on one and all of life's battlefields. But this creative endeavor, upon which the whole of our Christian culture hinges is above any human award; indeed beyond our powers to know and understand. Yet the survival of Christian culture wholly depends upon this communion of holy souls with God.

[2] John, 14:6.

Men and Symbols

Dorothy Donnelly

Mrs. Donnelly, author of The Bone and the Star, The Golden Well, *and essays and sketches for magazines like* Transition *(Paris),* Commonweal, America, Catholic Art Quarterly, *and* Pylon *(Rome), is also recognized as a poet. Her poems have appeared in the* Hudson Review, Poetry *(Chicago),* The New Yorker, Spectrum, *etc., and she has been a recipient of* Poetry's *Union League Award, as well as of the Harriet Monroe Memorial Award and the Longview Foundation Award. A volume of her poems will be published this year by the University of Arizona Press. Mrs. Donnelly is married to Walter Donnelly, and lives in Ann Arbor, Michigan, with her husband and three grown sons. Detroit-born, she has the degrees of A.B. and A.M. from the University of Michigan and is a member of Phi Beta Kappa.*

MAN IS A symbol-making animal and by his symbols you may know him. Wherever he exists, or has left remains of his existence, there are symbols to give evidence of him. They constitute a kind of informal record of man, indicating something of his beliefs, hopes, and achievements, and of the quality and direction of mind, spirit, imagination, and sensibility.

The term "symbol," today, is likely to call up, first of all, Freudian connotations: the technique of psychoanalysis and the dream-images which are its working materials. To some it may suggest the lurid or the sinister, but in general it seems to arouse an expectation of glamorous, exciting, or esoteric revelations. Occasionally, such expectations are abetted by advertising; a recent notice of a book about symbols said that it contained "over 1,000 signs, symbols, and pictographs, from prehistoric times to the atomic age, ranging from astrology and alchemy to today's arts, sciences and professions, from mythology to the world's great religions, from magic and the occult to symbols for holidays, love, and good luck." It makes one think of the gaudy little dictionaries of dream symbols one comes across mixed in with horoscopes and pamphlets on yoga, as well as of Mr. Eliot's more literary pack of Tarot cards with their Hanged Man and drowned Phoenician Sailor.

The word "symbol" lures the imagination because it seems to promise to reveal what is hidden and secret. Curiosity is human, and the taboo and the unknown have an understandable fascination. This urge to discover what is behind the door is immortalized in its grimmer aspects in the story of Bluebeard and his wives. However, I do not propose to talk about symbol dictionaries, Freudian interpretations of dreams, the sexual symbolism of architecture and poetry and painting, the interpretations of specific liturgical or Biblical symbols, like the four wheels the color of aquamarine, and the living figures full of eyes in the cloud of amber-colored fire in the book of Ezechiel, or the beasts and candlesticks and enigmatic numbers of the Apocalypse. What I am concerned with is the symbol in its broader and more basic aspects, the deeply human symbol which has perennial validity and which is capable of throwing light on the world and on man, his desires and his destiny.

A symbol is briefly defined as "something used or regarded as standing for or representing something else." This brief and colorless definition calls up out of the vasty deep of the unknown, interesting questions about world nature and human nature, and suggests the existence of a necessary unity at the root of being, if one thing can be called on successfully to stand for something else. I should like to talk about the symbol in two of its significant aspects: as a kind of universal speech and as an illuminative force in human life.

Each of us is born into a world already in full swing, and each from his own specific cluster of circumstances, gradually fans out into a wider participation in this world of things and ideas, becoming as he does so, more and more himself. Each is equipped with a sense of wonder and a consciousness which becomes richer over a lifetime — it becomes what Henry James calls "an inhabited consciousness." Since man is a social being and was not meant to live alone, he needs from the beginning to communicate with others. One of the greatest deprivations and punishments is to be placed in solitary confinement. Human communication is more or less indirect; that is, it is carried on by symbols, which always require interpretation. Smiles and frowns and tears are symbols which we learn to interpret early in life, but it is not long before we begin to understand and to use language which consists entirely of signs and sounds. Spoken language is an indispensable tool in normal life, and written language advances us a long step, enabling us to preserve our discoveries and make them accessible to others through its symbols of reference.

If there were one common language, not only would the problem of communication be a comparatively simple one, but the sense of the unity of men would be much stronger. Language differences tend to divide men and to wall them up in narrow and often hostile groups. The story of the Tower of Babel, whether one regards it as historical or symbolic, is a dramatic account of the splitting of the human race from a primeval oneness into myriad alienated groups, which become as strangers to one another because they were unable to understand each other's speech.

In spite of the diversity of language, the fundamental human qualities remained; there were the same needs and the same basic desires, with a consequent possibility of future unity on some other level.

Star differs from star, and we enjoy these differences. Much more do individuals and families differ, and the great variety of symbols which develop out of their differences can give us much pleasure and can enlarge our concept of the versatility of human gifts. We should be able to look with an interested eye on all symbolic manifestations if we want to understand our fellowmen. Even cookery is symbolic of a culture, and to some extent we can gauge the degree of sophistication and imaginative vivacity in a group according to its utilization of available flora and fauna: ostrich eggs in Africa, blubber in Alaska, barley and rancid yak butter fused in tea in Tibet, melons cooled with snow in Persia, or a French gourmet's dish of stuffed snails. We should not succumb to the naïve, local view — "Oh, that sounds terrible! My mother never made anything like that!" A sympathy for the alien and unfamiliar symbol is essential to an understanding of it, and it keeps us from becoming narrow and provincial. No one can learn all the languages of the world, but anyone who has a mind to can come to appreciate and learn from the symbols of other peoples, no matter how remote in time or place. Each group has something that the other has not, and it is to our mutual advantage to cultivate the generous spirit which enables us to receive as well as to give.

This basic type of symbol with which we are concerned is found in every culture and every phase of life. Wherever there is human making or doing there are symbols; we find them in stories, poetry, sculpture, and painting, in the dance, in tools, utensils, and all other artifacts. We find them in the speech and in the manners and customs of a group, in the various gestures of greeting for example: shaking hands, bowing (from the mere nod to the 90-or-more degree angle bend), kissing on the cheeks, rubbing noses, removing the hat. Each one is a symbol of courtesy, and courtesy is a reflection of one's regard for a fellow human being. Moreover each will reveal something of the social temper of the group — its exuberance or restraint, gusto, gaiety, or dignity.

What people make shows what they like, and what they like reveals their sense of values, their wit, their sensibility. And it is often the things which seem to have no practical use that are most illuminating and most pleasing — a carved ivory grasshopper from ancient Egypt, for example, or a cicada of greenstone from China, or the commemoration of a grasshopper in a Greek epigram. We can find any number of such charming and rather puzzling things: a tiny bronze fish or frog made by the Ashanti for weighing gold dust, a yellow ostrich painted on stone by some Bushman, surprising owls sketched by Picasso, as well as a plaintive one in an old Chinese poem: "A sad owl hoots in the yellow mulberries," and the pert, well-groomed owls on silver Athenian coins. From this preoccupation with animals as subjects, and the urge to refashion them in stone and paint and words, we can discover something important — not what the encyclopedia or natural history can tell us about insects and birds, but a knowledge of the attitudes of men, past and present, toward the creatures of the world. We see that they have always been objects of attraction and of affection with an aura of mystery about them, how they have been understood and misunderstood, and how the primitive, especially, felt that they held some secret of power which he would like to share.

These various creatures belong to the world of *things*, and they are clearly regarded, not as objects only, but as symbols. As Gerard Manley Hopkins puts it: "Each mortal thing does one thing and the same . . . myself it speaks and spells." And so it does, but it also radiates a multitude of other suggestions, because insofar as a thing is a symbol, it says something other than itself. God did not create the things of the world disparately, but all united in a bond of being; they appear in variety; they are rooted in unity. Since a thing which is made bears some resemblance to its maker we can say that created things are the fingerprint of God. They give us a clue to him. Or as St. Paul expresses it: "The invisible things of him, from the creation of the world are clearly seen, being understood by the things that are made; his eternal power also and divinity."[1]

And since men are made in the image and likeness of God, their actions have a likeness to God's actions. They, too, are symbol-makers, utilizing created things and devising others of their own. That is why everywhere in man's world we find transformations of plant and animal forms, the acanthus and the papyrus leaf, the lotus and the rose, painted on walls and carved in marble: the lion's image on rock-paintings in Africa and in Assyrian sculpture; in the Psalms: "I lie down in the midst of lions;" in folk-tales and poems, Blake's lion in a lamb's world: where "the lion's ruddy eyes shall flow with tears of gold;" in Eliot's and Auden's more intellectual turning to the lion in their talk about time: Eliot asking "Who clipped the lion's wings . . . ? " as he meditates on "Time's ruins," and Auden assuring us that though "The hour-glass whispers to the lion's paw . . . . Yet Time, however loud its chimes or deep, has never put the lion off his leap . . . ."

Probably the most universal of the natural symbols, and one of the few which compels our attention, in spite of its familiarity, is the sun. Sunrise and sunset are daily dramas, expected spectacles of which we never tire. One has only to look at the sun to see why it has often been chosen as a sign of divinity and sometimes as an actual object of worship (though I am inclined to think that the sun-and-moon and stone-and-animal worshippers more often than not worship the spirit behind the thing and so come closer than we realize to a spiritual concept of God). The Egyptians are probably unsurpassed in their expressions of praise and admiration of Rä, the sun. Though they sometimes seem to confuse the sun itself with the creative spirit, their purest concepts show that they are worshipping the God who brought everything, including the sun, into being. There is an explanatory passage in the introduction to the *Book of the Dead*[2] which says: "In the hymns to Rä the dead person apostrophizes the glory and the majesty of the One God, the creator of the world and all that therein is, who manifests himself to his creatures under the form of the sun, by whose heat and light men and women, beasts and feathered fowl, fish and creeping things, trees and herbs have their being." The darkness of night into which the sun disappeared when he set was per-

[1] *Epistle to the Romans*, 1:20.
[2] *The Book of the Dead*, translated by E. A. Wallis, (London: Budge, 1898).

sonified as an enemy of the sun, and the daily victory of light over darkness was hymned with gladness by his worshippers. From one point of view the Egyptian regarded the course of the sun as a type of his own life, and day symbolized life, and night, death; the conflict in which the sun engaged with the powers of darkness typified the struggle of the deceased with his enemies in the underworld, and man hoped that he would overcome them even as the sun vanquished all who opposed his course. Following are a few lines from one of the finest of these hymns: "Thou risest, thou risest, thou shinest, thou shinest, thou art crowned king of the gods. Thou are the lord of heaven, thou art the lord of earth; thou art the creator of beings celestial and of beings terrestrial. Thou art the One God who came into being in the beginning of time. Thou didst create the earth, thou didst fashion man, thou didst make the watery abyss and didst give life to all that therein is. Thou hast knit together the mountains, thou hast made the heavens and the earth. Thou dost travel across the sky with heart swelling with joy. Thou art unknown, and no tongue is worthy to declare thy likeness; only thou thyself canst do this. Millions of years have gone over the world; I cannot tell the number of those through which thou hast passed."

The sun is used in the Psalms also as a symbol of the divine. The same exuberance is there, but its expression is more restrained. "Our God is a sun," the psalmist says. He does not say *the* sun, but *a* sun, making it quite explicit that he is using *sun* as a symbol. This symbolic use is made even more clear by the balancing image; the complete line being "Our God is a sun and a shield." There is another psalm which in symbol and exuberance reminds one of the Egyptian hymn, especially the lines: "The heavens declare the glory of God, and the firmament proclaims the work of his hands. There he has set up his tabernacle for the sun, which goes forth like a bridegroom from his chamber and rejoices, like a giant, to run the course. From one end of the heavens is its rising, and its course ends at the other; nothing is hidden from its heat." One feels in these lines the stirring power of concrete things in their character as symbols.

What I have been saying has sounded a basic note of optimism, but optimism is not the fashion at present in the more avant-garde circles — regardless of the persuasive advertisements which show men, and especially women, perpetually smiling, with perfect teeth, perfect health, eternal youth, and no personality whatever. The prevailing philosophy seems to be skeptical and pessimistic, even though life presents a surface enameled over with an arrogant gaiety. It is a modern variation of the old eat, drink, and be merry for tomorrow we die; an expedient substitute for true optimism — and, from the evidence of mental and physical illness, insecurity, fear, and despair, obviously not a very convincing or satisfying one.

Existentialism, in its radical non-Christian form, is one of the more popular pessimisms of the day. I suppose one might define an existentialist as a man who says, "Here I am, but I don't like it." That is: "Here I am, thrust into a world not of my making or choosing, at a time when things are in a fearful tangle and I am obliged to live in this complex and incompatible nest of circumstances which I find thoroughly disagreeable and not at all up to my standards of what a decent world ought to be, unless I avail myself of the one course of free action open to me and end it all." Alexander Hertzen,[3] a hundred years ago, gave this attitude prophetic expression when he wrote: "Our ideas have led us to unrealizable hopes, absurd expectations; together with them, the last fruits of our efforts, we are caught by the waves sweeping over a sinking ship. The future is not ours; we have nothing to do with the present; we have no means of escape. For we are tied to this ship in life and in death. All that is left is to wait with folded hands for the waters to flood over us; anyone who is bored, or is braver than the rest, may jump into the sea."

The symbol of the committed existentialist is "nausea," and his appraisal of the world is that it is "a moldy crust of bread." The life urge is so persistent, however, that not only do most existentialists go on living, but they seem to find some pleasure in being a part of, and observing and writing about, the gruesome spectacle. It is only fair to add, that from a completely natural point of view, their attitude is partly justified.

The Christian attitude toward things and the world, no matter how horrible the concrete or the existential situation, is necessarily, optimistic, since the Christian believes that, in the words of Juliana of Norwich, "All things shall be well," that in spite of the often horrifying appearances, God exists and knows quite well what He is doing, that He can, as St. Augustine says, write straight with crooked lines. This optimism is expressed in the psalmist's great cry of faith "We do not fear, though the earth be overthrown and the mountains crash into the midst of the sea."

[3] Alexander Hertzen, an impassioned Russian writer whose writings both before and after his banishment in Siberia were a powerful influence.

There is abundant evidence of this affirmative attitude toward life in the symbols of men and in words symbolic of their underlying attitudes. Several have struck me with special force. There is a trenchant comment by Henry James, who said of an unhappy character in one of his stories, that after all he had had the *"chance of life."* James saw that this was the great thing, this chance of life which is the first and necessary gift and opportunity on which all the others depend, and which is pre-eminently worth having whatever risk is involved.

Then there is the remark made by Rilke, shortly before he died of leukemia and when he was suffering acutely. He said to someone who was taking care of him: "Never forget, dear friend, life is a glory." These two men were not, at least formally, Christians, but their concepts of the supreme value of life are Christian.

Ivan's dream in the *Brothers Karamazov*,[4] a highly symbolic passage, casts a bright light on the profound problem of temporary suffering (whether as punishment or not) in relation to eternal joy. The tone of mocking humor sharpens and brings into high relief the deeply moving climax. The story is told to Ivan by the devil who says that the story belongs to the Middle Ages and no one believes it any more. He says:

> This legend is about Paradise. There was, they say, here on earth a thinker and philosopher. He rejected everything, "laws, conscience, faith," and, above all, the future life. He died; he expected to go straight to darkness and death and he found a future life before him. He was astounded and indignant. "This is against my principles!" he said. And he was punished for that; that is, you must excuse me, I am just repeating what I heard myself, it's only a legend. He was sentenced to walk a quadrillion kilometres in the dark, and when he finished that quadrillion, the gates of heaven would be opened to him and he'll be forgiven. Well, this man, who was condemned to the quadrillion kilometres, stood still, looked round and lay down across the road. "I won't go, I refuse on principle!"
>
> "Well, is he lying there now?"
>
> "That's the point, that he isn't. He lay there almost a thousand years and then he got up and went on."
>
> "What an ass!" cried Ivan, laughing nervously. "Does it make any difference whether he lies there forever or walks the quadrillion

[4] Fyodor Dostoevski, *The Brothers Karamazov* (New York: Random House, 1950) pp. 782-3.

kilometres? It would take a billion years to walk it."

"Much more than that. But he got there long ago and that's where the story begins."

"What, he got there? But how did he get the billion years to do it?"

"Why, you keep thinking of our present earth!"

"Well, well, what happened when he arrived?"

"Why, the moment the gates of Paradise were open and he walked in, before he had been there two seconds, he cried out that those two seconds were worth walking not a quadrillion kilometres but a quadrillion of quadrillions, raised to the quadrillionth power."

This is not theology, but it conveys theological truth made sharp and vivid by the repetition of the symbolic term "quadrillion," evocative in its dramatic context. The examples show a faith in the intrinsic value of life in spite of its darkest appearances.

Auden states the case with his usual adequacy:[5]

Defenceless under the night
Our world in stupor lies;
Yet, dotted every where,
Ironic points of light
Exchange their messages:
May I, composed like them
Of Eros and of dust,
Beleaguered by the same
Negation and despair,
Show an affirming flame.

Man's affirmative attitude toward life includes in it an attitude toward *things* that the Chinese call the Ten Thousand, that is, created things in general. He finds things good and expresses this discovery in his symbols which are not limited to one time or one country or religion but are found everywhere, uncovered by the archaeologist's shovel, preserved in museums, in homes, in books. This fragmentary but sufficient evidence of things that men have made and said assures us that an appreciation of the good, the true, and the beautiful has been in man as far back as we can find any sign of him. We and our works are inseparable, and our works speak clearly for us. They pro-

[5] "September 1, 1939," *The Collected Poetry of W. H. Auden* (New York: Random House, 1945), p. 59.

vide a universal speech which tells us all sorts of things about our-selves, what we like and believe and hope, and how with more or less success, we are all going the same way, in search of truth and joy.

Symbols not only speak their own eloquent language; they have other powers. They emit light; they can illuminate life when it shows itself common and dull; they have a tonic effect on sluggish spirits; they can enlarge the boundaries of our vision which tends to shrink inward and narrow the view.

Everyone knows the dull, dark day when life loses its color and savor, when it is *reduced* to its meanest proportions. This state is characteristic of the human condition in which we are obliged to keep ourselves going by the literal or psychological sweat of our brows, so that we lose sight of what a Chinese writer calls "the gleam on the mountain." In these dim moments some symbol can come to the rescue, simply by catching our eye. Shakespeare knew it, for he said: "How far that little candle throws its beams: so shines a good deed in a naughty world." In our case the good deed is the effective symbol.

Not all symbols have the same power. Some are one-candle power, some are suns. The primitive sought the stone with the greatest "mana" or force, or what we might call symbolic power. He recognized such power by the shape. If the stone had the right contours he planted it in a field of tubers to increase their fertility, or he made a fetish or a talisman of it. Some primitives found special power in the sunflower root and said to the root (before they ate it) "You are the greatest of all in mystery!" This symbolic efficacy is found in slight as well as extraordinary symbols — in the glimpse of a familiar face, a phrase of music, a letter from a friend, in the greenness of a tree, or the flight of a bird. Or in an image in a poem. Picasso knew how to light up a whole scene of horror by sketching on his canvas a single flower. Things have power in so far as they rouse us to a sense of the depths and radiances of life.

We give shape to the stream of time by dividing it into centuries and years and weeks, and the weeks into days. Of these the first day of our week, the Christian Sunday, is high in symbolic value. Set apart from all the other days, a special significance attaches to it; it is different; we expect of it something finer than other days offer. On a natural level it is different because it is a free day on which one doesn't (perhaps) work. On a supernatural level this appointed and mysterious day of rest is a kind of image of the life to come when there will be rest without oblivion and activity without labor, when "night shall be no more" and the light of the Sun shall make an eternal day.

Clearly, man is by nature not only a symbol-maker but a symbol-reader. He not only finds delight and use in the symbols he creates, but he recognizes and enjoys and is enriched by those of other men. In every group there are some people who have imaginative power beyond the ordinary; these are the poets, musicians, artists, sculptors, etc. They are not a group apart; they are the spokesmen, the delegates of the people, because they are delegated by their gifts to the task of seeing, hearing, and recording what others want to see and say, but have not the power to do so. By reading the symbols which the artist creates, others can share in what he sees, can participate in his larger vision. In Marianne Moore's words, someone's "illumined eye has seen the shaft that gilds the sultan's tower," and by our reading we see what his eyes see.

Art, which is a kind of magical distortion, is based on symbol, and it is the distortion of the symbol, which abstracts and accents the thing, that corrects the distortion of everyday appearances in the world. For there is all about us a distortion in the direction of the commonplace and the ugly which *misdirects* us as to the quality of life by seeming to make little of it. It makes molehills of mountains. The work of art, on the other hand, distorts in the direction of the beautiful and the strange. Art does not hide; it reveals — anything, everything — man, God and objects through its transfigurations.

In poetry it is metaphor which distorts. Belloc says in *The Path To Rome* [6] "There was a sturdy boy at my school who, when the master had carefully explained to us the nature of metaphor, said that so far as he could see a metaphor was nothing but a long Greek word for a lie." But it is not a lie; it is a light. A metaphor makes use of symbols; by bringing two or more of them together it allows them to throw light on one another, thus actually creating a new symbol. This power of unlike things in conjunction, throwing light each on the other, is strangely impressive.

Take as an example a tiny poem, a Chippewa love song: [7]

A loon I thought it was
But it was
My love's
Splashing oar.

[6] *The Path To Rome* (New York: Longmans Green, 1902).
[7] Astrov, Margot, "Love Song," *The Winged Serpent* (New York: John Day Co., 1946), p. 79.

Two sounds are suggested and a complex image of night, love, a human situation, a geographical milieu, a culture, are evoked. The few things said, conjure up many others unspoken. As a Papago Indian once said to a translator, "The song is so short because we know so much." The understanding of the song depends on the background of knowledge in the reader; the economy of the poem demands that many things be unsaid. But it is this very accent on chosen detail and the suppression of others which helps to create the effective symbol.

Another more sophisticated example of this power of the metaphor's conjunction of unlike things to bring into focus a profound emotional and intellectual experience occurs in a poem by Po Chu'i (ninth century A.D.) called "Climbing the Ling Ying Terrace and Looking North":[8]

> Mounting on high I begin to realize the smallness of Man's Domain;
> Gazing into distance I begin to know the vanity of the Carnal World.
> I turn my head and hurry home — back to the Court and Market,
> A single grain of rice falling, into the Great Barn.

In all symbol-things, whether an African mask or a shape of music or a poem, one finds that the sense of beauty is involved. The love of beauty is not esoteric; it is a fundamental part of the human character, for the works reveal the man. To find signs of beauty in ordinary things we have only to look at the artifacts of primitive people. Men seem never to have been satisfied with the merely necessary. They did not stop when they had found a stick to stir the soup; they made beautifully shaped and proportioned spoons and ladles; they developed elaborately woven baskets; they dyed their fabrics and carved the lintels of their doors and the prows of their boats. One of the earliest known artifacts is the prehistoric arrowhead, not the crudely sharpened stone we might have expected to find in a 30,000-year-old weapon, but a flint meticulously chipped, of an elegant leaflike appearance which cannot be duplicated today.

The problem of the what and why of beauty is an intriguing one. Natural things like a star and the rose and the lion have each its proper beauty; and the things made by men tend toward beauty. But

[8] *A Hundred and Seventy Chinese Poems*, translated by Arthur Waley (London: Constable & Co., Ltd., 1918), p. 162.

what is beauty for? That is the question. It causes delight, certainly, but is that its only end?

There is a passage in a story by the Basque writer Miguel de Unamuno, which presents one fairly common point of view. The conversation between two men goes as follows: "And whoever told you that the real purpose of medicine was to cure illnesses?" "What is it then?" "Knowledge; a knowledge of diseases. The end of all science is knowledge." "And the end of art, what is it? What is the end purpose of this sketch you have just made of our grandchild?" "That is its own end; it contains its purpose. It is an object of beauty and that's enough."

This is one of the standard conclusions: beauty is an end in itself; it is a delightful experience of the eyes, but beyond that it means nothing. This seems to me not so much an end of beauty, as simply a dead end.

There is another more integral view of beauty. It sees that though beauty of itself is a true and immediate delight, it sends out a ray which points to beauty's source; if one follows a ray, one finds a Sun. Plotinus, in his first *Ennead* [9] said about beauty that it "is something . . . perceived at the first glance, something which the soul names as from an ancient knowledge, and recognizing, welcomes it. . . ." But then he adds, "What is there in common between beauty here and beauty *There*?" It is the ray which connects the two in our thought. Plotinus could not conceive of beauty as an isolated experience that ends in itself. As to what he means by *There* he says, "The Fatherland to us is There whence we have come, and There is the Father." One is reminded of St. Augustine's statement, that Christ Himself is our native land.

Plotinus moves step by step toward the Beauty *There*; he says, "There is the beauty conferred by craftsmanship, of all a house with all its parts, and the beauty which some natural quality may give to a stone," and he concludes that the material thing becomes beautiful "communicating in the thought that flows from the Divine."

Then he sees a higher kind of beauty "the face of Justice and Moral-Wisdom, beautiful beyond the beauty of evening and of dawn," and beyond that, the "ultimate splendor." He warns: "never can the soul have vision of the First Beauty unless itself be beautiful. Therefore,

[9] *Plotinus: The Ethical Treatises*, translated by Stephen McKenna (Boston: C. T. Branford Co.; no longer in print).

first let each become godlike and each beautiful who cares to see God and Beauty." Beyond the Intellectual-Principle is "the nature of Good radiating Beauty before it. . . . The Good is the Fountain and the principle of Beauty; the primal Good and the primal Beauty have the one dwelling-place, and thus, always, Beauty's seat is There." These are noble concepts; here, indeed, is splendor but in the end it remains a cold, proud, detached splendor.

In contrast we look again at the familiar created things which are *God's* symbols; seas, stars, crystals, flowers, animals. And we name over the symbols used by Christ — the cup of cold water, the mustard seed, a broom, a candle, a moth, a bottle, birds and grass and lilies. We understand that these humble things are always of value, that we are not and never need be completely detached from them, for they are part of the human situation. That is Christian humanism — respecting and loving and using the things of this world, not as finalities but as transparencies revealing other truth.

One can find in Gerard Manley Hopkins' poems clear evidence of his concern with beauty and its symbolic values; "The world is charged with the grandeur of God," he writes, and though he calls beauty "heaven's sweet gift" he urges us to wish for "God's better beauty, grace."

There is pain as well as delight in the experience of beauty, because of its transience; it passes away, and we can't bear the thought of losing it. One thinks of Thoreau who said, "May I gird myself to be a hunter of the beautiful, that nought escape me. I am eager to report the glory of the universe." Hopkins explores and solves the dilemma of transiency in his poem, "The Leaden Echo and the Golden Echo."[10] The heavy leaden echo states the hopeless case:

How to *keep* — Is there any . . . latch or catch or key to keep
Back beauty, keep it, beauty, beauty, beauty, . . . from
vanishing away?

Is there no

waving off of these most mournfull . . . messengers of grey? No there's none, there's none. . . .

And the echo concludes

since, no, nothing can be done
To keep at bay

[10] *Poems of Gerard Manley Hopkins* (New York and London: Oxford University Press, 1948; also D. 15 in Penguin Books Inc., Baltimore, Md., 1958), p. 52 in latter.

Age and age's evils . . .
Be beginning, be beginning to despair . . .

Then the golden echo catches the last syllable of sound and transforms it:

Spare!
There *is* one, yes I have one . . .
Only not within the seeing of the sun
. . . Yes I can tell such a key, I do know such a place,
Where . . . The flower of beauty, fleece of beauty,
    too too apt to, ah! to fleet,
Never fleets more.

If that is the case we can resign what is lovely and watch it fade, without hopelessness for we see that we shall have it again. "Give beauty back," he says,

beauty, beauty, beauty, back to God, beauty's self and beauty's giver.
There it is kept with
Fonder a care than we could have kept it.
And we are already on our way to where it is:
We follow, now we follow. —
    Yonder, yes yonder, yonder,
    Yonder.

The "Yonder" of course is the "There" of Plotinus; but it is a more accessible There and it transforms but does not destroy the human element.

The optimism of the "golden echo" is asserted by the unbroken line of affirmative symbols that begin with the earliest men of whom we have a sign, and continue throughout history. It is there in the touch of red ochre on the face of a person buried in a primitive grave, a symbol of the love of life, and of faith, and hope in its everlastingness. It is in the chants of the Egyptian *Book of the Dead* which sing of life lived forever among the starry deities. It is in all the luminous symbolic things fashioned by men in the teeth of adversity, in a world plagued by illness, injustices, wars, and innumerable personal sorrows. There things comprise a chorus which everywhere sounds assent and affirmations of praise.

There is some quality in the finer man-made things which sets them apart; something about them attracts us, as the color of a fruit or the smile on a face attracts. It is something which distinguishes them from ordinary commercial or mass-produced things. They have about them a kind of radiance as if they bore the seal of the personality which created them. When the very fine carvings of the Africans began to be appreciated, there was an attempt to have them made in quantity, to be sold for money. They immediately began to deteriorate in quality. The radiant something in them, the sincerity of intention which was one cause of their beauty was lost. To produce the truly fine thing — chair or table or house or garden or song or painting — not only time and patience are necessary, and a labor which does not count the cost, but ardor which is at the very root of the making.

The true maker loves what he makes, and as Dante says, it is Love that moves the sun and other stars. Men, too, make stars which light up for us a darkened world. They shine — as God's works shine — because like His they are works of love.

Art and Faith

Ivan Mestrovic

Ivan Mestrovic, the world-renowned sculptor, was born in Croatia in 1885. He was once called by Rodin "the greatest phenomenon among sculptors." He is considered by Father John LaFarge, S.J., as the greatest religious sculptor since the Renaissance." Professor Norman Rice of Syracuse University, where Mestrovic was resident artist for many years after World War II, wrote in his mammoth volume, The Art of Ivan Mestrovic, *"His sculpture is an affirmation of profound belief — born of conviction in the dignity of man and the need of his recovery of faith........a rebuke to the materialism which places expediency before human good, and it searches for the purposes of life through dedication to the purposes of Christianity." This volume published by Syracuse University Press in 1948 contains, besides full biographical details and a critical appreciation of the art of Ivan Mestrovic, 158 full-page reproductions of his works. Mestrovic is a patriot who refuses to compromise with evil, not a politician; yet he has been forced more than once, because of devotion to principle, to spend years in exile from his native Croatia, where he is a hero in the minds and hearts of his people. He refused Tito's invitation to return permanently to Croatia, and he insisted that the national chapel there, which contains some of his special works, be first dedicated by a priest. Since the Fall of 1955, he has been on the staff of the University of Notre Dame, where a special studio was built for him and where he teaches and continues to create masterpieces. His famous, more than life size, marble* Pietà *was brought to Sacred Heart Church, Notre Dame, in the university, where it will remain permanently. Among his recently completed works are the Madonna of the Immaculate Conception that stands above the entrance of the new Basilica of the Immaculate Conception in Washington, D.C., a* Pietà *in Miami, and a twenty-four foot bronze sculpture called "Man and Freedom" at the Mayo clinic, Rochester, Minn. The recipient of many honors, Ivan Mestrovic received the 1954 Christian Culture Award and wrote his first address in English for the occasion.*

MY MEDIUM of expression is the plastic form. Though even in my native tongue the spoken word has not been my most effective way of expressing what I think and feel, and though my English is still clumsy, yet I shall try to express in words some of my convictions on art and religious inspiration.

Even in my first creative days I was aware that sculpture is a way of expressing one's feelings or the feelings of the national and ideological group to which one belongs. However, I must admit that in my youthful passion for creating, I had no time nor desire to subject these feelings to a closer scrutiny for analysis. For my works I selected the themes from life as I saw or imagined it to be, but soon became aware that a wide gap existed between my views and those of the ideological group to which I thought I belonged. Moreover, noting a wide divergence of views among those supposed companions of mine, I was prompted by a further thought: was it possible to accomplish anything significant and lasting in the field of creative art if one's feelings and basic convictions are chaotic, if they are not anchored in some unifying idea that transcends time and outlives both us and our epochs? May I say parenthetically that many modern artists seem not to realize that expressing one's own subjective and ephemeral feelings without some deeper philosophy of life results in nothing enduring. Their works seem to be the product of this state of mind: "I want to create something different but do not as yet know what . . . ," or, "I want to express myself but I am uncertain as to what self is . . . ."

I discovered very early in my development that I could not subscribe to the slogan "L'Art pour L'Art," the view which was then almost universally held; that art should serve beauty and esthetic pleasure only. I wondered: What constitutes beauty? Is every aspect of life beautiful? Is everything beautiful that has been created in visual art and poetry? Is everything beautiful in Dante's *Inferno* or Michelangelo's "Last Judgment?" Obviously not, if by beauty we mean that which is pleasing to the eye and delightful to the mind. What is beauty? Is it the same as goodness, as the Greeks thought? Or, should not the order be reversed so that the good embraces the beautiful, *i.e.*, that the beautiful is only that which is good, or more precisely, that which aims at the greatest common good?

The artistically effective then is not the same as the beautiful. Besides the forms and lines which give joy and delight to the eye and the mind, there are those which are not pleasing. The latter are needed to make the former stand out. Discords are there to throw harmony into focus.

Such questions have tormented my mind, as they probably have many of my contemporaries in the beginning of our century. In vain did I search for answers to these problems in the books of professional estheticians and philosophers. Despite their best intentions, I could clearly see that they themselves had no solution.

Meanwhile some momentous events were taking place in the world, in which I took an active part. Before and during World War II, I had thrown in my lot with one side of the conflict, in the conviction that it fought for human ideals, a more humane social order, equality, justice, and freedom for all men and all nations. But my experiences during that war convinced me that this was not true even for my side. Cruelty and false propaganda tainted both sides. Evil cannot be thwarted with evil; harmony does not arise from sowing discord, preaching hatred. War, regardless of who wages it, is a common evil reducing man to the status of half-animal, destructive of all human values, material and spiritual.

Perplexed and confused, I returned to a small neutral country to try to find, at least, a solution to my personal spiritual problem.

With me I took the book which in my childhood I had read without a great deal of understanding; only the memory of its poetic beauty had still lingered in my mind. But now I understood it: I knew then that this book contained not only unmatched beauty but also the profoundest wisdom. The book was the *New Testament.*

Inspired by the great drama of the Son of God becoming Flesh, I started to work on the themes taken from the life of Jesus of Nazareth. It was then that I carved in wood the scene of the Crucifixion. Many people did not like it, because it was not esthetically pleasing. They found the Crucified Christ too emaciated and disfigured. But the Crucifixion scene was not meant to represent the historical Jesus nor His supreme sacrifice. It was intended to depict the crucifixion of His idea, the perversion and disfiguration of the teachings for which He came into this world and for which He died on the Cross.

There are more and more people today who have reached the conviction that one main cause of the tragic events of the recent past, and of those which loom on the horizon, is the fact that contemporary man has all but forgotten the great teachings of the Sermon on the Mount. For this blame rests not only on our contemporary despotisms, but, unfortunately, on a long list of talented men of science and art who have not foreseen the corroding implications and destructive consequences of their doctrines. This atmosphere of unbelief, this tragic state of man isolated from the very axis which holds and moves everything, has had repercussions on all domains of human activity, including art, which in the most significant periods of civilization worked hand in hand with religion—an ennobling and spiritualizing factor in human life.

Christian civilization, in our days, finds itself locked in a mortal struggle with the forces of secularism in varying forms and degrees. Too many people still fail to realize that Christianity, by waging the fight for its principles, defends also the foundations of the democratic way of life: for the concept of the dignity of each man and the equality of all men stands and falls with the Christian view that man is created in the image of God. Thus the Church is in the front lines of the battle against the onslaughts on human freedom.

May I mention again my wood carving of the scene of the Crucifixion, for the piece of wood on which I carved the Crucifixion has an interesting story. I was in Geneva, Switzerland, when I was seized by the desire to carve the Crucifixion. Every available oak had been bought by the factory which manufactured rifle butts, presumably for both warring sides. It was difficult to acquire from the factory even a few boards for reliefs. The whole piece of a trunk was unavailable because all the boards had been sawed off; but eventually, I discovered one whole trunk, withered and standing there with roots still in the soil—considered unsuitable for rifles as its wood was probably decayed. When I started to work on it, it was found to be solid and whole. The lumberman told me that it had been imported. I asked from where. I was surprised to learn: from Croatia, my native country.

That same piece of wood was later returned to Croatia, transformed into the Crucifixion scene. Today it stands there in a small chapel, in that country where the Catholic Church is being crucified daily, including the head of that suffering Church, Cardinal Stepinac,[1] my compatriot, my dear friend, of whom I and all Croats are proud. Our feelings are shared not only by all the Catholics throughout the world but also by all men of good will who cherish freedom of spirit.

In vain do the godless and restless men, who are today making

[1] His Eminence, Cardinal Stepinac, has died since [Ed. note].

weapons in the hope of enslaving the world, think that the trunk of the Christian tree is withered. It will outlive and outlast the forces of evil in my native land and throughout the whole world. He who has conquered death will conquer the destruction of His teaching.

I am happy and grateful that my modest artistic efforts have been considered a contribution to Christian culture, which I would define with Paul as consisting of three things: Faith, Love, and Hope. Faith in God, love of Him and our fellowmen, and the hope of final victory of good over evil.

The Book as Book

Hugh Kenner

Hugh Kenner was born in Peterborough, Ontario, and attended the University of Toronto and Yale University. He taught English at Assumption College (since Assumption University) in 1946–48, and appeared on the Christian Culture Series in 1957. His books include Paradox in Chesterton, The Poetry of Ezra Pound, Wyndham Lewis, Dublin's Joyce, The Invisible Poet: T. S. Eliot, *a collection of essays,* Gnomon, *and a textbook,* The Art of Poetry. *He has also published over one hundred essays and reviews in periodicals here and abroad. He is a Fellow of the Royal Society of Literature, and held a Guggenheim Fellowship in 1957–58. He now lives with his wife and five children in Santa Barbara, California, where he is Professor of English and Chairman of the Department at the University of California.*

We shall be looking into more than one century before we have finished, but I want to start in the present, with a particular book, and with an obvious fact about that book, a fact that was more obvious to the author than it has been to most of us who have followed after him. The book is *Ulysses* by James Joyce,[1] and the fact is simply this, that the reader of *Ulysses* holds a book in his hands. Homer envisaged no such possibility. Consider for a moment what it makes possible. On page 488 we read, "Potato preservative against plague and pestilence, pray for us." Now just sixty pages earlier, if we were alert, we may have noted the phrase, "Poor mamma's panacea," murmured by Bloom as he feels his trouser pocket. And fully 372 pages before that, on the bottom line of page 56, we have Bloom feeling in his hip pocket for the latchkey and reflecting "Potato I have." The serious reader's copy of *Ulysses* acquires cross-references at these three points; and Bloom's potato, it is by now a commonplace to remark, is but one trivial instance among hundreds of motifs treated very briefly at two

[1] (New York: Random House, 1934).

158

or three widely separated points in the book, and not even intelligible until the recurrences have been collated. It is customary to note that Joyce makes very severe demands of his reader. The point I want to develop is a corollary of this. The demands Joyce makes on the reader would be impossible ones if the reader did not have his hands on the book, in which he can turn to and fro at his pleasure. And more than that: the whole conception of *Ulysses* depends on the existence of something former writers took for granted as simply the envelope for their wares: a printed book whose pages are numbered.

Literary criticism, like mathematics, frequently makes progress by discovering what the mathematician calls a tranformation: by which he means an unexpected but useful way of restating some truth already known. What I am proposing to you is a transformation, in that sense, of something we have heard often enough, namely the proposition that Joyce disrupts — abandons, even — the familiar processes of prose narrative. Narrative, it is evident, implies that someone is talking. It is an art that unfolds its effects in time, like music. It holds us under the spell of a voice, or something analogous to a voice, and (again like music) it slowly gathers into a simplified whole in the memory. The supreme vividness of the present instant drops continually into the memory: words fade, past scenes blur, scenes and characters we had forgotten reappear with studied *éclat* in some late phase of the adventure; the voice presses on, and the effect is completed as the final words set up resonances among our recollections of all that has preceded. No one understood this better than Joseph Conrad, who is at such pains to subject us to the spell of the teller of a tale. Conrad, with his studied apparatus of spoken narrative discharged into a reflective silence, attempted to carry to some ideal limit the convention under which Dickens, for instance, had operated with such confidence: the convention that a tale is something told, an act of intrepidity on the part of the teller, who is venturing where he has really never been before; and that the tale is a whole only in the hearer's memory; and that the writen book is simply a record of the telling, or purports to be such a record. If we press back to Dickens we find an even simpler convention: the written book is a script, to be brought to life in oral delivery, by some middle-class Englishman reading aloud at his fireside, or by the author on an American tour. Far back of Dickens, again, lies Homer, whose book is simply a graph of what the bard recited: something that lived exactly in his memory, and gets transferred to the listener's memory less exactly. A manuscript or printed book, entitled *The Odyssey* has simply this function, that it takes the place of the rhapsode's memory, somewhat deadly, somewhat mechanically.

Homer, of course, also lies behind *Ulysses*; and the most profound of all Joyce's Homeric transformations is this, that the text of *Ulysses* is not organized in memory and unfolded in time, but both organized and unfolded in what we may call *technological space*: on printed pages for which it was designed from the beginning. The reader explores its discontinuous surface at whatever pace he likes; he makes marginal notes; he turns back whenever he chooses to an earlier page, without destroying the continuity of something that does not press on, but will wait until he resumes. He is manoeuvred, in fact, precisely into the role of the scholiasts whose marginalia encumbered the Alexandrian manuscripts of Homeric texts; only here is a text designed, as Homer's was not, precisely for this sort of study. It really *does* contain, as Homer's work was reputed to contain, a systematic compendium of arts, sciences and moral teachings; symbols, rituals, and practical counsels; Irish history, and the geography of the city of Dublin. If we are agreed that Homer's text does not designedly contain all the things that symbolic exegesis used to find there, it is because we are convinced that Homer spoke and sang but did not fuss over a manuscript. The Alexandrian scholars lived in a manuscript culture, whose conventions they projected onto their author. Joyce, however, did fuss over a manuscript, and a manuscript designed for a printer and he pored over galley proofs and page proofs also. Joyce is acutely aware that the modern Homer must deal with neither an oral culture nor a manuscript one, but with a culture whose shape and whose attitude to its daily experience is determined by the omnipresence of the printed book.

He was very careful, therefore, to reproduce in his text the very quality of print, its reduction of language to a finite number of interchangeable and permutable parts. We have the impression, as we read the Circe episode, that we have encountered all its ingredients before, only in a different arrangement.

Dennis Breen, whitetallhatted, with Wisdom Hely's sandwichboard, shuffles past them in carpet slippers, his dull beard thrust out, muttering to right and left. Little Alf Bergan, cloaked in the pall of the ace of spades, dogs him to left and right, doubled in laughter.

This combines Mr. Breen, the Mad Hatter's hat, the sandwichmen from page 152, a shuffling gait and the phrase "dull beard" from page 157, Breen's dream of the ace of spades from page 155, and Alf Bergan who on page 157 is named as the probable sender of a disturbing postcard. (This is a hasty census: I may have missed a few items.) There presides over this phantasmagoria precisely the faith that presides over the 18th century rationalism, the faith that we can register all relevant phenomena in some book where we can find them again: in a dictionary, where human speech is dissociated into words which can be listed in alphabetical order, or in an encyclopaedia, where human knowledge is broken up into discontinuous fragments to be registered on a similar principle.

The Rev. Walter J. Ong, S.J., has argued brilliantly that printing was the efficient cause of those intellectual movements which in the 16th and 17th centuries destroyed the hierarchies of knowledge and rearranged the things we know for the sake of pedagogic convenience. Certainly it was printing which led us to think of speech as being composed of interchangeable parts, if only because printing and its by-product levicography enforced a uniformity of spelling which gave each separate word a stable identity to the eye, whatever its equivocal status for the ear. After that, writing becomes a matter of locating and arranging words, and Joyce, sure enough, spent a day, as he told Frank Budgen, trying out different arrangements of fifteen words:

Perfume of embraces all him assailed. With hungered flesh obscurely, he mutely craved to adore.

He made these words lie within the gestures of the spoken voice, while conveying tensions that speech, which manipulates phrases rather than words, would never have discovered for itself.

Printing also leads to the manufacture of books, and to the nuisance of untalented authors. And here we encounter one of those loops in time, uniting the 18th and the 20th centuries, which the student of Joyce's Dublin learns to anticipate, welcome, and explore. For the first author of talent to have been forcibly struck by the *nature* of the printed book appears to have been a compatriot of Joyce's and a great denizen of *Finnegans Wake*, by name Jonathan Swift.

There are many ways of describing *A Tale of a Tub*; I propose to call it a parody of the book as a book. For its method is to emphasize to the point of grotesqueness exactly those features which distinguish the printed book *per se*, the printed book a technological artifact, from a human document. Human documents Swift is prepared to understand, though looking around him in 1704 or thereabouts, in the first dawn of the bookseller's paradise, he can discern precious few.

Between a human document and the thing that Gutenberg's monster typically disgorges, a distinction may be discovered which turns on the intimate nature of what the brain thinks and the hand writes. For Swift, a piece of writing is by its nature something that exists in a personal context, where one human being is seeking to gain the confidence and understanding of another. Pamphlets like the *Modest Proposal* or the *Argument Against Abolishing Christianity* depend for their effect on our understanding and approving this fact: their supposed author reposes in a state of bland rapport with readers who will respond suitably to his insinuations and share his notions of rational conduct. Though the pamphlet is anonymous, its effect is not to depersonalize the supposed author but simply to efface him; he is the obedient humble servant of whatever reader is jackass enough to find him congenial. The rapport between them, while it depraves the rational intercourse of honest men, is still an intercourse between persons: as much so, Swift might add, as an act of sodomy. By contrast Swift finds in the typical contemporary printed books as much of the inviolable human person as would transfer from an animated-cartoon version of the *Coy Mistress*. *A Tale of a Tub* is not at bottom a civil letter, as a pamphlet is essentially a letter. It is anonymous because it is written by nobody, by no person, but by the autonomous book-compiling machine itself; and it addresses itself, like a public speech from the scaffold, to the public at large and to posterity — that is, to no one. *A Tale of a Tub* is the first comic exploitation of that technological space which the words in a large printed book tend to inhabit. Commerce and capital have recently discovered that printing is not simply a way of disseminating manuscripts, but that a book is an artifact of a new kind. This discovery has brought with it a host of technical gimmicks which Swift regards with fascinated disquiet. We have discovered in our own day that the motion picture is not simply a way of recording plays, but a different medium; and that television is not simply a way of disseminating motion pictures, but a different medium; and each of these discoveries has brought with it an embarrassing swarm of new techniques. So it was, in Swift's day, with the book: and *A Tale of a Tub* is the register of Gutenberg technology, discerned by a man who regarded each of the bookmaker's devices as a monstrous affront to the personal intercourse which letters in a dialogue culture had served to promote.

The book as book entails, then, Introductions, Prefaces, Apologies and Dedications; Headings, Subheadings; Tables, Footnotes, Indices. The way in which some of these help mechanize the act of discourse is perfectly plain. The footnote, for instance — I do not mean the scholar's footnote which supplies a reference, but the footnote that supplements, qualifies, parallels, quips, digresses, or elucidates — the footnote's relation to the passage from which it depends is established wholly by visual and typographic means, and in a typical case will evade all efforts of the speaking voice to clarify it without visual aid. Parentheses, like commas, tell the voice what to do: an asterisk tells the voice that it can do nothing. You generally cannot read a passage of prose aloud, interpolating the footnotes, and make the subordination of the footnotes clear, and keep the whole sounding natural. The language has forsaken a vocal milieu, and a context of oral communication between persons, and commenced to take advantage of the expressive possibilities of technological space.

This ventriloqual gadget, the footnote, deserves some attention, partly because Swift became a great virtuoso on this new instrument, and Joyce later devoted a whole section of *Finnegans Wake* to ringing changes on the footnote and its cousin the marginalium. One would like to know when it was invented; it is as radical a discovery as the scissors or the rocking chair, and presumably as anonymous. The man who writes a marginal comment is conducting a dialogue with the text he is reading; but the man who composes a footnote and sends it to the printer along with his text, has discovered among the devices of printed language something analogous with counterpoint: a way of speaking in two voices at once, or of ballasting or modifying or even bombarding with exceptions his own discourse without interrupting it. It is a step in the direction of discontinuity: of organizing blocks of discourse simultaneously in space rather than consecutively in time. We encounter its finest flower in the immense scheme of annotation to the final edition of the *Dunciad Variorum*, a project in which it is customary to discern Swift's hand. *The Dunciad*, like *A Tale of a Tub*, is not only a satire against the abuses of the Gutenberg era, but an exploitation of technical devices made available by that era. Because print enables us to distinguish verse from prose at once by eye, we may here observe, page by page, an Attic column of verse standing on a thick pedestal of miscellaneous learning. Or the verse plunges majestically forward amid a strangely orderly babel of commentaries, assailed at random by every fly in Grub Street. Very often the note is needed to complete a poetic effect; Mr. Empson has analysed a famous instance of this. And Pope's intricate mosaic of allusions to other poems, it is pertinent to remark, depends for its witty precision on a prime assumption of the Dunces, namely that poetry is to be found exclusively in books, that the texts of past classics are as stable as mosaic tiles (having been quick-frozen by the printer), and that with a little scissors-and-paste work one can thus rearrange the general stock of literature to produce new beauties. The Dunces themselves, of course, do this all the time; Pope is always careful to imitate their very mannerism with insolent fidelity; and it is the easier to do because metrical varieties have become so standardized, like that standardization of machine-screw threads which today makes possible an international technology.

If we return from this vantage-point to *A Tale of a Tub*, we shall be in a position to throw a great deal of light on Joyce. We said of the foonote that it is a device for organizing units of discourse discontinuously in space rather than serially in time. The same is true of the Introductions, Dedications, and Digressions with which the *Tale* is so lavishly equipped. They all of them instance and exploit the essential discontinuity of the book as book. The introductory matter expands to a heroic scale certain printers' conventions. A conventional heading in large capital letters suffices to legitimize the presence in a book of almost anything the author and bookseller choose: flattery of some patron, for instance, which we can incorporate into any book at all simply by heading it Dedication. Swift allows the eponymous author of the *Tale* to plume himself mightily on his own capacity for sheer miscellaneousness, and carries this theme into the text itself by the device of interpolating immense Digressions, each headed "Digression" to prevent any earnest reader from supposing that he is losing the thread. The first section of the book proper (headed Section One: the Introduction) makes a great pother about the various conditions for the oral delivery of wisdom: from the pulpit, the stage itinerant, the scaffold, and perhaps the bench; but nothing is clearer from the beginning of this book to the end than the fact that all conceivable modes of oral discourse are totally unrelated to it. The Digressions, indeed, treat not of speech or dialogue but of every aspect of bookmaking: notably indices, tables of contents, anthologies, compilations, the art of disgression, the practice of criticism, and the improvement of madness in the commonwealth.

We have mentioned Pope's witty precision, and we should mention Swift's in turn, for the two of them generate a stylistic curve which passes axially through *Ulysses* and *Finnegans Wake.* If their exactness of language pleases and surprises, it is by a sort of analogy with deft manufacture; we acknowledge as much when we apply a word like "precision," which in the twentieth century is a technological metaphor. The *mot juste* is a beauty we owe to the omnipresence of the printer, because oral delivery tends to blur it. Our interest in the *mot juste* is a function of our concern with the single word, its look, feel, weight, history, range, and denotation: a concern first fostered by the 18th century interest in lexicography, which interest in turn belongs to the age of the book. A scholiast writing marginalia to the *Odyssey* may pause over a single word to consider how Homer is using it here; but a lexicographer abstracts it from all particular usage. Samuel Johnson may be described as the first writer to have examined individually in turn each of the words he employs, and without actually compiling dictionaries, writers have followed his example ever since. Certainly Joyce does. And in Johnson's lexicography there is crystallized an attitude to language already for half a century prevalent and dominant, sponsored by the concern of a whole society's intelligence with the production of printed books. (A word assembled from leaden cubes in a type-case, as Father Ong has indicated, is already well on the way to being an interchangeable part). When Pope writes of a herioc Dunce diving into the Thames,

Furious he sinks, precipitately dull,

we know that the word "precipitately" has received from Pope a kind of attention which the word "incarnadine" did not receive from Shakespeare. Pope's wit consists in the exactness with which the word's etymology is being re-enacted in the line. Swift in the same way, reflecting on the posthumous fame of authors, is careful to arrange each of his individual words, clearly defined, into scintillation and balance:

. . . whether it is that fame, being a fruit grafted on the body, can hardly grow, and much less ripen, till the stock is in the earth, or whether she be a bird of prey, and is lured, among the rest, to pursuit after the scent of a carcass: or whether she conceives her trumpet sounds best and farthest when she stands on a tomb, by the advantage of a rising ground, and the echo of a hollow vault.

We hear "carcass" start out from among the ceremonious euphemisms of decease, and hear the smart "advantage" offset the Virgilian "echo," and hear "rising ground" paralleled by "hollow vault," and no blur surrounds any of these effects, etched with lexicographic clarity. The effect is quite different from the effect that a similiar terminology might have in a sermon of Donne's because it is queerly unrelated to oral delivery: an eerie life stirs among words that have been briskly laid out to fill categories and complete tropes, in the stunned neutrality of print. Each term snaps magnetically into its place in the inviolable whole; each sentence is levelled like a course of bricks. To contrast these smartly articulated figures of thought, each one displayed and delimited like a little algebraic calculation, with some Shakespearean image groping obscurely among the roots of language for its own bases of relevance:

Witness this army of such mass and charge

is to perceive the kind of clarity that works by analogies with visual clarity and with the fact that we have before us a page to look at, where the backward glance to the beginning of any phrase, clearly indicated by the punctuation, will confirm the accuracy of every epithet. This is the precision which Joyce inherited from the first heyday of the book, and exploited as no one ever exploited it before out of some connatural awareness of the nature of a civilization structured by print.

It is noteworthy, for example, that though Bloom's knowledge, most of it traceable to books, is extremely inexact, it never produces on us an effect of confusion. There is no loss of outline: perfectly distinct words, each clearly remembered, have simply gotten into the wrong categories, or else sentences of which he has gotten the beginnings fixed in his memory are incomplete because he has forgotten the endings.

Where was that chap I saw in that picture somewhere? Ah, in the dead sea, floating on his back, reading a book with a parasol open. Couldn't sink if you tried: so thick with salt. Because the weight of water, no, the weight of the body in the water is equal to the weight of the. Or is it the volume is equal of the weight? It's a law something like that. Vance in high school cracking his finger-joints, teaching. The college curriculum. Cracking curriculum. What is weight really when you say the weight? Thirty-two feet per second, per second. Law of falling bodies; per second, per second. They all fall to the ground. The earth. It's the force of gravity of the earth is the weight.

Whatever the deficiencies of Bloom's understanding, there is no blur surrounding any of these words, any more than Swift's. The sentences do not achieve the formulations to be found in the physics textbooks Bloom is half remembering, but each word is clearly enunciated, and so far as lexicography can tell us, clearly understood. In fact the criterion of intellectual adequacy Bloom has inherited, the criterion to which he does not succeed in living up, is a criterion based on the authority of the book. One is not expected to understand the phenomena; one is expected to get the formulas right, to lay hold of all the words and arrange them in the order in which the textbook arranges them. This proposition is easily tested: one need only note that we do not need to understand the physical laws involved to be sure that Bloom does not understand them. We need only note the incompleteness of his sentences, and their bathetic, anticlimatic rhythms. For words are interchangeable parts to be arranged, and there are authorized arrangements the recitation of which evinces confidence. Stephen Dedalus may understand what he is talking about or he may not, but he enjoys the confidence of the born word-man:

> Ineluctable modality of the visible: at least that if no more, thoughts through my eyes. Signatures of all things I am here to read, sea-spawn and seawreck, the nearing tide, that rusty boot.

That these examples touch principles which underlie the whole conception of *Ulysses*, is a principle obscurely recognized by the very large amount of critical energy that has been devoted to making wordlists for Joyce's books. The books, it is felt, are permutations of a stock of words which can be counted, enumerated, and classified. You can of course count, enumerate and classify Shakespeare's words, if you are so minded, but you are unlikely to attach any importance to the fact that a given word occurs in the canon, say, seven times. Or if you do attach importance to this fact, as the scholars who do explore Shakespeare's image-clusters, will explain the fact on psychological grounds rather than assigning it to deliberate technique. One does not think of Shakespeare as a man conscious that certain words, a large but finite number of them, enjoyed a proper existence, whereas any other words that came to his fancy were coinages. Joyce on the other hand, in a world where the dictionary and the printing press suggest limits to the authorized vocabulary, functions with a peculiar sardonic awareness of the fact that "catalectic," "consubstantial," and "costdrawer" are citizens in good standing of some large dictionary, that "contransmagnificandjewbangtantiality" is a molecule synthesized by him out of several such words, and that on a wholly different principle "lovelorn longlost lugubru Blooloohoom" is a comic coinage because it freezes in visual space some gesture of the tongue, the voice and the breath.

These auditory coinages deserve a bit of attention. Bloom's cat meows, and Joyce writes out the sound: "Mrkgnao!" Davy Byrne yawns, "Iiiiiichaaaaaaach." The paperfolding machine speaks in its own way:"sllt." The fact that the dictionary gives no help to an author who wants to register phenomena of this kind attests to the divorce between printing-case language, inhabiting technological space, and acoustic language, the intelligible creation of human speech. The ordinary words we speak inhabit both dimensions, and we shift from the visual to the vocal manifestation of some word with the negligence of lifelong habit. But let an intelligible sound which the dictionary has omitted to register be transcribed according to approved phonetic rules, and the result is taut, arbitrary, and grotesque: something living has been imperfectly synthesized out of those 26 interchangeable parts to which every nuance of human discourse can allegedly be reduced: as though technology were offering to reproduce Helen of Troy with an Erector set. There is something mechanical, Joyce never lets us forget, about all reductions of speech to arrangements of 26 letters. We see him playing in every possible way with the spatial organization of printed marks: inserting headlines; reducing the themes of an intricate Augustinian music to 59 grotesque permutable phrases, each printed at the head of the Sirens episode on a separate line; entrusting the enervate languor of Eumaeus to grey unbroken paragraphs that numb the mind by tiring the eye; printing the questions and answers of the great catechism with emphatic intervening spaces, and the ultimate monologue of Mrs. Bloom with neither paragraphs, commas, nor full stops; and delivering what one would expect to be the very epitome of the free and fluid, an immense drunken phantasmagoria a fifth of the book in length, into the keeping of the most rigid typographic formality he employs anywhere: discrete speeches, capitalized speakers, italicized narration: the status of everything visible at a glance.

What he thus freezes into a book is the life of Dublin, chiefly its vocal life. Ireland, it is relevant and even commonplace to observe, is unique in the west for the exclusiveness of its emphasis on oral rather than typographic culture, and *Ulysses* is built about the antithesis between the personal matrix of human speech and the unyielding formalisms of the book as book. It can hardly be accidental that two Irishmen, Swift and Sterne, exploited as long ago as the 18th century the peculiarities of the book as book to an extent no Anglo-Saxon has ever thought to emulate: nor is it accidental that the two of them link arms throughout *Finnegans Wake* like a pair of tutelary deities. Both of them were detached, as Joyce himself was later detached, from the assumptions of typographic culture: detached by the richer assumptions of a culture that thinks not of words but of voices, of the voice that states rather than the book that contains, of person confronting person in a matrix of speech rather than of fact and language delivered over to typographic storage. The Irish tradition of emitting pamphlets and broadsides rather than treatises, a tradition to which Joyce himself contributed in his youth, is an extension of these assumptions: the broadside is inalienably personal. It would be tempting to base a modern history of Ireland on the fact that the country has never sustained a large-scale publishing industry to erode its vocal and rhetorical bias, and polarize its sense of language toward the immutability of print rather than the coercive evanescence of breath. Even today it is customary for Dublin tavern wits to despise Joyce for practising a lesser art than the talker's, a contempt sustained by something more than jealousy.

We seem indeed to have picked up the trail of some literary presence that is, if not an Irish tradition, then a tradition sustained chiefly by Irishmen. Swift, we have seen, reached his most frenetic flights of ingenuity in the presence of the bookman's arsenal of technical devices. Laurence Sterne availed himself of a hundred devices totally foreign to the storyteller but made possible by the book alone: not only the blank and marbled pages, the suppressed chapters represented only by the headings, the blazonry of punctuation marks and the mimetic force of wavy lines, but also the suppression of narrative suspense—a suspense proper to the storyteller who holds us by curiosity concerning events unfolding in time—in favor of a bibliographic suspense which depends on our knowledge that the book in our hands is of a certain size and that the writer therefore has somehow reached the end of it—by what means? Nothing more completely separates typographic from oral narrative than the fact that, as we turn the pages, we can literally see the end coming: a fact that should never be left out of any reckoning of the effect on, say, Dickens' novels, of their publication in monthly parts. Following Swift and Sterne, Joyce shut a living world into a book, a heavy book that contains Dublin, kills it, and sets it into motion once again on a new plane: but a technological plane and a comic because finically precise motion. Dubliners tell discreditable stories about their enemies, and all Dublin knows the stories; but Joyce's revenge on Olive Gogarty was to shut him into a book: a deed that crushed Gogarty more, despite the limited number of Dubliners who inspected the result, than any number of rumors: for in a book Buck Mulligan enacts the same formal ballet of irreverence, and emits the same delimited witticisms, for ever: always on schedule, always in the same context, always on the same pages: a precise definition of imaginative hell, ineluctable, unstoppable, unmodifiable. This preoccupation of Dublin wits with the book continues: both Flann O'Brien in *At Swim-Two-Birds* and Samuel Beckett in his great trilogy of French novels capitalize on the anti-social quality of literature, the fact that the writer is not speaking, is not drinking, is confronting nobody warming and warming to nobody, but exists shut away in a room setting on pieces of paper word after word which once they have passed through Gutenberg's machinery no afterthought will ever efface: a deed the very antithesis of everything that Irish culture prides itself on being.

Joyce went on, of course, to *Finnegans Wake*, a book that even more than *Ulysses* is inconceivable without the mediation of print. Print is the very *form* of this last work. It is print that fixes and defines the fluid metamorphoses of all the voices in Europe, constantly tugging the vocal into the magnetic field of alphabetical, permuting vowels according to plan, alpha and omega, a, e, i, o, u: coolly insisting on the power of just 26 letters over all of speech, and according each deliquescent dream-coinage the delimitation, the *status*, of a printed word. This book of words that are not words employs to a still greater extent than *Ulysses* those discontinuities first explored by Swift: discontinuities which the format of the book itself will serve to unify.

Passage is juxtaposed with passage, phrase with phrase, not in the economy of speech but on the page. And still more than *Ulysses* it dispenses with narrative in time. Time-ridden according to its own proclamation, time-obsessed because it distills voices that search forward in time, it yet inhabits typographic space, drawing not towards some narrative finale but towards its own last page, next to its back cover, and then circling forward to do the only thing the reader who has reached the end of a book and has no other book can do: begin again.

Nothing is more characteristic, finally, of the book as book than its obliviousness to chronological pressure. Time is not its currency, time is what the reader brings to it ("the ideal reader suffering from an ideal insomnia"). The book is a spatial phenomenon, an affair of pages that turn when we please to turn them, incorporating no hurry, no impatience. In technological space the word, as we have seen, is self-sufficient; so in the ultimate book are paragraphs, chapters, sections: *Ulysses* has 18 and *Finnegans Wake*, 17, succeeding one another with economy and necessity but no urgency, like Pound's *Cantos*, the sections of *The Waste Land* (a poem with numbered lines and footnotes), or the static effects in Wyndham Lewis's *Childermass*. In an expansive quiet which has led some writers to consider oriental analogies, the book as book deploys its blocks of type, incorporating all that the writer knows, or all (it tries to convince us) that mankind has thought or said, in its soothing unhurried arrangements and rearrangements of twenty-six bits of type.

Hilaire Belloc

Robert Speaight

Robert Speaight, distinguished British actor, biographer, novelist, and critic, was born in England in 1904. He is a Fellow of the Royal Society of Literature. In 1958 he was appointed a Commander of the Order of the British Empire. At the age of 24, after winning an Honors Degree in Literature at Oxford, he began a career in the theatre. He created the part of Hibbert in Journey's End, *and he appeared in many leading Shakespearian roles at the London Old Vic. Like Maurice Evans and John Gielgud, he played* Hamlet *in its entirety. He was chosen by T. S. Eliot, originally, to play the part of Becket in Eliot's play* Murder in the Cathedral, *a part he has played more than one thousand times in English and French. He played the role of Christ in Dorothy L. Sayers' famous series,* The Man Born To Be King. *He has made world-wide tours as a lecturer for the British Council, and he has had extensive experience in broadcasting, directing, producing and adjudicating. In the last twenty years Mr. Speaight has devoted much time to literature, biography, and criticism. Among his novels are* The Legend of Helena Vaughan *and* The Unbroken Heart. *The biographies for which he is best known are* St. Thomas Becket *and* Hilaire Belloc. *He is a regular contributor to London literary reviews, and his books of criticism include* Acting *and* Shakespeare and Nature. *He has recorded poetry by Belloc, Shakespeare, Hopkins, Eliot, and Merton. Mr. Speaight received the Christian Culture Award for 1957 and on the occasion dedicated his acceptance address to the late Hilaire Belloc, a sincere exponent of Christian culture.*

THE DEATH of Hilaire Belloc defies the conventions of obituary. What is the point in speaking of death where so much is alive, or of passing where so much is imperishable? In the active and literary sense Belloc had died more than ten years ago when the triple disaster of the French defeat, his son Peter's death, and his own nearly mortal illness stilled his energy forever. He remained a gentle, patriarchal figure living with the memories of his youth; fixed in the conclusions of a lifetime; enjoying the care of his family and the company of his friends; singing snatches of old songs; forgetful of injury and entrenched in prejudice; always capable of the lightning phrase and the occasional Rabelaisian rhyme; simple in his faith, steadfast in his affections, and calling for wine upon his death-bed. It is thus that I remember him from many conversations over more than a decade, and from two Christmases spent in his family circle. But what I knew and loved was like the ghost of a great wind that had blown itself out into the calm of a summer evening. Those who had known him longer could still hear the overtones of the tempest. I was among the much larger number who had caught the blast of his creative energy mainly from his books.

It is easy but altogether accurate to say that Belloc's place in English literature will be unique. Men will always argue about his excellence in one or another genre of writing. But when criticism (which often means no more than the whims of contemporary fashion) has been allowed for, it is possible, without any exaggeration of *partipris*, to ask the following questions. Is there a better biography in the English language than *Marie Antoinette*? Is there a better essay than *Autumn and the Fall of Leaves*; a better pastiche than *Belinda*; a more exact political prophecy than *The Servile State*; a more trenchant polemic than his retort to Wells? If you take the body of his epigrams and his lighter verse, is there anything comparable in the same kind? Is there anything, in the Parnassian vein, better than the best of his sonnets? Are not *The Path to Rome* and *The Four Men* quite new kinds of books which only Belloc could have written? I do not see how any sensitive reader can escape an affirmative answer to these questions, whether he is sympathetic or hostile to Belloc's opinion and personality. If you are calculating the English achievement in these various expressions of literature, then you are bound to admit him among the masters. He may go violently against your grain; but you cannot deny him entrance.

It has been said that he wrote too much; and he, who set too low a price upon his trade, would perhaps have agreed with you. Among one-hundred fifty-three separate publications, not to mention a host of uncollected articles, some are naturally better than others. When Belloc took to dictation, he wrote less well; although his orations to the Saintsbury Club and his *Heroic Poem in Praise of Wine*,[1] both carefully and deliberately wrought, showed that his powers had not declined. He could always write magnificently when he wanted to; but, except in the matter of his verse, he was careless of his reputation. He did not mix in the literary crowd, and he was indifferent to what they thought of him. He was concentrated as a man, but dissipated as a writer. His books, even at their best — and their best was unsurpassed — were the largess of his personality; they were not, like the poetry of Yeats or the novels of Hardy or Henry James, their "raison d'etre." To say this is not to disparage the literary "devot"; it is only to say that Belloc was a different kind of man.

He was never a great reader, though he had a considerable knowledge of the classics. He admired Homer and Virgil; Catullus and Theocritus; Rabelais, Milton and Molière; and the poets of the Pleiade ("Avril" is an excellent introduction to them). He admired the prose of Edmund Gosse and Dean Inge, and the imagination of H. G. Wells. He enjoyed the novels of Trollope. Maurice Baring used to say that any Trollope from the London Library which was not out in his own name was out in Belloc's. But he rarely read the books even of his best friends. Someone was discussing with him the merits of *The Everlasting Man*, by Chesterton, and he had to admit that he had never read it. And when he wrote his essay on Gilbert Chesterton's place in contemporary English letters he chose for illustration a collection of ephemeral articles — presumably because he had read nothing else. What he admired in Chesterton was the man and the mind; he thought the writer, with his incessant paradox, was too anxious to titivate the palates of a middle-class reading public. Belloc, when the matter in hand was unsuitable for rhetoric or satire, was never afraid of being dull. You might dispute his facts, but he knew when not to embroider them.

Although he was prolific, he rarely achieved what writers understand by popularity; that is to say, women did not besiege the libraries for his books. He quite lacked the sophistication which sells, and regarded the intimate themes of private life as a matter for mirth, perhaps, but not for psychological dissection. He could be, when he chose, a grand entertainer, but his purpose generally was to instruct; so that it has become difficult to discuss Belloc at all without discussing his opinions. Now there is something forbidding about a man who is always laying down the law; who is always saying exactly the

---

[1] *Sonnets and Verse* (2nd ed., London: Duckworth, 1954), p. 172.

same things. We may or may not agree witht Montaigne that *opin-ionâtre* is the *signe exprés de bêtise,* but we tend to be bored by it. I will not say that those nearest to Belloc were never bored by his thousandth repetition of a familiar truth — that the English peasant was robbed of his land at the Reformation, that Socialism didn't mean handing over property to the people, but handing it over to the politicians; but they were less exasperated than they might have been because his pursuit of truth was so plainly disinterested. It had no tincture of vanity. This may sound surprising when we remember how prejudiced he could be. But he was a man of strong attachments, and he would no more have deserted an idea than he would have betrayed a friend. He was a man for whom truth was ever new and ever lovable, and there was in him a strain of chivalry which made him go on praising it to the same tune.

He had a lucid, powerful, and subtle — not too subtle — mind; and he had a boundless appetite for reality. Certain things came home to him with overwhelming force, but he saw them so vividly that their balancing or contrasting opposites were generally excluded from his vision. It would be absurd to suggest that he understood, in any general way, the Church of England, but he did understand one enormously important thing — that the power of Anglican Christianity was literary. "Prevent us, O Lord, in our doings with Thy most gracious favor and favor us with Thy continual help, that in all our works begun, continued and ended in Thee . . ." — this had become part of the English religious psychology with which Belloc wrestled to his dying day. Cranmer had possessed the mind of a Cambridge modernist, but his ear was indefectible. English Christianity was bound up with two masterpieces of English prose, and even in New-man's room at Edgbaston, preserved as in his lifetime, it was the Authorised Version which lay thumbed upon his desk. The deep, intimate associations of the Anglican past compose a suasion against which the logic of Catholicism generally breaks its teeth in vain. But Belloc never desisted from the frontal assaut. He was more an antique Roman than a Greek, and the tactics of the Trojan horse were not in the curriculum of St. Cyr.

Belloc would have liked to think that his criticism of the modern world was a critique of pure reason; and indeed no man of our time did more to uphold the rights of the intelligence unbemused by emo-tion, in its own domain. But in fact his thoughts and preaching were both profoundly conditioned by experience; at their most nakedly geometrical, they were clothed in flesh and blood. His childhood at St. Cloud was passed in the shadow of the great defeat, and against a repetition of that recent shame the army was the only insurance. When, therefore, the General Staff decided upon the guilt of Dreyfus, the young Belloc felt no temptation to join hands with those who had decided upon his innocence. In this respect, at least, he was perhaps the most illustrious victim of Maurras's *nationalisme integral*. But the Republic was in his blood; through his own Bonapartist forebears and his study of the Revolution; through his service in the Army that the Revolution had made; through his adherence to the doctrine of democracy, as Rousseau had expounded it in another masterpiece of style. In this allegiance to the Revolution, as the men of 1789 had imagined it, he never wavered. You can read his vision in *The Girondin*,[2] and here the vision is defeated; but though defeated, it is not lost. The last time I saw Belloc, I put to him the most torturing of all historical questions — had the Revolution done more good than harm? Undoubtedly more good, he replied; without it society would just have withered up. Like his friend, Duff Cooper, I should have answered the other way. But there is no more endearing quality in a man than fidelity to an ancient dream, and it was this virtue, more than anything else, which, even through enfeebled age, kept Belloc young.

When he came up to Jowett's [3] Balliol, he had one foot in the camp of clerical reaction and the other in the camp of revolutionary progress. He was bored by the Royalist and intolerant of the Faubourg.[4] Like any self-respecting young man, he was contemptuous of respectability and riches. He was by nature sceptical, and though his family were Catholic in the tradition of the *bourgeoisie*, it would seem to have been touch and go on which side he finally stood in the great French quarrel. We do not know very much about the process by which he made up his mind, but it was of the very essence of his Catholicism that it had conquered doubt, although it was strengened (through his marriage) by a Catholicism which never had any doubts to conquer. The one was wholly French, the other wholly Irish. United, they shook the prosperous and complacent Protestantism of Edwardian England like the wind of Pentecost. The young

[2] (New York: Nelson and Sons, 1911).

[3] This world-renowned classical scholar was a dominant influence at Oxford for over fifty years, especially at Balliol where he was Master [Ed. note].

[4] The French urban and quasi-proletarian class as opposed to Belloc's favored peasants [Ed. note].

Belloc had looked behind him into history, and about him into life (his essay, *The Arena*, shows vividly the span of his inquiry), and he decided that the Catholic Church was not of this world. Having made this discovery, he proceeded to communicate it, in a very loud voice, to the educated Englishmen of his time.

They did not thank him for it. His naturally forgiving manner never forgot the rejection of All Souls,[5] and he always attributed this to the militancy of his beliefs. The Common Rooms can accommodate a Don who goes to Mass discreetly, and is an influence for good in the College; such exceptions, provided they are rare, can be welcomed as a signal of broad-mindedness. But a man who seriously set about to overthrow Gardiner and Froude and who would have dismissed Acton as a Whig, was perhaps a little sanguine in expecting a Fellowship in History. There are times, even at Oxford, when brilliance is not enough. "The trouble with you, Belloc," remarked F. E. Smith (later Lord Birkenhead) after listening to one of his scintillating speeches in the Union, "is that you will always play the fool." Had the excoriating rhymes about what Belloc, in a fatal phrase during a debate in the House of Commons, was to call "the Anglo-Judaic plutocracy" already begun to circulate? In any case it is instructive to compare the careers of Belloc and Birkenhead — each combative, courageous, and loved to idolatry by his friends. In the one case there was success limited by cynicism, in the other failure lightened by faith. And Belloc's frivolity was immeasurably more serious than the perorations of those for whom government was a game, and the platitudes of those for whom justice was a joke.

He made his friends among those educated upper classes whom it was his particular pleasure to deride. "The English country house," he said to me once," "was one of the jolliest things in Europe." But the gulf which separated England from the Catholic tradition never ceased to exasperate him. Here, he would say, was the thing which had determined the destiny of Europe; the thing recognized, even when it was hated, by every educated man or woman on the continent. The thing which had to be taken into account in deciding any large issue of politics or morals. And yet it was persistently ignored by the finest intelligences of the country, the country he had made his own. "Their ignorance of the Catholic Church!" I can still hear the characteristic emphasis with which he bit out these words as I

[5] In competition for the Fellowship at All Souls College, Oxford, Belloc was unsuccessful [Ed. note].

was escorting him to the funeral of Father Vincent McNabb. So long as he had breath in his body he would try to explain to people what it meant to belong to a living, teaching and continuing Church. And he was correspondingly intolerant of what they preferred to call "Christianity" — a vague cloud of inherited sentiments and selected doctrines, interpreted by particular inclinations. What he did not quite understand was the quality of Christian life which could still be lived in communities outside the Church. He would not have denied that this existed, but it was something outside his experience; and just as it was part of Belloc's fecundity to have experienced a great deal, so it was a corresponding defect in him not to imagine sympathetically or easily the things that were beyond his range. His intelligence, unclouded by emotion thought it was, was vital, never academic. No prophet more abundantly lived his preaching.

But his insistent dogmatism still left a false, an unfavorable impression on minds which did not share his certitudes. He never troubled to prepare his listeners for the shock; they were stunned rather than seduced into acquiescence. But when you talked to him in the flesh, you were surprised by his patience and courtesy. He listened well and argued quietly. (I remember, when we were performing *The Four Men* through Sussex, how an actor tried to persuade him of the social benefit of television — he would not have a telephone in the house!) He was generally fond of his opponents and of the people he was supposed to disapprove of. I never, for example, heard him say a word against the Germans or the Jews. For years he had a Jewish secretary and I can remember him summing up the Jewish tragedy in a sentence. "Poor darlings, I'm awfully sorry for them, but it's their own fault; they ought to have left God alone." Contrarily, he often expressed his impatience with French reactionaries, Irish clericals, and the old English Catholics. There was a certain distinction to be observed between his private preferences and his public attitudes. You felt this when you were privileged to be invited to his house, still lost among the meadows of the World. The memento cards in the little chapel upstairs, the faded photographs, a framed sketch that he had done on the path to Rome, the miscellaneous litter of a lifetime — all these proclaimed a public man who had known how to guard jealously yet never ungenerously, the sanctities of the private life.

It was inevitable that his influence among English Catholics should have been strong, because it is only rarely that genius flourishes in our midst. His convictions and his energy would always have carried him a certain distance, but it was the power of his personality as well as the variety of his gifts which enabled him to impose on so many people a way of thinking and of feeling the Faith. It was his own way, robust and idiosyncratic, high-spirited and tender, and it did not always suit his disciples. Those who were not his disciples reacted against it with irritation and occasionally with anger. His simplifications were often vulnerable. Parliaments could be corrupt, but despotisms were not necessarily better. Aristocracies could be insolent and absurd, but they fostered liberty more than he ever allowed for. In England, at least, the only alternative to the accustomed social relationships has not been the better distribution, but the brutal displacement of property; not the yeoman farmer but the socialistic bureaucrat. The Polish were not invariably angels; the French military mind could occasionally make mistakes; and the English cohesion in disaster was at least a plausible argument of what Belloc would have called the myths of English patriotism. I took a French priest down to see him once, who remarked afterwards "j'avais l'impression d'un prophete qui se trompe toujours." This was not a fair comment and when I repeated it to Etienne Gilson, he vehemently disagreed. The point about Belloc was that he was so triumphantly right over a few major matters, that he could afford to be wrong over a few minor ones. His error was to misjudge, very often, the audience he was trying to convince.

But his way of being a Catholic — the humanist way, radical and traditionalist, militant and humble, obedient and free — was still a good way, and it will survive the spurious imitation. There are few men of genius of whom it is natural to say, even after knowing them a little, that they are good men. And it was further true of Belloc that he was sane before he was inspired. There is no necessary connection between sanity and sanctity, and genius is often marked by aberration. It was perhaps a limitation of Belloc's genius that he did not comprehend perversity. And if we are to find his companions in English letters, we must go back to Cobbett and Johnson, and beyond them again to Chaucer. Yet because he was sane in a world distraught by lunacy, and happy through much personal misfortune, we should not think of him as a bouncing optimist or an insensitive stoic. By nature he was inclined to pessimism. He met and lived his sorrows, and the whole of his later life was passed in the company of his beloved dead; of his wife, and the two sons whom the wars had taken from him. In this steadfast reminiscence he was very French, and the last time I saw him, only a few weeks before he died, I had the sensation of speaking to one who already stood himself within the shadow. When a number of his friends met in the house he loved so well, after the committal of his body to the earth and the commendation of his soul to its Creator, the rooms were serene with his presence. The tribute of Chesterton was recalled; that no man of our time had fought so consistently for the good things.

New Media and the New Education

Marshall McLuhan

Herbert Marshall McLuhan was born in Edmonton, Alberta, in 1911. After receiving his B.A. and M.A. from the University of Manitoba, he studied at Cambridge University, England, receiving from there the degrees of B.A., M.A., and Ph.D. He has taught at the University of Wisconsin, St. Louis University, Assumption University of Windsor, and the University of St. Michael's, where he is full-time Professor of English. His well-known book The Mechanical Bride: Folklore of Industrial Man *grew out of a lecture he gave in the Christian Culture Series. He is married and has six children. One of the recipients of a large grant from the Ford Foundation some years ago, he became co-founder of the magazine* Explorations *and also co-editor. This past year he has been devoting full time to research on communications, helped by a grant received for his work, through the National Association of Educational Broadcasters and the United States Office of Education, under Title No. 7: Concerning Military Matters. One of the Kenyon Critics, his essay on Gerald Manley Hopkins has been widely acclaimed. He has contributed close to one hundred papers to scholarly magazines and has several books in preparation.*

"THE ARTIST," wrote Wyndham Lewis, "is engaged in writing a detailed history of the future because he is aware of the unused possibilities of the present." It is quite literally true that since the advent of printing it has been the poets and painters who have explored and predicted the various possibilities of print, of prints, of press, of telegraph, of photograph, movies, radio and television. In recent decades the arrival of several new media has led to prodigious experimentation in the arts. But, at present, the artists have yielded to the media themselves. Experimentation has passed from the control of the private artist to the groups in charge of the new technologies.

That is to say, that whereas in the past the individual artist, manipulating private and inexpensive materials, was able to shape models of new experience years ahead of the public, today the artist works with expensive public technology, and artist and public merge in a single experience. The new media need the best artist talent and can pay for it. But the artist can no longer provide years of advance awareness of developments in the patterns of human experience which will inevitably emerge from new technological development.

The painters of the fifteenth century explained perspective or *fixed* point of view to the public when print was scarcely known. Aretino became "the scourge of princes" when print was young, and long before the newspaper took up its inevitable republican role. Petrarch developed the Sonnet as a mode of self-expression and of self-analysis before print and long before Montaigne revealed the artistic meaning of the printed page in his *Essays*.

In a word, the artist discerns the forms of technological change in their full cultural dimensions before the technicians actually take over.

But to-day, for the first time in human history, our technology includes an external projection of each of our senses. Nobody has considered the significance of this development which confers on our technology an inclusive organic relation to mankind for the first time. From the invention of the wheel and alphabet, onwards, we have been accustomed to conceive technology as a progressive splintering and dissociation of what in nature is integral and organic. Thus the wheel was an abstraction from animal form, since a running animal is in a sense rotating. And the first movie ever made was of a running horse.

To-day radio, telegraph and television, have no moving parts. The electronic age abandons mechanism for the movement of light and information only. Viewed in the crudest quantitative terms, the shift from mechanism to electronics presents the character of total revolution. It is inconceivable that school and society alike should not receive the full impact of this change.

Looked at more closely, the electronic mode of shaping situations reveals its bias towards *field* structure. But even "field," preferred by physicists, can mislead by suggesting a flat, single plane. But a multidimensional field is intended, an "everyway roundabout with intrusions from above and below." Thus, for example, "point-of-view," so inevitable in print culture, is alien to electronic "field" and the affiliates of such "field." For "point-of-view" originates in the discovery of a fixed position such as creating perspective, or vanishing point. It was this discovery in the fifteenth century that we associate with the end of medieval art. It was the same discovery taken up by map-makers and by navigators that made the world voyages possible. For prior to this discovery of space as homogeneous and lineally continuous, it was not known that one could simply proceed on and on in a straight line on a single plane. Mircea Eliade's *The Sacred and the Profane*[1] is a study of the contrasted ideas of space and time as between modern and premodern man. And Harold Gatty's *Nature is Your Guide*[2] provides much illustration of premechanical relation to time and space. The methods and procedures in organizing our lives, in time and space, which are still accepted as "natural" derive almost entirely from the introduction of mechanism into teaching and learning by means of the first teaching-machine which is the printed page.

In providing the first complete mechanization of an ancient handicraft, print created an explosion in learning in the sixteenth century. But the technology by which the mechanization of writing was achieved also invaded every phase of teaching and learning during the past five hundred years. It will repay us to consider, briefly, what happened, if only because we are to-day involved in a much greater technological change which concerns the nature of teaching and learning more pervasively than print ever did or could.

Basically, the mechanization of writing involved the inspired step of segmentation. Movable types are a kind of static analysis of the movements of the scribal hand. And whether we regard the differential calculus or assembly-lines, science and industry have since the sixteenth century, and until recently, extended the principle of segmentation to all procedures of investigation and of applied knowledge.

It is all the easier to observe the patterns of knowledge and of human association. It may seem baffling that in the electronic age there should be such an increase of books and printing. But the same paradox occurred after printing had ended the constitutive role of manuscript and scribe. For everybody began to write a great deal after printing. And now that print has ceased to constitute the major basis for teaching and learning and is no longer the dominant technological form of our world, there is much more printing than ever

[1] (New York: Harcourt Brace, 1959).
[2] (London: Collins, 1958).

before. So far as my studies have taken me, the reason for this is that a new medium splinters the older ones into a variety of new forms and roles. The typewriter merges composition, writing and print publication in a single act. To-day the book has many new roles and functions, as had the manuscript in the sixteenth and seventeenth centuries.

Here, then, is a brief indication of the new patterns that entered teaching and learning as a result of printing. There was first, uniformity and repeatability which conferred the power of speed and silence on the reader. The manuscript was read slowly and aloud. The speed, uniformity, and repeatability of the printed book entirely altered patterns of study. It was then possible for the first time to read *widely*. And repeatability and accessibility of the book made it unnecessary to memorize all that one read as the manuscript reader had tended to do for purely practical reasons.

For the inaccessibility and nonrepeatability of the manuscript made memorizing a need as it made oral learning and disputation a natural thing, capable of much greater speed and range than manuscript reading could achieve. (To-day we encounter the reverse situation in which film, videotape and even photography permit the rapid grasp of complex cultural *gestalts*, past and present, which the printed word cannot convey even slowly.)

The portability of the book, shared with its repeatability and cheapness, created on the one hand the habit of privacy and silence, and on the other hand made possible the class room in which all have ready for use the same data and texts. By contrast, the pre-print classroom expended much time in enabling each student to make his own text while the teacher did aloud the work of the ancient exegete and the modern editor. All kinds of rhetorical analysis, word by word, went hand in hand with minute considerations of variant readings and punctuation (Baldwin's *Small Latin and Lesse Greek*).[3] Thus there arose from print a new kind of corporate life in the school and a new kind of privacy in the study. The curriculum was revolutionized to include a great range of authors and several languages, such as never could have been encompassed by manuscript means.

But print at once gathered another group of changes, namely the related habits of self-expression and self-investigation. Print as a mass medium offered a sort of launching pad for the projection of the

[3] *Wm. Shakespeare's Small Latin and Lesse Greek* T. W. Baldwin, Vol. I and Vol. II, University of Illinois Press, 1944 and 1956.

private person into the role of public institution. Pietro Aretino and Rabelais were perhaps the first to explore these new dimensions for the individual ego. Ego enlargement via print, at the same time created the sense of fame and self-perpetuation by means of the repeatability and indestructibility, as it were, of the private self. Marlow's *Tamburlaine* and his *Doctor Faustus* are excellent types of the new megalomania arising from print.

Publication for Chaucer, by contrast, meant only a private reading of his works to friends. Self-expression and self-portraiture and self-analysis swiftly merged in the sixteenth century in the great figure of Montaigne. He revealed another feature inherent in the segmental analytic patterns of print, namely "systematic doubt." After Montaigne, print laid few further patterns on the private self and began to release its powers in the reshaping of society and politics as the newspaper developed.

There is scarcely a feature of print culture which can to-day be discerned in the over-all field of our new electronic technology. Static fragmentation as a means of analysis and of production and expression are not to be found. Jacques Barzun in his *House of Intellect*,[4] which he assures us is built on the alphabet (and print), has provided a handy testimony of the total incompatibility of the new age with the typical values and procedures of the print age. Art, science and philanthropy to-day, he says, represent a team destructive of all intellectual values. (He is careful to dissociate intellect from intelligence.) Perhaps he might have written a different book had he understood the private and social consequences of print as print. For one of the curiosities of print and literature is an obsession with "content" as opposed to "form." It is easy to see why the blank page awaiting an imprint should appear to "contain" things of good or ill use and report. It is in fact this formal, structural aspect of the page that obliterates awareness of the page itself as a structure. To a lesser degree, this oblivion of the structure of the page, and of print itself, extends to writing in the ancient world as well. For the alphabetic translation of the audible into the visible had huge consequences such as mark off Greece and Rome from all other societies which lacked phonetic means of codifying and translating experience into analytic, visible terms.

Let us suppose for a moment that a team of present-day testers had been available in the year 1500 to find out whether the new book or

[4] (New York: Harpers, 1959).

reading machines and instructional materials were capable of doing the plenary traditional job of education in the future. Would not this team, even as it would today, ask whether the privately read word could measure up as a means of teaching and learning to the memorized manuscript and its formidable extension in oral exegesis and group disputation? Since we know that printing wiped out the educational procedures of the preceding centuries, we can say that the testers would have been quite wrong in asking whether the new could compete with the old when the new had only one mode of procedure, namely to erase and to brainwash the older culture. Our testers today are still geared to the static assumptions of the print *form* and ignore the structural dynamics of the electronic form. In 1500, as in 1960, they could report variations in the facility with which educational skills in a wide range of subjects are achieved by print or by television. But they have no regard for the new patterns of perception and sensibility which are subliminally imposed on us by new structures for codifying and moving information. For the new structures modify our means of apprehending past and present. They recreate our sense of space and time, of teaching and learning. Basically I should say that in the electronic situation there is a great new stress on learning (creativity) and a corresponding relaxation of teaching stress.

Again let the artists of the last ten decades be our guide. The Romantics reacted strongly against the book as book, spotting it as the enemy of nature and of natural modes of learning. They insisted upon the creative imagination as the birthright of all, and began a ceaseless quest for the inclusive and integral Image. This arduous search was taken up with great intensity by the Symbolist who realized that it could not be a merely visual image, but must include all the senses in a kind of dance. En route to this discovery, Hopkins and Browning, Poe and Baudelaire, ended the print-fostered dichotomy between author and reader, producer and consumer, and swept mostly unwilling audiences up into participation in the creative act. After Poe, and since Cézanne, poets and painters devised ever new modes of speaking not *to* their readers and viewers, but *through* them. As the voice of art resonated within and through the print-cultured audiences, the cry went up, and still continues: "the artist is using a private language." The artists' demand that the audiences enter the artist role as co-creators was not welcome to the consumer mind. Such is the meaning of the abstract art and the do-it-yourself kits which artists have for a hundred years been carefully preparing for their affronted public.

Of course, children love abstract and symbolist art, and experimental films. But by the time they have been given in late adolescence the cookie-cutter patterns of the House of Intellect they freeze up in the presence of the playfully abstract cartoons of Picasso and James Joyce.

That situation is easy to understand. The educational establishment is also built on print and ABC-mindedness. But today we are asking what will be the shape of things to come educationally. The answer is simple. The artists have told us in minute detail this past hundred years. They have built endless models of our challenge and our needs, and of how to live with the new instructional materials. They have told us that there will be no more consumer packages in education — not at least if education is to have a relevance to our new world. The dialogue will replace the guided tours of data provided by the book as teaching machine. In the dialogue there is no maintaining of a "point of view," but only the common participation in creating perpetually new insight and understanding in a total field of unified awareness. For dialogue is not light *on*, but light *through*, which is the difference between film and television.

Let us note that in all forms of electric circuit and appliance, whether telegraph, radar, or guided missile, we are confronted with the give and take of dialogue and not the one way song of lyric self-expression. Even the various forms of electric appliance impose a large measure of do-it-yourselfness, whether the electric toaster, the vacuum-cleaner or the washing-machine.

I say, therefore, with impersonal assurance, that unless we choose to abandon all electric forms of technology we cannot possibly retain in our teaching and learning the modes of instruction and apprehension associated with the mechanical forms of print and its innumerable cultural progeny. Even if we are zealous, like Dean Barzun, to retain and to maintain the characteristics of print culture we shall need to know much more than he does about the cultural dynamics of print in individual society; and also it would be necessary to have a very complete knowledge of the new dynamics of our new technology in order to harmonize the twain. It is characteristic of the semi-aware products of print culture that they prefer to take a strong *moral* stand on one or another horn of a dilemma. They love dichotomies. They point with pride. They view with alarm. They then feel that duty has been done by spiritual values. But of understanding and, therefore, of control of new situations they are bereft.

I am not optimistic about saving any of the traditional qualities in education from the electronic bombardment. It could be done by those who had a firm hold of both old and new situations. And since these of the older print culture are not morally or mentally prepared to tackle the new, it behooves the products of the new electronic culture to seize and to maintain some of the needful qualities from the wreck of the House of Intellect. If this sounds like Robinson Crusoe revisiting the wreck, it will be a Robinson Crusoe equipped with electronic technology.

Earlier I listed some of the basic characters and consequences of printing in teaching and learning. It seemed a useful way of moving from the known to the less well-known. I have insisted that any new structure for codifying experience and of moving information, be it alphabet or photography, has the power of imposing its structual character and assumptions upon all levels of our private and social lives, even without benefit of concepts or of conscious acceptance. That is what I've always meant by "the medium is the message." Moreover, a new medium bombards older media and awareness, stripping the older forms of experience to their bare bones or basic codes. That is why, today, when we are already living through intense nuclear bombardment from within our own cultures, we have achieved almost total clairvoyance of our own condition and of our debts to earlier ages. Today, we master languages and whole cultures faster than men formerly mastered an author. Our children live in a world museum of cultures from infancy, even while we continue to educate them as if they were bolted into only one of these cultures. And these changes, or this acceleration of change to the point where change itself becomes the very matrix and foundation of society — all this is owing to our century-old shift into the electronic mode of information-shaping and movement. We have left the one-thing-at-a-time of print and mechanism for the all-at-once of the inclusive "field" of electricity. And it is the very structure of this all-at-once inclusive mode in teaching and learning which automatically ends what we until now called "subjects." The electronic alters the contours of math and physics and "nature" even as it abolishes literature. The nature with which we will henceforth be *engagée* is one whose lines of force we will travel and explore with the sensitivity of the greatest artists. The split between art and nature ends now, as surely as the division between culture and commerce. So far as the young are concerned, all these things are already accomplished. Their sensibilities have been formed almost entirely and exclusively by electronic modes of experience. Even the film, that last mechanical link with the Gutenberg era, they experience mostly as translated through the medium of television.

I put the matter this way in order to confront the educational point: "What is the difference between movie and television after all?" Just to heat up the issue a bit more, let me answer that they have scarcely anything in common except the fact that both are visible. The structure that is seen, however, is another matter. The movie is a mechanical way of rolling up the world in a sequence of small still shots, not unlike the way in which print captures the movements of an author's mind in a sequence of black and white still shots. Played back, these still shots recreate or reconstruct an earlier action. The movie has built-in perspective and is superb in details to fill the pictorial space of its perspective. In contrast, the television image is a continuously formed mosaic with no still shots, no reconstruction of actions, no perspective and very little detail. The television mosaic is so poor in data, in fact, that it must be mostly filled in by the viewer. And moreover it has no light *on*, but only light *through*. So that, typically, the television viewer is conditioned to expect much activity and to expect knowledge to be a kind of total revelation of illumination from within both subject and himself. As some medical and dental users of television in teaching point out, television in medical instruction has shown that the speaker, instructor, or lecturer must efface himself, and also that the viewer, in operations for example, was less a spectator than the scalpel. The viewer does not so much see as do the operation. Even the surgeon watching the monitor while actually performing the operation frequently is surprised by aspects of the operation which the television camera picks up beyond his immediate visual range. Or rather the operation is translated into another medium, and so revealed in another mode, much as the newspaper translates our ordinary social and political lives into a special mode, providing quite new dimensions and meanings for them.

Let us say, then, that television, like radio, states much less than it suggests. That is the symbolist or do-it-yourself phase of this electric medium. Book and film, in contrast, state very fully and suggest much less than electric media. That is another way of saying that electric media deal with experience *in depth*, rather than spelling it out on the single plane of flat statement. The radio listener takes for granted the action of providing a visual world for the sound experiences. The television viewer must have an image he can complete for himself. So that even persons appearing on television must not be too definite or one-sided types. The vague, ambiguous, uncommitted person, whether in politics or entertainment, will survive on television. But the definite classifiable figure who satisfies the film or newspaper medium as a right guy will frustrate the television viewer who wants to complete his own image. The flood of Jack Paars, Mort Sahls, Shelley Bermans, has scarcely begun. But a similar noncommittal, ironic whimsicality will appear more and more, not only in television figures, but will evoke many persons and forms of expression, not directly related to television. The newspaper man and reader are just as baffled by these changes emanating from television depth suggestion as the bookmen. Yet a century ago, the poets and painters began to unfold in detail this whole complicated story which has now become part of the educational drama.

The "square" and the "egghead" are the bookmen as seen by the new television generation. In the sixteenth century, the new book generation saw the oral and oracular, previous generation much as Polonius appeared to Hamlet. The razor precision of the oral schoolmen appeared to the new literary humanists as "words words words." They called the schoolmen not squares, but dunces.

The new criticism (or reading in depth) which has appeared in our electronic era is often called scholastic in form by the literary humanists. Is it not terribly wasteful of values and opportunities, as well as destructive of harmony that unwittingly men should so embroil themselves in civil feuds arising from media change? In our age the onset of multiple media changes makes impossible the older patterns of gradual adjustment and oblivion of the obsolete. There is no time to adjust. We simply have to know, and understand, exactly what is happening; and indeed, as educators we can avail ourselves of the artists to help us to become contemporaries of ourselves. Rather we must all become creative artists in order to cope with even the banalities of daily life.

The Meaning of Mass Production

Peter Drucker

Peter Drucker, author, professor, and management consultant, was born in Vienna in 1909. He became a naturalized American citizen in 1943. For the period between 1942–49 he was professor of philoso. phy and politics at Bennington College; in 1950 he was professor of management at New York University. In 1957 he received the Parlin Memorial Medal of the American Market Association, and in the same year he also received the gold medal of the International University of Social Studies of Rome, Italy. Among his well-known and challenging books are The End of Economic Man, Future of Industrial Man, Concept of the Corporation, The New Society, America's Next Twenty Years, *and* Landmarks of Tomorrow. *Mr. Drucker is indeed one of the most highly respected observers of the American scene.*

THE REAL revolution of our times has been the worldwide sweep of industrialization since World War I. Before 1914 industrialization was confined by and large to the immediate hinterland of the North Atlantic. Today there are few areas of the inhabited globe which are not under its full sway. More than any of the social upheavals of the last thirty years, it is industrialization that has been uprooting ancient societies like the Chinese, that has been changing ways of life and of culture older than recorded history, and has shaken if not broken ancient institutions such as the caste system of India or the Chinese family system. The basic conflict of our time is that being waged over the control of this new revolutionary force and over the order that will emerge from it.

This revolution is based on a new principle of social organization: mass production. To most people "mass production" seems nothing more than a matter of techniques, the application of a few machines and tools or even one tool, the conveyor belt. But today the mass production principle is not confined at all to manufacturing even though

191

it originated there. Mass production has shown its application in farming, in office work, and in the organization of scientific research. Even the way in which the great invasions of Europe were organized by the Allies during World War II was nothing but the application of the mass production principle to the organization of military forces.

In other words the mass production principle is quite independent of any given tool, machine, or of any given technique. It is, like any proper technique, conceptual rather than technical. And the essence of mass production is not the production of large numbers of uniform products. It is the very opposite — the ability to produce an infinite variety of final products from uniform and standardized parts. The best proof of this is the fact that American industry today has a variety of final products such as Europe has never known.

Nor does mass production rest on the substitution of unskilled for skilled work — another fallacy still generally believed. In the United States, where mass production has become the universal principle of organization, unskilled laborers are practically a dying race, to be found primarily in the poorest farming areas of the country. Even the men who run a machine — and that requires a considerable amount of training — are declining both as a proportion in the labor force and, despite our rapidly growing population, in total numbers. The groups in the population that have been growing most rapidly all require a considerable background of training and education: executives and technicians, skilled workers, foremen and clerical workers. The unskilled worker on the assembly line, whom novelists and movie-script writers did so much to make a figure of popular myth, is rapidly becoming obsolete.

This is of the essence of mass production. For the principle of mass production is precisely that the actual work is done before the job of production is begun. It is done in the idea, by using theories, on paper and conceptually. For instance, it takes two to four years work and something like four thousand tons of theoretical engineering drawings before an airplane, even a small airplane, can be put into production; after that, production moves so rapidly that at the end of another half year thousands of airplanes can have been produced. But without the years of theoretical work no airplanes can be produced at all. A mass production economy, in fact, can never have enough educated and trained people.

Above all, mass production is not a technological principle but primarily a new social order, a new concept of organizing joint human effort. And while not without precedent — the human organization that built the great Gothic cathedral was essentially based on the same principle — mass production is a radical innovation. In mass production no one person actually produces. It is the group, the whole that produces. But no one person is unessential, since the work of the whole cannot be done unless everyone works and con tributes. Mass production creates a true society in which everybody is a citizen because everybody is absolutely essential, and in which, at the same time, no one can be productive without all the others.

This means in effect that mass production rests not so much on specialization — the thing all the technical writers talk about — but on the very opposite, on integration. It rests on the ability of people to see the whole before the work even begins, to visualize the whole as the relations of all its parts and then create the whole — all before a single hand is put to a machine or a single nail is pounded in by a single hammer. The integration of mass production requires man's most human qualities, his imagination and his ability to apply generalization to the specific and the concrete.

But the industrial revolution is not only based on a new social principle. It also is based on a new social institution — the modern business enterprise. Legally this new modern business enterprise looks exactly the same as the business of fifty or a hundred years ago which it succeeded. Socially and philosophically it is something different. The modern business enterprise is an institution in the sense that it is a social unit of its own. It is the productive factor in the economy. Neither the machine nor the human being by themselves would be productive. They are productive only in the organization of the enterprise.

It cannot be emphasized too strongly that there is no essential difference in the nature, requirements and structure of the business enterprise in the various political systems. It is essentially the same in a free enterprise society, a Communist or fascist totalitarianism or under social democracy. This fact has a most important consequence for our time. It means simply that the basic problems of social order do not lie in the organization of the State.

From the nineteenth century we inherited philosophies which preached that by changing the juridical order and the form of government, society can be basically changed — for better or worse. Today such philosophies are simply obsolete. They are reactionary; they are a hundred years behind the times; they are — and this is the worst one can say about an ideology — irrelevant. Whoever bothers with them, whoever puts his faith in them, simply worries about the problems of today. He may come to power — by using bayonets or exploiting the misery and suffering of the masses. But he can stay in power only by brute force and terror. For he cannot possibly deliver what he promises — a new social order. The problems of social order lie within the modern business enterprise.

This new institution, the modern business enterprise, has produced new basic organs which are the new social leaders of our modern age — business management and labor union leadership. These new organs of society have emerged during the last fifty years. As far as I know, never before have new basic social organs grown so rapidly as these two have from the most obscure beginning within the memory of many people still alive to their present dominant position. They are the social reality of a modern industrial society.

In estimating the political meaning of this change the first thing to be noticed is that management has become the new socially-leading group in an industrial society.

I do not say "capitalist." That term has become meaningless since we have no "capitalists" in the traditional sense of the term. Something like fifteen million families — forty per cent of our population — are the owners of our industrial and business corporations with very few of them being either rich or deriving the main income from their ownership in business enterprise. Nor am I talkng of "employees," since the new "manager" is himself usually an employee.

Management is a functional classification. It is an organ of the enterprise. It derives its power, its importance and its authority not from property but from what it does. Primarily, it is a professional term and every day management in the United States assumes more of the character of a profession — a certain fundamental theoretical education, a basic code of mores and morals, a concept of social responsibilities, and a growing body of systematic theoretical knowledge rapidly assuming some of the characteristics of a genuine science.

The first duty of management is to the enterprise, to maintain the enterprise as a productive organization. But that also includes duties to all the groups which stand in a relationship to the enterprise — whether they be the owners, the workers, the customers or society in general.

Management is indispensable. Soviet Russia has no more been able to do without it than would any other country that industrialized to any extent. In fact Soviet Russia has learned that no matter what Marxist theory says about it — and obviously Marxist theory would not accept the existence of management — the integrity of management, its authority, its responsibility and its function must be protected and must be preserved.

But industrial society also requires the labor union — otherwise management can never be a "legitimate ruler." Management must always put the interests of the enterprise first. It cannot be government primarily in the interest of the employees who are subject to its rule. Therefore the employees require a counterforce to offset, to limit, to balance management's power.

Such a counterforce is not unknown to history — a close parallel is the *tribunus populi* of ancient Rome. But it is not something that is too easy. For while the union is absolutely needed — in fact it can be suppressed only by totalitarian government, and its suppression makes totalitarian terror and dictatorship absolutely inevitable — the union will always be secondary and limited in its function. For it can never become the management itself.

In the interest of a strong and constructive trade unionism — something every industrial society needs badly — we must insist that the union not corrupt itself by assuming the functions of management. A very good example of what happens to a union that ceases to be a counterforce to management and becomes management itself may be seen today in Great Britain in the nationalized industry.

Only a few years — and yet long established and greatly popular union leadership has become, in the eyes of the workers, a "tool of management" and has lost their confidence and, increasingly, their allegiance. The union leaders in the nationalized industries are in their jobs today only because of the thirty or forty years of personal loyalty they have built up; once they are gone their successors will hardly be able to be both members of management and accepted union leaders. For participation in management of the enterprise means inevitably that the union leader will himself have to put the interest of the enterprise first and it is his job — as it was the job of the *tribunus populi* — to put the interest of the employees first.

Because both management and unions are necessary, the worker himself will insist — and increasingly does so — on a relationship between the two that enables him to give allegiance to both. In an industrial society it is the worker above all who cannot exist in a situation of "class war." He cannot survive in a conflict of loyalty that requires him to take sides permanently.

Most especially, the business enterprise is a social order. For its employees, it is increasingly the community in which they spend the major part of their waking hours and from which they therefore expect the fulfillment of the social promises of their society. Its employees expect from the enterprise the status and function which make a person a citizen, and they expect to find the equal opportunities of a democratic society. In other words, the workers look upon the enterprise as the place in which they realize both freedom and justice.

But the enterprise too must insist that its employees are citizens. It is absolutely clear that industrial society cannot afford to employ proletarians, people whose sole interest in the work is the wage they get out of it. It must insist on people who take not only an interest in the whole but who have something much rarer and much more difficult — a view of the whole, that is, a "managerial view."

And it is equally to the interest of the enterprise to establish a relationship between its own profitability and the economic interest of its employees. The more complicated and complex our technology becomes, the greater the dependence of the enterprise upon the desire of the employee to make the enterprise a success. Therefore he must himself have a real stake — in terms of employment stability, protection against the hazards of life, of old age, of retirement, etc. — a stake that is grounded in the success of the enterprise.

Finally in its internal community life the enterprise in its own interest must give the worker adequate opportunities for the discharge of local self-government responsibilities. It must draw on the worker to run those affairs inside the plant community or the office which are predominantly of interest to the employee and which are not really in any way connected with the economic profitability and survival of the enterprise.

For our society, the new institution of the enterprise has important consequences. In it we have the first new autonomous institution that has emerged in Western society since the collapse of the medieval order. The enterprise is not a creature of the state — even though the laws which govern it and set its limitations are of course laws of the state. The enterprise has a nature and logic of its own. It is the local self-government of modern society, the logical successor to manor, village and town. Thus for the first time in four hundred or five hundred years we will in the future again have a society in which local self-government is absolutely necessary and in which only tyranny can establish a centralized state. We have to learn again to be pluralists in our political thinking.

The nineteenth century believed profoundly that economic activity is a-social or anti-social activity. It saw in the self-interest of the individual or of the business a force that was in no way directed towards social goals. One philosophy believed — though without any real evidence — that by the sheer magic of the "Invisible Hand" of the Manchester school of Liberalism this purely a-social activity would be turned into the social good. The other school, rapidly growing since it first appeared a little over a hundred years ago, believed that in order to save society economic self-interest had to be suppressed. On neither assumption could a modern industrial society possibly exist; if either theory were correct, we would have a schizophrenic society, bound to disintegrate rapidly.

Today we know that those two approaches are nonsense, that they are obsolete, that they are irrelevant. For the modern business enterprise, nothing is fundamentally profitable in the long run, unless it is constructive for society. What society requires in the relationship between management and labor, between enterprise and employees, is also the one and only way to get more production, greater profits, and greater competitive strength. The distribution system that will give the highest standard of living to the greatest number of people — and will especially tend to increase the standard of living of the lowest income groups the fastest — is also the distribution system that will give the enterprise the biggest market. Above all, we now know that the production of wealth in such a system will rapidly tend to promote economic equality and the justice of equal opportunities.

During the last twenty-five years in the United States — through a tremendous depression and a tremendous war — the differential between the upper income group and the lowest income group has been cut by some seventy per cent and almost entirely by the raising of the standard of living of the lowest income group. The United States today is the country in which equality of income and equality of opportunities are the most nearly realized, while the Soviet Union — with its basic assumption of the conflict between economic interests and the interests of society — has probably the greatest inequality of income of any major country today.

What this means is that we again have a moral society. For no society can be a moral society in which the self-interest of the individual does not also promote the best interest of society, in which the fullest development of the personality of the individual does not promote the greatest perfection of society, in which competition and co-operation are not equally needed and equally socially productive.

I am not saying that an industrial society automatically and by itself realizes any of these goals. Far from it; it requires a very great effort from all who live in it, as every good society does. But we have today, in the challenge and the opportunities of industrial society, the possibility of creating harmony, establishing again a moral community. In this possibility lies the real meaning of industry, and also the best chance for the survival of Western society as a free, strong and prosperous society, and for the survival of Western Man as a free man, a citizen and a person.